Sacred Markets, Sacred Canopies

Sacred Markets, Sacred Canopies

Essays on Religious Markets and Religious Pluralism

Edited by
Ted G. Jelen

ROWMAN & LITTLEFIELD PUBLISHERS, INC.
Lanham • Boulder • New York • Oxford

ROWMAN & LITTLEFIELD PUBLISHERS, INC.

Published in the United States of America
by Rowman & Littlefield Publishers, Inc.
4720 Boston Way, Lanham, Maryland 20706
www.rowmanlittlefield.com

12 Hid's Copse Road
Cumnor Hill, Oxford OX2 9JJ, England

British Library Cataloguing in Publication Information Available

Library of Congress Cataloging-in-Publication Data

Sacred markets, sacred canopies : essays on religious markets and
religious pluralism / edited by Ted G. Jelen.
p. cm.
Includes bibliographical references and index.
ISBN 0-7425-1186-3 (alk. paper)
1. Religious pluralism—United States. 2. United States—Religion.
I. Jelen, Ted G.
BL2525 .S235 2002
306.6—dc21

2002002370

Printed in the United States of America

∞™ The paper used in this publication meets the minimum requirements of American National Standard for Information Sciences—Permanence of Paper for Printed Library Materials, ANSI/NISO Z39.48-1992.

Contents

Preface

As I write this in September of 2001, I am nearing completion of a four-year term as editor of the *Journal for the Scientific Study of Religion*. In that capacity, I have received and reviewed numerous manuscript submissions related to "supply-side," "rational choice," or "market" theories of religious adherence. Briefly, the controversy with which these manuscript dealt, and which forms the rationale for the present volume, involves the applicability of economic reasoning to religious behavior. Can individual decisions concerning whether or where to attend church, to contribute time or money to religious organizations, or to forgo certain temporal activities be described or explained as a special case of economic theory? Can religious choices be understood as responding to the same laws of supply and demand as other forms of consumer behavior?

Processing the large number of submissions in this general area, I was struck by two related facts. First, much of the work being done in this area is of very high quality. As readers of this book will see, some very smart people have devoted a great deal of time and energy to promoting or debunking the application of economic theory to religious behavior. If for no other reason than to observe good minds in action, the issue of religious markets merits the attention of scholars of the social scientific side of religion. Second, this debate has been going on for some time. This came as something of a surprise to me (a political scientist) who became aware of this literature only rather recently. Many of the manuscripts I was reading as editor of *JSSR* invoked a growing and formidable literature, which could strike students new to the controversy (like me) as somewhat intimidating.

When it occurred to me that other readers of *JSSR* might have the same reaction, I began to formulate the idea for this book. It seemed (and still seems) to me that work in the area of what I have chosen to call "religious markets" is likely to continue for some time, and that younger scholars will come to find working in this area very attractive. My hope with this volume is to provide a starting point for students and scholars approaching this set of problems for the first time, and to supply a concise source for the arguments, evidence, and criticism of the market model of religious economies. I hoped that it was possible to provide a sort of "roadmap" for people seeking to navigate the previous literature in the field, as well as a guide to the issues, controversies, and concerns which are likely to emerge from this continuing scholarship.

To the extent that I had a strategy for this book, it was perhaps best expressed by Claude Raines, who, at the end of *Casablanca,* instructed his police sergeant to "round up the usual suspects." Readers already familiar with the religious markets literature will see that I have done precisely that. The contributors to this collection are among the leading scholars in the sociology of religion generally, as well as constituting an excellent representation of the best contemporary work on economic models of religion. It has been a pleasure to work with every one of the contributors, each of whom provided me with first-rate work in an organized, timely manner. I thank them for their efforts and for their sense of cooperation. I also thank Steve Wrinn for having some faith in this project and for guiding it to a successful conclusion.

1

More Progress on the New Paradigm

R. Stephen Warner

Almost a decade ago, I proclaimed that progress was being made on "a new paradigm" for "the sociological study of religion in the United States."[1] I said that current trends in American[2] religion are continuous with the past[3], but we[4] need a new way of thinking to appreciate that fundamental continuity. This chapter recapitulates and clarifies the argument of the "new paradigm" article (Warner 1993) and traces additional progress.

By speaking of a "new paradigm," I meant to highlight (1) the fact that religion in the U.S. was disestablished from the time of the nation's founding, with the consequence that the U.S. has had an "open market" for religion for over two hundred years. The open market means that anyone can set up a religion or a church in the U.S.; to that extent, American churches operate in a competitive environment. Additional claims of the new paradigm are (2) that religion flourishes in conditions of cultural pluralism in America because churches provide social space for cultural particularism, (3) that competition promotes change in American religious institutions to accommodate to new realities, (4) that American religion serves as a vehicle of empowerment, and (5) that Americans' evidently increasing proclivity to choose whether and where to be committed to a religious community does not mark a fundamental break with the American past.

WHAT "PARADIGMS" ARE

The first clarification needed is that I announced a new "paradigm," not a new "theory," but didn't explain what was meant by a "paradigm."

A paradigm[5] is, in the words of historian of science Thomas Kuhn, a "gestalt" (Kuhn 1970: 112, 122, 204); it is a way of seeing the world, a representation, picture, or narrative of the fundamental properties of reality. For our purposes, paradigms may be regarded as metanarratives:

In astronomy, the earth can be seen as the stable center of the universe, as it was by Ptolemy, about which the sun, the moon, the planets, and the stars orbit, or it can be seen as one of several planets that revolve about the sun, as Copernicus insisted.

In geology, the earth may be imagined, as it was until a generation ago, as a once-hot, slowly cooling ball, developing a fixed, thickening shell of continents and sea floors as it cools, the shell cracking and fissuring, the continents rising or falling. Or, as taught by plate tectonic analysts, the earth may be imagined to be still hot and churning inside, so that the thin shell is continually renewed and destroyed by convection, hunks of it floating on the surface until they collide and are consumed, edgewise, in its depths.

In biology, evolution by adaptation may be conceived of as a matter of organisms struggling with their environment (in Lamarck's view) or struggling with each other for the best exploitation of their environment (as Darwin saw it).

The Copernican, plate tectonic, and Darwinian paradigm shifts represent radical changes in point of view. So also does the new paradigm in the sociology of religion in the U.S., although it is by no means as momentous an intellectual revolution. Here are the contrasting points of view:

The old paradigm metanarrative of religion begins more than eight hundred years ago in medieval Europe, when, by state sanction ever since the days of Constantine, a monopoly church commanded sacred authority over the whole society. There was only one provider of religious meaning and religious services, only one place to approach God and only one institution to confer legitimacy on rites of passage. Since the church was a protected monopoly, assent was assured by the fact that there were no ideological alternatives, and the church's viewpoint, it is said, was unquestioningly taken for granted. The church's monopoly status was the "plausibility structure" of medieval religion.[6] Since the heyday of this system (roughly the thirteenth century), its hegemony has slowly eroded (which is called the process of "secularization"), both because other powers rose to challenge it and because the sacred answers it provided became less plausible. The increasing implausibility of religious ideas is the result of ideological and cultural competition—Islam, the discovery of the New World, the success of the Protestants, the Enlightenment—which offered alternatives that had more plausibility or simply, *as* alternatives, invalidated the claims of the church.

The new paradigm metanarrative begins two hundred years ago in the early republican United States. Most people were not church members, and the dominant ideology, including that represented in social theory, was largely secular. At about that time (between 1776 and 1835), religion was disestablished, and a majoritarian political system was instituted. Thus religion no longer enjoyed the support of the state, but also the state made no room for the representation of minorities. Some religious bodies (e.g., the Anglicans) found disestablishment a challenge, but others had already been outsiders to the older establishment and quickly adapted to the new circumstances. Eventually no one body could successfully rule another claimant out of the system. People had to be persuaded to give assent to religious bodies, and religious entrepreneurs and operatives criss-crossed the country to save souls, anathematizing each other and offering a great variety of alternatives to their audiences (Heyrman 1998). Especially on the frontier, people made religious choices, joining up with congregations led by one or another of these competitors (Hatch 1989). The result within a generation was the creation of a huge, popular, quasi-public social space that women, and later racial minorities, could appropriate to their purposes. Eventually, religious profession became as much an identity marker in the U.S. as language, accent, and social class were in Europe.

The old paradigm says that secularization (meaning declining religious conviction) is a function of the increasing implausibility of religious doctrines, which is in turn due to the demise of religious monopoly, which was the normative status of religion for the old paradigm. Old paradigm thinkers say that under condition of pluralism, one religion's claims tend to invalidate another's. The more competing religious beliefs, the less plausibility any one of them will have.

The old paradigm is not groundless. Although very little evidence is ever provided for the "plausibility" dynamic (whose theoretical persistence seems to rest ironically on its own plausibility to intellectuals), Europe's monopolistic religious regimes did experience erosion concomitant with modernity. Having become, in the ten years since I drafted the new paradigm article, a regular visitor to Greece, now sharing a grandchild with a Greek family, I can see how the old paradigm could be applied to the Greek religious system, one of the oldest and latest-to-modernize provinces of Constantinian Christendom. It is "taken for granted" in Greece that for religious purposes everyone is Orthodox, and it is the norm that socially acceptable marriages must be solemnized and babies baptized within the monopolistic church. There's little choice about it. The civil and religious calendars coincide to a far greater extent than in the U.S., and businessmen look forward to the commercial opportunities afforded by Easter, Annunciation (which is also Independence Day), Assumption, and local saints' days. At the same time, in most towns for most purposes on most days, piety is not much in evidence, the ubiquitous churches treated as cultural decor except on the infrequent occasions when they're actually in use, usually for a rite of passage. The highly visible priests are greeted in the town square as civilly as anyone else—"good morning" and good evening"—but receive little more in the way of diffuse respect when not performing their liturgical duties. The church's position is increasingly threatened by secularizing forces—successful in gaining full entry into the European Union, the socialist government of Greece has decided to implement a decree prohibiting religious profession on citizens' identity cards (Molokotos-Liederman 2001)—and it may well be that over the next few decades we will be able to witness in Greece a version of the secularization process as it took place over the past five hundred years of western European religious history. Within a generation, analysts may be saying that the Greek church *no longer* enjoys the position it once had; that it *no longer* provides an unassailable sacred canopy over Greek society.

But that nostalgic expression, "no longer," so often used by old paradigm thinkers to conceptualize change in the status of religion from some robust golden age to the presumably tenuous present (Warner 1993: 1053–54), simply doesn't apply to the case of the United States, which never had a monopoly church and in which religion's high point (in the 1950s, if we have indeed yet passed it) was gained through the competing efforts of a huge plurality of religious organizations. The remarkable growth of religion in the U.S.—including the many accomplishments that old- as well as new-paradigm thinkers credit it with—*began* when religion was disestablished.

New paradigm thinkers stress continuing high levels of religious interest in our society, and they direct our attention to "supply side" factors and structural conditions as variables to account for ups and downs in religious activity (Finke 1997). Here is some evidence. In social survey data, people who don't go to church are not particularly those who express disbelief; many believers are not in church (Ammerman 1997a). Doubters and defectors cite perennial, not particularly modern grounds for their doubts (e.g., the problem of theodicy, endemic to monotheism, not the problem of others' beliefs); most of them are disappointed in religious institutions, not disbelievers in God (Smith 1998: 154–173). Yes, it helps to solidify one's beliefs if they receive validation from associates and authorities, but religious beliefs are no more vulnerable in this regard than other beliefs, including scientific beliefs, and in some way less vulnerable because so many religious beliefs draw on ineffable, highly intimate personal experience (Smith 1998: 173–177) rather than on arcane experiments conducted in remote laboratories.

THE NEW PARADIGM AND ECONOMIC THEORY

It is clear that new paradigm analysts willingly employ economic imagery and reasoning ("market," "religious suppliers," "monopoly," "competition"), but, as I said before (Warner 1993: 1053), the new paradigm is not *defined* by economic imagery; nor is it identical to rational choice theory. This was especially important to me a decade ago because Peter Berger, whose early theory (in *The Sacred Canopy*) I took to be the very exemplar of "old paradigm" thinking, himself used economic reasoning to understand what he saw as the degeneracy of American religion. He pointed out that American denominations had to compete with one another. They therefore could not assume the status of protected monopoly that he thought religion required for its plausibility and instead had to erect more or less transparently contrived "plausibility structures" to coddle their vulnerable belief systems. For Berger, competition was injurious to religion, but he used economic theory to make his point. Other old paradigm thinkers, including Max Weber, make extensive use of rational choice reasoning (Warner 1970, 1972).[7] *The contrast that sets the new paradigm apart from the old is not therefore the use of economic theory but the concept that disestablishment, the beginning of the end for European religion, is the beginning for American religion.*

Because of disestablishment, religious groups must persuade their constituents, they cannot command them. Moreover, the religious field is open to anyone. Religion is in principle not the property of the whole society, its ruling class, its patriarchy, its gerontocracy, or its dominant ethnic group. When, as is true of the United States, the society is culturally and structurally pluralistic, religiously organized groups can enjoy a great deal of autonomy to define themselves. Constitutive disestablishment is the crux of the new paradigm.

A paradigm is not a theory (Warner 1997b). Geologists who adhere to the newer paradigm of plate tectonics do not discard the knowledge of the chemical composition of rocks that their predecessors gained nor the theoretical tools of physical chemistry that they used. They use many of the same tools and adduce much of the same knowledge but arrange them in new ways, beginning with different presuppositions about the sequence in which things happened and arriving at different prognoses for the future. Similarly, new paradigm sociologists need not jettison knowledge gained by old paradigm analysts nor to forswear the tools of survey research and ethnography or the theories of cultural affinity that they used.

For example, in my own attempt (Warner 1988) to understand the appeal of evangelicalism to the hundreds of new members who flocked to the Presbyterian church of small-town Mendocino, California, in the mid-1970s, I found invaluable Wade Clark Roof's excellent but old-paradigm-influenced analysis of religious "cosmopolitans and locals" (Roof 1978) among North Carolina Episcopalians in the 1960s. But where Roof presupposed that the "locals" (who found "plausible" the brand of Protestantism that I call evangelicalism) had to be an embattled and declining constituency in our modern and mobile society—that the stable small-town life that protected their mindset had to be a thing of the past—I found that Mendocino attracted hordes of "*elective* parochials," people with cosmopolitan backgrounds who were drawn, by choice, to the values of small-town life (and to whom the local Presbyterian church's newly minted evangelicalism hugely appealed). Thus a congregation that turned its back on its denomination's modernized and rationalized religion appealed mightily to people with the cultural wherewithal to choose (and help perpetuate) a lifestyle that only appeared to be the way of the past. Under evangelical leadership from 1973 on, the Presbyterian church of Mendocino was a social space for the religious expression of the particular culture that I dubbed elective parochialism.

Insofar as my own argumentation in the foregoing paragraph stresses the cultural awareness of and options available to Mendocino's evangelicals, a rational choice perspective on human action has obvious resonance. The overlapping companies of rational choice theorists and new paradigm analysts of religion have in common a bias that it is a mistake to assume that religious people are, to put it bluntly, benighted. We are inclined to think that people are religious for good reason[8]. We also think that no more than the common run of humanity—citizens, family members, even scientists—do religious people desperately need their ideas to be protected from a culturally alien world, even as we recognize that, like most people for most purposes, religious people enjoy the company of those with whom they fundamentally agree. Far from being threatened by other belief systems and needing protection from them, adherents of American religions have typically defined themselves in contrast to their rivals, and their communities have flourished as particular repositories of truth within a world full of error. Thus, in contrast to the old paradigm, we think that the plausibility of Americans' religious ideas does not depend on their being sheltered so that they can be taken for granted from time out of mind; it depends rather on their being aggressively asserted, generation after generation. Thus nothing is gained theoretically by saying that the "plausibility" of religious ideas is a special problem for religious people, and a great deal of valuable scholars' time is wasted by looking around for the "plausibility structures" that solve such a banal "problem."

Yet in my determination to contrast the new and old paradigms, I overstated the case in the "schematic comparison" that was printed as Table 1 (1052) of the 1993 article. Insisting that religious meaning systems are not as vulnerable as old paradigm thinkers make them out to be, I seemed to say that the provision of meaning was not a key function of religion. That was a mistake on my part. *Of course* the new paradigm recognizes that religions provide meaning. It's just that the meanings they provide are, from our point of view, one of their strengths, a solid foundation they build on, as did Mendocino's evangelicals, instead of being their particular point of vulnerability, the flimsy roof they have to ensure doesn't leak and dampen their "plausibility," as the old paradigm has it. If there is a "theoretical" difference between the old and new paradigms, it is our rejection of their "plausibility" problematic. But we have no intention of leaving a focus on religious culture to the old paradigm. For example, religious meaning systems are one source of the empowering, mobilizing potential of religion which we stress (Pattillo-McCoy 1998; McRoberts 1999).

To repeat, the "new paradigm" as I define it makes five claims about the American (i.e., United States) religious system:

1. Disestablishment means that there is an "open market for religion" in the U.S., which in turn means that "barriers to entry" are low (it's easier to open a storefront church than an auto dealership, let alone an airline), and churches therefore operate in a competitive environment.
2. American religion flourishes in conditions of cultural pluralism because churches provide social space for cultural particularisms.
3. Religious competition promotes structural change to accommodate institutions to new realities.
4. American religion promotes individual and group empowerment, serving as a vehicle for popular democratic movements.
5. Americans choose whether and where to be committed to a religious community; this has been implicit all along and especially overt in the early-nineteenth-century Second Great Awakening as well as today. Whatever we may think of it, religious individualism is traditionally American.

THE RELIGIOUS "MARKET"

The concept of a "religious market" has invited the most misunderstanding of the new paradigm. First of all, the new paradigm does not require the economist's "rational choice" assumptions, the idea in other words that ordinary people behave religiously just as they presumably behave economically (Warner 2001b). Such assumptions *are* made by sociologist Rodney Stark, and before these ideas are rejected out of hand I especially recommend Stark's brilliant and entertaining book, *The Rise of Christianity* (1996), where the reader can appreciate how much explanatory "mileage" Stark gets out of such assumptions (see also Stark and Finke 2000: 46–55). Rational choice assumptions are also made by economist Laurence Iannaccone, who (1991) uses the theory of inefficient monopolies to explain why religious participation in pluralistic America is so much higher than in monopolistic Scandinavia and who (1997) presents an algorithm of the place of such assumptions in explanatory theories. But other new paradigm thinkers like Nancy

Ammerman (1997b), Andrew Greeley (1989), Mary Jo Neitz (1990, Neitz and Mueser 1997), Christian Smith (1998), and myself employ less economistic models of human psychology. All we insist is that American religious leaders, operating in an open market since about 1800, have always had to work to persuade their constituents to follow them; to speak of a "market" means that they couldn't coerce assent or participation on the part of their charges.[9]

What new paradigm talk of a religious "market" does *not* entail is that religious leaders simply devote themselves to "market research," asking around what religion people want and then simply giving it to them, "marketing" services in the most vulgar sense. There are church-watchers and church consultants who recommend such an approach, seeming to countenance religious pandering, but they are not following the new paradigm.

Let me spend a moment with this seeming paradox: "new paradigm" market theorists of religion are not the ones who talk about the need for religious leaders to kowtow to the vagaries of public opinion. In fact, Stark and Iannaccone, and Stark's collaborator Roger Finke, have proposed that it is "strict" churches, led by people who stick to their religious guns, that are most likely to grow, and lenient ones, ones that sway and waver, to decline (Finke and Stark 1992; Iannaccone 1994). These "new paradigm" analysts don't say that churches flourish when they say, "anything goes." Quite the contrary: they flourish when they make things tough.

The reasoning behind this "strictness" theory is that strict churches will succeed in weeding out "free riders," the half-hearted "let George do it" people who exploit and undermine others' enthusiasm. Strictness will tend to generate the high levels of human and material resources that church growth demands. Other analysts (Chai 2001; Sherkat 2001; 1486) claim that churches flourish when they offer their adherents identities and opportunities that are not so much strict as distinct from those of the surrounding culture.

Here's an example of what a new paradigm market perspective means drawn from Chicago's famous (or infamous) Willow Creek Community Church.[10] Some twenty-five years ago, Bill Hybels and his early followers did a door-to-door canvass to find what was keeping his fellow baby boomers out of church (hypocrisy and trappings like gloomy statuary, dark buildings, and musty hymnals), and in the design of his church Hybels lowered the barriers to appeal to the type of person he called "unchurched Harry." The church he designed doesn't "welcome" people with a handshake. Visitors are left alone to explore church on their own time, and they are conspicuously not asked for their money during the offering. The auditorium (not sanctuary) has clear glass and no religious symbols. There is no dress code, no hymnals, and no arcane liturgy. (That was no great sacrifice for Hybels, who was Reformed to begin with.) But Hybels didn't dumb down the service. Services are very thematic, with music, skits, and readings that all prepare the congregation for the message, which is evangelical, thoughtful, and lengthy.

Now, having successfully reached a huge clientele, numbering in the tens of thousands, Hybels can respond, as any Protestant pastor does, to their concerns. One of those concerns has to do with the fragmentation of modern life, something that I will return to. But Willow Creek elicits great financial and volunteer commitments from its members, on the basis of which it has built a huge plant and offers an astounding array of services. In that sense, it's relatively strict, not an example of pick-and-choose, cafeteria-style, religion "lite."[11]

The new paradigm says to any would-be religious innovator, "follow your calling, but strive to spread the word." Operating within a religious market may require religious innovators to determine who wants what they are called to do. The only thing they cannot count on is people being required to pay attention to them. But the message is theirs to spread.

SOCIAL SPACE FOR CULTURAL DIVERSITY

New paradigm analysts argue together against the old paradigm that religion and pluralism go hand in hand in America, which is at once the most religiously diverse and one of the most religiously active societies on earth. We differ among ourselves on the dynamics. Some, like Stark (1997), are inclined to say that the open religious market *begets* religious diversity; others, and I am among them, say that the open religious market *makes room for* cultural diversity, whatever the source of that diversity. I am also inclined to stress *cultural distinctiveness* rather than *sectarian strictness* as a key to church strength (Warner 1988, 1998a, 1997b).

The U.S. has known many kinds of religiously relevant cultural diversity: social class (occupation, education, income, etc.), region (the South and the West are different), the urban-rural continuum, national origin and ethnicity, language, race, sexual orientation, aesthetic taste, even religio-ethnic identity (e.g., the Anabaptists). Internal migration of gays and lesbians, the retired, and religious seekers is another source of religious differentiation.[12]

Over the past decade, I have worked on international immigration as a source of religiously relevant cultural diversity. At a minimum, immigrants want to worship in their own language, which is often not English; more urgently, when no co-religionists reside in the area to which they have moved, they need to establish their own houses of worship, which is the case for many new immigrant Muslims.

But even when there is already a church of one's own faith worshipping in a language one can understand, people often still want to be among their own kind. A sociologist friend of mine, an immigrant from China and a Christian, told me that he is often warmly received in "white American" churches but that he prefers to worship in Chinese churches: not just for the language, but for the taken-for-granted assumption of Chineseness as the norm. Instead of responding to the well-intentioned "hello, where are you from?" question with "China" (instead of, for example, "Korea") he (and others like him) can give the particular province, territory, or expatriate community (Singapore, Malaysia, Indonesia, etc.) that they call home and can then delight in sharing stories of the enormous complexity and profound unity of the Chinese diaspora. My friend enjoys that Chinese cultural space.

I got an inkling of what my friend had in mind when, as an enthusiastic singer, I reflected on one of the things that felt right about a nearby Lutheran church when, a few years back, my wife and I took up a friend's invitation that we come for a visit. It turned out to be one of the first churches I'd been to in years where someone did not turn around after the service to say, "My! You ought to be in the choir." My wife and I are now members of this church, Immanuel Lutheran, where it is assumed that *everyone* participates in the sung liturgy. Immanuel is, among other things, a social space for the musically inclined, and, like my friend's Chinese church, it is also a Christian church with sound doctrine, dignified liturgy, and erudite preaching.[13] Churches provide social space for cultural diversity, but they are not reducible to those cultural particularisms.

As I said, immigration has been a perennial source of cultural diversity in America, and today's immigration, which at a rate of about one million per year matches that of the last turn of the century, is bringing more diversity than ever before to our society, with the great majority of new immigrants coming here from non-European countries, especially from Latin America, east and south Asia, and the Middle East. Nevertheless, my inclination (Warner 1998a), which is not uncontested, is to stress continuities between today's immigration and that of the past, including the likelihood of widespread cultural assimilation of immigrant progeny over two to three generations.

First of all, although they differ racially and linguistically from what is still the dominant white English-speaking American majority, the new immigrants are overwhelmingly Christian. A plurality are from Mexico and other deeply Christianized Latin American countries. Those from Asia are likely to come from dominantly or partially Christian countries like the Philippines or from Christianized sectors of religiously diverse societies like Korea and Vietnam. *Immigration is not random with respect to religion* (Warner 1998b, 2000). Whether or not Christian, their religion is often highly salient to immigrants, as it tends to be especially for the Christians, Buddhists, and Muslims from, respectively, Korea, Thailand, and south Asia.

Second, although one hears a great deal about "multiculturalism" and although we are bound as a society to respect religious diversity, new immigrants are inclined to be quite conservative socially. (I sometimes think that if inside-the-beltway politicians knew how conservative new immigrants tend to be on family-related issues, the Democratic and Republican parties would switch sides on maintaining high levels of immigration.) In one study of the social impact of the new immigrants, sociologist Edwin Hernández (1995), himself a Puerto Rican Seventh-Day Adventist, has spoken of "the browning of Adventism" as entailing a slowing, or even a reversal, of the Adventists' trajectory from conservative sect to relaxed denomination (see also Lawson 1998).

Third, although some do not have the skills they would need to compete in our increasingly information-based economy, many, coming under occupational preference provisions, have skills that are in high demand, and others are finding entrepreneurial niches and bringing needed services to inner-city neighborhoods. With some exceptions (I am concerned about the Hmong and about refugees from Guatemala and El Salvador) they are by no means clustered at the bottom of the social ladder, and many immigrant communities have resources to facilitate help from one family to another as they settle in to life in America.

For these and other reasons, I expect that many new immigrant communities, whether Christian, Muslim, or other, will follow something like the Americanization path of earlier groups (Warner 1994, 1998a, 2000, 2001a). As I see it, Korean churches are in the early stages of the transition from the dominance of home-country language speakers to that of their English-speaking offspring, maybe where Swedish Lutherans were eighty years ago and Japanese were sixty years ago (Goette 2001). But that does not mean that Korean churches are about to disappear, or that we white Protestants can expect a mass influx into our churches of Americanized Korean young people. English-dominant Korean American youth also want social space for their cultural, racial, and religious particularities (Chai 1998, 2001). One religious growth industry in the next generation is likely to be planting mono-ethnic and pan-Asian churches for English speaking Asian Americans. American religious pluralism is robust.

While the idea that either the new paradigm or rational choice theory counsels clerical pandering is a popular misconception, the controversy over our claim that religious diversity is conducive to religious vitality is more substantial in the scholarly literature. Already in 1992 (Warner 1993; 1055–1057), I indicated that this was a live issue, the question whether a multiplicity of religious options, or "pluralism" as it is usually called, tends to promote religious participation. Beginning with the obvious point that the U.S. religious system is both highly mobilized and diverse and that both religious mobilization and religious diversity expanded in the nineteenth century, new paradigm advocates are inclined to expect a positive correlation between pluralism and participation. Because modernity and cultural diversity coincided with the slow decline of religion in Europe, old paradigm exponents expect the correlation to be negative.

As I wrote (1993, 1056–1057), the main thrust of new paradigm analysts' thinking about the pluralism/vitality correlation is the "supply-side" understanding of pluralism as a concomitant of disestablishment and proxy for competition, that when there are a multiplicity of religious suppliers (or other forces that prevent religious suppliers from becoming "lazy monopolies"), they will work harder to attract and maintain adherents (see also Stark and Finke 2000; 201–202). The importance of immigration for American religion must be understood from both the demand and the supply side. The religiously relevant cultural diversity that immigration brings increases the level and diversity of religious demand; disestablishment means that suppliers will have an incentive to meet these demands. The resultant hypothesis is, the greater the religious diversity, the greater the religious participation.

The old paradigm understanding of their pluralism/decline expectation has been recently and sympathetically summarized by Paul Fitzgerald (2001; 15): Religious pluralism means

> the relatively peaceful coexistence of different religious groups in a single society . . . such that cognitive contamination is a regular occurrence: different lifestyles, values, and beliefs mingle. . . . [A]long the way, believers will notice that their manner of perceiving reality, shaped as it is by a given religious tradition, is not the only plausible explanation for the way things are. . . . A taken-for-granted religious worldview first becomes questionable, then doubtful. The end point of this process is supposed to be pervasive relativism and finally complete unbelief.

Thus, for the old paradigm, the greater the religious diversity, the less likely that people will be involved in religious institutions.

The extensive literature that has been generated by these competing hypotheses (see the bibliographies in Finke and Stark 1998 and Chaves and Gorski 2001) has been less than fully satisfying, in both substantive and methodological terms. Substantively, religious "pluralism" (measured by the probability that two individuals in a given social unit will be adherents of different religions) is for neither side in the debate the actual theorized causal factor in the production of higher or lower levels of religious involvement. For the old paradigm, that factor is the psychological implausibility of their belief system presumably instilled in church members by their awareness of belief systems alternative to their own. For the new paradigm, that factor is the organizational energy presumably instilled in church leaders by not being able to take their members for granted. In a careful analysis of the religious pluralism/involvement literature (to which he is a major contributor) Daniel Olson (2000) has suggested that demand-side organizational processes may stand behind the alternatively positive and negative correlations that investigators report. Olson argues (2000; 9) that "to the extent that religious pluralism diminishes the proportion of coreligionists in one's *close personal networks*, the pluralism of an area should . . . reduce rates of religious involvement" [emphasis added], one reason being that coordination costs rise. Olson's analysis thus suggests that while the effects on participation of pluralism of intimates are negative, the pluralism in the locality means that religious groups supply more churches in their attempts to enroll a given population. When members of one's own family adhere to different religions, it's more difficult to get everyone out to church on Sunday. But, other things being equal, if there are more churches to go to, distances are shorter and it's easier to go. "Thus more people participate because they don't have to walk or ride as far to reach a church" (Olson 2000; 16; see also Stark and Finke 2000; 223–224).[14]

Methodologically, agreement has been elusive on what should be the local unit of analysis (are counties too large? does the answer to that question change over time as transportation improves?) and whether the presence of a single extremely large and internally diverse but embattled minority denomination (the U.S. Catholic church) itself provides the competition that presumably increases religious activity; if so, the equation should control for percent Catholic. Most recently, Olson and his associates (Voas et al. 2001) have argued that most of what purport to be empirical findings on the association of religious pluralism and religious participation may well be a series of mathematical artifacts of the way that pluralism and participation are measured. They show how "findings" very similar to those reported in the literature could be generated through a random process. If Voas et al. are correct, very little can be said one way or the other about the effects of "pluralism" itself given present measurement techniques. Thus, research on the effects of religious pluralism on individual religious participation is far from decisive for the claims of the old and new paradigms (cf. Chaves and Gorski 2001).

STRUCTURAL CHANGE

A third proposition of the New Paradigm is that the open religious system in the U.S. promotes ecclesiastical structural change to accommodate to new realities. Based on the American experience, the new paradigm recognizes the American religious system as an arena of chronic organizational creativity. In the absence of an established authoritative "church," American religious activists had to innovate other forms for the organizational expression of their faith, of which I spoke of three in the 1993 article: denominations, congregations, and special-purpose groups.

In Richard Niebuhr's (1929) judgmental analysis, the denomination—an American invention—was neither socially universalistic nor ethically principled, but partial and compromised, enrolling people of a particular social class, region, national origin, or race and assuming a stance of comfortable accommodation toward the wider society. Be that as it may, as a supra-local organization that allowed like-minded Christians (and later, Jews) to carry out programs on a national and international scope and to compete and cooperate with select similar organizations, while recognizing informally at first but over time quite firmly the legitimacy of similar organizations as coequals, the denomination was a nineteenth-century innovation well suited to the increasingly pluralistic religious system of the United States, the kind of innovation the new paradigm expects.

However, by the 1950s, the high tide of respectable religion in America, many of the large and socially prominent (so-called "mainline") American Protestant denominations, having come together in the National Council of Churches and thereby abandoned a good deal of their distinctiveness, had assumed in their own minds something of the status of a privileged religious establishment (Hutchison 1989), the sort of quasi-monopolistic taken-for-granted national religious elite that the old paradigm regards as, well, paradigmatic. When, in 1965, these denominations (Methodist, Presbyterian, Episcopal, northern Baptist, and other) went into a period of decline from which most of them have yet to recover, old paradigm analysts saw in their fate the fate of American religion in general, identifying with their self-diagnosis that secularization had come at last to America. But new paradigm thinkers, recognizing the historical contingency of the denominational form and not identifying the fate of religion with but one of its organizational expressions, looked elsewhere for continued religious vitality, one direction being to those denominations whose officers had not forgotten the distinctive identities on which their original organizational success had been premised (Finke and Stark 1992; Ammerman 2000; Sherkat 2001: 1486). Other analysts, without prophesying the end of religion, maintained that the denominational form, *per se*, is declining (Wuthnow 1988).

A second direction that new paradigm sociologists looked for organizational religious vitality was to another early organizational invention of religious Americans, the congregation (Warner 1994). Unlike the "parish" (the geographically defined local outpost of the universal church and its imitators), the "congregation" is the socially defined local base of the denomination, indeed the organ out of which denominations were originally constructed (Smith 1998). With its typical particularism and face-to-face interaction, the congregation was a religious form well suited to a pluralistic, mobile, and democratically inclined populace. With the rapid social (and especially cultural) changes of the 1960s and 1970s, American congregations, with their smaller size and huge numbers, were one place that religious innovators could forge adaptations to meet new conditions. Some independent congregations have been so successful that they became models for other congregations who have joined them in associations that may prove to be the denominations of the near future (Miller 1997; Stark and Finke 2000: 268–271). Some denominationally affiliated congregations flourished, even as their mislabeled "parent" denominations were declining (Warner 1988), some adopting hymnals and Sunday School materials that met their religious needs instead of their denomination's priorities, others insisting on greater faithfulness to their denominational traditions than they perceived on the part of their denominational officials (Ammerman 2000). Immigrant groups adopted, de facto, the congregational mode of organization regardless of the canonical organizational form their religions took in the old country (Warner 1994; Bankston and Zhou 2000).

Congregations within the same denomination are often so different that their members have more in common religiously with members of other denominations than of their own. Indeed one thing that many Presbyterians have in common is that their bitterest religious enemies are Presbyterians in other congregations who take the wrong side on cultural issues such as gay rights. Strong, successful congregations (whether acknowledged as such *de jure* or autonomous of their denominations) were both a cause of the declining significance of denominations and a structural alternative to them. The growth of the field of congregational studies (e.g., Ammerman et al. 1998) may be seen as another aspect of new paradigm progress.

Yet the world does not stand still, and people who want religion may not want it in the congregational or denominational packages; some look to a third nineteenth-century organizational form for religion, the "special-purpose group" (Wuthnow 1988). Often national in scope, interorganizational in genesis, and increasingly professional in staffing, special-purpose groups from the American Bible Society and Focus on the Family to People for the American Way and Clergy and Laity Concerned mobilize focused inputs, especially constituents' donations of money and time and staffers' expertise and coordination, toward defined ends. Insofar as affluent religious people wish to substitute their abundant money for their precious time (Chiswick 1995), such organizations are a rational solution.

Having first brought special-purpose groups to the attention of sociologists of religion in *The Restructuring of American Religion* (1988), Robert Wuthnow in *Loose Connections* has recently (1998) aided our understanding of what their increasing significance says about religion in America. Wuthnow broadens his gaze to look at institutions of all sorts in our society, religious and otherwise, which he sees as increasingly "porous," increasingly vulnerable to the complexities of modern life. Not only denominations and congregations are in jeopardy, he says, but other full-service, multipurpose organizations with a high sociability component—from Rotary and Kiwanis clubs through the League of Women Voters and the PTA to the Girl Scouts and the NAACP.[15]

The pressures of middle class life—the evolution from the two-person career to the two-career family, with the resulting difficulty of scheduling family activities; the need to get the kids off to their lessons and their teams; and the greater freedoms we all have to indulge our multiple leisure-time involvements—make it harder to organize time around the demanding and inflexible schedules of old-fashioned civic societies, including but not confined to churches. Meanwhile, new work pressures, including the insecurity of careers and need for childcare, added to awareness of new needs—for example, coming to grips with childhood trauma or substance abuse—make people's needs for social support more specific and less diffuse. The result is it is harder and harder to get people together in the same place at the same time, and when they do get together, they wish to do so for specific purposes under terms of involvement that they closely circumscribe (Wuthnow 1998).

Wuthnow doesn't think that people are necessarily getting more stingy with their time, and in fact they still volunteer in impressive numbers. But he thinks they don't want to sit around for chit-chat, and that they don't want to be responsible for running things. One result within the growing roster of not-for-profit organizations is that one of the key paid staffers is the volunteer coordinator. Here are three implications of Wuthnow's new analysis, which is not itself focused particularly on religion, for our story.

First, our society does present challenges to religious institutions, but, as stated earlier, the evidence is that *those challenges are not particularly to the plausibility of religious teachings but to the organization of religious work*, in Nancy Ammerman's felicitous phrase. Churches that are intentional about their identity can succeed (see Ammerman 2000).

Second, churches can enter into cooperative arrangements with each other for the provision of services that no one of them could afford on its own. Wuthnow recommends this, and Nancy Eiesland's ecological analysis of congregational life in exurban Atlanta (Eiesland 2000) talks about how such arrangements can look from below, from the side of church members who worship at their own church, take their young children to another church for weekday childcare, go to a support group at yet another church for grief counseling, and whose older youth take advantages of activities in still another.

Third, the trends that Wuthnow, Putnam, and Eiesland document help account for a feature of megachurches like Willow Creek that has been widely misunderstood. Many observers are struck with the very wide range of services and activities that Willow Creek features—from a gymnasium and a book store to a food court featuring a half dozen types of cuisine—that make the place look more like a shopping mall than a European-style cathedral. As new paradigm sociologists see it, these innovations do not represent capitulation to secularism but an antidote to it that allows families to stay at church all day Sunday. Willow Creek is not competing to be the best provider of food services; it's competing for its members' time, trying to combat what Wuthnow calls "porousness" with full-service, one-stop, it's-all-on-the-campus diversity of services. In effect, it is a modern sect.

RELIGIOUS INSTITUTIONS AND POPULAR MOVEMENTS

The fourth proposition of the new paradigm is that American religion promotes individual and group empowerment, serving especially as a vehicle for popular and change-oriented democratic movements, the most important recent example being the civil rights movement (Morris 1984). One reason that denominational particularism is not the scandal for new paradigm thinkers that it was for Niebuhr and his generation is that many of us lived through the civil rights movement during our formative years and saw how the Black church, as the only institution African Americans controlled of, by, and for themselves, was the necessary foundation for the movement. The empowering potential of the Black church rests in part on its "macro" or structural resources—indigenous leadership, meeting places, membership rosters, fund-raising capacity, communication networks—but also on its psycho-cultural or "micro" resources, the religious symbols and language it enshrines, and the sense of efficacy and community-consciousness they instill (Harris 1999; Pattillo-McCoy 1998). The Black church makes space available for people to meet but it also enshrines a gospel of hope and determination.

Instead of asking the plausibility question—in effect, "how can they believe these things?"—studies of the Black church are increasingly focused on accounting for variation in the extent to which these American religious institutions live up to their empowering potential. African Americans' involvement in churches they control is more predictive of their participation in the political process than is their individual religiosity, and such church affiliation promotes reformist rather than separatist and revolutionary activities (Harris 1999). The mobilizing potential of the Black church is not confined to the historic Black-controlled mainline denominations as long as the local congregation is Afro-centric (Cavendish 2000) and led by an activist pastor (McRoberts 1999; Cavendish 2001), which may in turn be effects of de facto congregationalism (Warner 1994). Churches that are part of an overchurched "religious district" produced by the abundance of cheap rental space instead of local religious demand have difficulty joining together to address the needs of the community (McRoberts 2000). Far from being a hindrance to activism, the theological conservatism that is so characteristic of the Black church—the conviction that a supernatural God is active in earthly affairs, that Jesus is Lord and the Holy Spirit speaks today, that the Bible is God's word and that there is power in prayer—has empowering potential, instilling, as it does, hope and a sense of personal and collective efficacy (Pattillo-McCoy 1998; Harris 1999; McRoberts 1999).

To call churches a "vehicle" for anything is to court the misunderstanding that the real impetus for change lies somewhere outside the church and that the church is only being used by those external forces to further their fundamentally irreligious agendas. This complaint is seldom applied any more to the civil rights movement—most American Christians now affirm that Martin Luther King was an agent of the advance of God's kingdom—but it is still a widespread response to demands on the part of feminists that the church open leadership opportunities to women, including the privilege of ordination to the ministry of word and sacrament, where pressures for change are seen as secular forces and resistance is blamed (or praised) as fundamentally religious.[16]

It is worth spending time on this issue with respect to a topic that I have studied in some depth (Warner 1995), the religious movement for the recognition of gay and lesbian rights.[17] When one encounters the irreligion of much of the Gay, Lesbian, Bisexual and Transgendered movement, it is easy to assume that the movement is basically foreign to the churches, at best an outside force with no use for religion, at worst, one trying to push its way in. Yet the pressure for the acceptance of non-celibate gay and lesbian Christians as full participants in the church began for our time with a gay pentecostal named Troy Perry, who, inspired by a vision in which he experienced God's love for him as for a man God created gay, opened a church for homosexuals in Los Angeles in October 1968, nearly a year before the birth of the modern gay liberation movement at the Stonewall Bar in New York. Perry is an evangelist for the gospel as he has heard it and experienced it. "God is all powerful and God loves his creation" he learned in the Florida pentecostal churches in which he grew up, and "homosexuality is innate" he learned from reflecting on the yearnings of his own body. So he began to preach that "The Lord Is My Shepherd and He Knows I'm Gay" (Perry 1972: Perry and Swicegood 990). When word spread along the west coast about what Perry was doing, gay lapsed Baptists and Catholics and defrocked Protestant ministers showed up to share in the good news and, not incidentally, to help Perry shape the Biblical hermeneutic and ecclesiastical structure of what quickly became a new denomination, the Metropolitan Community Church.

Inspired by Perry's example, gays and lesbians in many other faith communities—Catholic, Episcopal, Presbyterian, Methodist, Mormon, Seventh-Day Adventist, Jewish Reform—began to speak out for recognition within their faith communities of their being as children of God and homosexuals. Uncounted numbers of other unacknowledged homosexuals continue to participate loyally in their churches despite the pain of feeling their being denied by those who represent them to God. These loyalists are not the type to create a ruckus, but they look forward to the time, as expressed to me by one highly involved Chicago Catholic gay layman, that his parish might some day belatedly celebrate the union of him and his partner, the man with whom he owns a home on the city's north side. Because I know people like him, I do not doubt that theirs is a truly religious longing, the desire to share fully in the catholicity of the church. Meanwhile, whether "out" or still "closeted," gay Christians overwhelmingly reject the key "social constructionist" tenet of the secular Queer Movement in favor of their own "essentialist" conviction that sexual orientation is God's immutable gift (Wilcox 2000; Warner 1995); it is clear that theirs is not a movement outside the church.

Although the Religious Right is prone to seeing the gay movement as an ungodly (and secular) movement, so secular liberals are inclined to regard the feminist movement in the churches as equally secular (and thereby emancipated from religion). Both are in thrall to the old paradigm which (1) credits (whether with approval or disapproval) the claims to religious authenticity of old-line heterosexist and patriarchal establishments and (2) regards (again, whether positively or negatively) religion as inherently establishmentarian and therefore incapable of representing the voice of insurgents. Progressive change, in this view, must come from without. Neither party sufficiently reflects on the fact that the nineteenth-century women's movement had its roots in women's religion and that, for example, some holiness and pentecostal churches granted ordination rights to women long before most mainline churches did so (Chaves 1997: 16–17). As anti-religious as it may appear today, feminism is not an inherently secular force.

Although old paradigm reductionists like to see capitulation to secularism in contemporary liberal Christians' incorporation of feminist and lesbi-gay perspectives, the Christian tradition has long recognized without scandal the role secular interests played in the development of the Constantianian old paradigm itself. From the Council of Nicaea onward, Christian orthodoxy was shaped, in part, by the political interests of Constantine and his successors (Armstrong 1993: 110–111; Fletcher 1997: 22–24). Christian tradition affirms that the Emperors' political motives were put to God's purposes. Because of disestablishment and popular mobilization in the early republican period in the United States, the very process that new paradigm analysts identify as the crucible of the American religious system, religion here is not the preserve of an elite, whether ecclesiastical or political. Thus, Americans have been religiously entitled for two hundred years, and, from a Christian point of view, God's kingdom in our country had to be furthered by motives other than dynastic ambitions, using popular visions that are no more Godly in themselves than Constantine's reign, but have Godly outcomes. Only at the cost of inconsistency can old paradigm advocates regard the impact of political interests (usually of the left) on religion as evidence for "secularization."

THE "NEW" VOLUNTARISM

I now turn to the fifth and final element in the new paradigm as I have defined it, the American tradition of religious individualism. Ever since the early republican period, Americans have been free to choose whether and where to be committed to a religious community, a choice that must have been widely exercised in the nineteenth century (as evidenced by the rapid growth of "upstart denominations" like the Methodists, Baptists, and Churches of Christ, growth that could not have been the result of inherited identities from birth or immigration [Finke and Stark 1992]). More overtly today, religious choice is both widely exercised and positively asserted. At my public university in heavily Catholic Chicago, about half of the students in my sociology of religion classes are cradle Catholics, but half of them claim no longer to be Catholic, many of them affirming no religion at all. There are also scatterings of students who say they were "raised Lutheran" or "raised Methodist" but now "don't practice" or affirm no religion. Some affirm another religion. It feels insufficiently self-actualizing to say that one just "happens to be" a Catholic, a Lutheran or a Methodist; one's religion is supposed to mean more than that.

Religious individualism does not, of course, require that one flees from religious involvement; one can embrace it. As I said, half of the cradle Catholics in my classes at the University of Illinois at Chicago claim to have left the Catholic fold, but half of that half say that they have done so in order to become "Christian." These students are very likely to be Hispanic—especially Mexican and Puerto Rican—and the Youth and Religion Project probed what students like them mean by their new "Christian" identity: they are now participating in fairly rigorous, indeed sectarian, evangelical and Pentecostal churches that encourage the discipline they need to succeed in college. It is not that their Catholic churches would be inimical to such discipline. Rather, what they seem to find in their Protestantism is some leverage against strands in their culture that they feel do hold them back and that they experience as inextricably bound up with the Catholic tradition.

Similarly, the UIC campus today abounds in Muslim women who have newly adopted the *hijab*, or head scarf, as a badge of their seriousness. In a Youth and Religion Project focus group, we heard women like them say that they did not learn these practices from their mothers; they decided on their own to observe a discipline of their faith. I imagine that they are destined to lead adult lives that are far less in tune than are their mothers' lives with the patriarchal Middle Eastern and south Asian cultures from which their families derive. (For details on this and the previous paragraph, see Warner, Martel, and Dugan 2001; Williams and Vashi 2001.)

Although I have used today's jargon ("self-actualized") to characterize today's spirit of religious individualism, that spirit does not represent the advent of a new age of enlightened secular individualism that the old paradigm (as well as some of my students) make it out to be.

- Although religious individualism is rampant at the close of the twentieth century, one major source of American religious individualism was itself the evangelicalism of the early nineteenth century (Bellah et al. 1985).
- Although in George Gallup's effort to understand the "unchurched American," an astounding 80 percent of Americans agreed with the proposition that the individual "should arrive at his or her religious beliefs independent of any church or synagogue," the difference between the churched and the unchurched on this opinion was small, with three quarters of the "churched" agreeing with this individualistic proposition. Among Americans, religious individualism is religiously conventional (Princeton Religion Research Center 1988).
- Although baby boomers left the religion of their upbringing in enormous numbers, largely accounting for the membership decline of the mainline Protestant denominations, many, including those who once felt most alienated from the church, have returned to religion, and more often to conservative than to liberal or moderate Protestantism (Roof 1999).
- Although the proportion of religious non-affiliates in the U.S. population has tripled or more since a low point in the 1950s, irreligion is an identity much less stable than Catholic, Baptist, Jewish, or Mormon, and those who grow up with no religion are disproportionately likely to turn to varieties of conservative Christianity as they mature (Sherkat 2001).

Two lessons are clear for scholars and church leaders. *No church can take the loyalties of its young people for granted. But religion is not on the way out.* The new paradigm asserts that such has ever been the case for American religious institutions.

Robert Putnam's exhaustive research into the fortunes of America's civic institutions (Putnam 1995, 2000) sheds considerable light here. During the last third of the twentieth century, the enrollment of most membership associations in the U.S.—Rotary, Elks, 4-H, American Legion, Business and Professional Women, Eastern Star, PTAs—and not just the mainline churches, declined drastically as a fraction of their target population (what religious economy scholars call their market share). And they declined for broadly similar reasons, foremost among them their failure to enroll the baby boomers and their offspring. Thus, it is not only the churches that are having trouble keeping their young people. "Looking for root causes or solutions only within the religious sphere is like the man who, faced with a flooded basement, looks for the leak in his own pipes, not realizing that the water main has broken and every house on the block is flooded" (Chaves 2000: 755). Moreover, Putnam does not see these society-wide declines as part of a longer-term secular trend—they do not represent what "modernity" does to churches and other such associations—because the during first two-thirds of the twentieth century both modernization and association-building flourished. The trajectory is one of ups and downs, "*not just downs*" (Putnam 2000: 25). Something drastic but relatively short term and potentially reversible happened in the U.S. after World War II. The associational jig is not up.[18]

In the American religious system, traditions do not simply persist. They have to be nurtured in youth, and they may be adopted by adults whose own religious nurture was insufficient or did not suit them. One thing we have learned about "religious switching" in the postwar period is that it is decreasingly related to social status and increasingly related to moral culture and religious distinctiveness (Roof and McKinney 1987; Sherkat 2001). Since the 1970s, it has been less true than it was in the 1950s that upwardly mobile people move from low-status to higher-status religious communities, the Baptist salesman eventually becoming the Episcopalian vice-president for marketing. Instead, people seem to be switching into religious communities that match their moral convictions, whether conservative or liberal, or that have something religiously distinctive to offer them. That bit of sociological knowledge should offer encouragement to religious leaders who know what it is they stand for.

The point of these observations is the paradox, if you will, that people can choose to embrace tradition, or, in other words, that tradition can be modern. For example, Reform Judaism is liturgically much more conservative today than it was a generation ago in the use of Hebrew and ritual clothing; young Reform Jews are more likely to observe Jewish religious customs (lighting Hanukkah candles, attending Seder, fasting on Yom Kippur) than are their elders (Stark and Finke 2000: 274). Yet Reform temples have many gentile converts (often wives of Jewish men) and these and other women in the congregation are now religiously enfranchised to read Torah, wear prayer shawls, and be ordained as rabbis. The Reform movement is not simply turning back the clock. Other young Jews have chosen to "return" to an Orthodoxy they had never before known (Davidman 1991). In my book on the Mendocino Presbyterians (Warner 1988), I tell the analogous story of "elective parochials," small-town people by choice with like-minded friends all over the country.

With respect to my own newly adopted church, the ELCA, "Lake Wobegon"–style ethnic Lutheranism, although strong, seems ultimately doomed in a society where ethnicity is optional. Yet Lutheranism's distinctiveness does not rest only in bland Scandinavian cooking and cool Nordic manners. Religious institutions in the U.S. flourish in part because they provide space for distinctiveness, but religious distinctiveness is more than the social grounds on which it may have arisen. I am one of those for whom, in Ammerman's words, Lutheranism is not "taken for granted . . . [as] a matter of enclave and birth" but "chosen . . . [as] a matter of faith and practice" (Ammerman 2000: 307). Congregations like mine "see their theological heritage as a gift, intentionally teach newcomers about the faith, and celebrate their own unique worship traditions" (Ammerman 2000: 307), a heritage and traditions that, in the case of my own congregation, include rich hymnody, observance of the church calendar, communion at the altar rail, Sunday evening compline, long-standing practices of religious nurture, and learned preaching. Lutheranism, as I see it in my church, entails cultural elements than can be embraced regardless of ethnicity or language, traditions that, stripped especially of any scent of racial or gendered privilege, can serve as cultural magnets to twenty-first-century Americans who did not grow up with them, as well as a treasured legacy for those who did.

NOTES

This chapter is greatly revised from its origin as a plenary address to the Lutheran Educational Conference of North America (LECNA) in Washington, D.C., on February 6, 1999. I am grateful to the staff and members of LECNA for the stimulation provided by their invitation to deliver the address and by their response to it. Thanks also to Nancy Ammerman, Lina Molokotos-Liederman, Daniel Olson, and Rev. Frank Senn for their help.

1. The article, "Work In Progress Toward a New Paradigm for the Sociological Study of Religion in the United States" (Warner 1993), appeared in *American Journal of Sociology* in March 1993. However, I began circulating it widely as soon as it was accepted for publication the previous spring. By November it was the featured work at the fall symposium of the Center for the Study of American Religion at Princeton University, attended by scores of scholars. Being cited before it was published, it has been part of "the literature" since 1992.

2. Properly, "religion in the United States." In default of a suitable adjective to refer to the U.S., I shall occasionally use "American" in this restrictive fashion.

3. For this reason, although I am pleased that Donald Miller (1997) found my ideas useful for the understanding of what he calls "new paradigm churches" (e.g., Vineyard churches), I must part company with the view the such churches represent anything truly new in American religion.

4. The "we" refers particularly to sociologists, for whom the Eurocentric "old paradigm" is more seductive than it is for American historians, for whom the ideas of the "new paradigm" are not new at all; see, e.g., Mead 1963; Carpenter 1997.

5. The following paragraphs are adapted from Warner 1997b, which contains citations to the literatures on scientific revolutions.

6. The allusion is to the "old paradigm" theories of Peter Berger (1969), for whom the concept of a "plausibility structure" is a key component in religious viability.

7. Although Weber's sociology of religion was in part intended as a refutation of Marxian theory, Weber identified himself as a political economist, and his explanatory models relied heavily on notions of individual interests and culturally defined incentive structures (Warner 1970; Warner 1972, chapter 4). Weber's *Protestant Ethic and the Spirit of Capitalism* is properly understood as a primary source document for the old paradigm, However, his companion essay on the religion he saw on his 1904 visit to the U.S., "The Protestant Sects and the Spirit of Capitalism," can be understood as a contribution to the new paradigm (Warner 1993: 1052).

8. In their most recent comprehensive overview, Stark and Finke (2000: chapters 1–2) present this idea—that religion doesn't rest on human irrationality—as the core of the new paradigm.

9. I allude to the writings of Sydney Mead (1963), another mentor of the new paradigm, whose work is hardly recent and was in fact foundational for Will Herberg's classic analysis of American religion (1960). To repeat: the "new paradigm" is a novelty in sociologists' way of looking at religion; it is not a claim about novelty in religion itself.

10. Observations about Willow Creek are based on field trips taken by my sociology of religion classes over the past fifteen years, as well as the church's own self-presentations.

11. *Caution*: Hybels's formula, how to meet the needs of "unchurched Harry," may well be specific to heavily cradle-Catholic Chicago and the baby-boom generation. Even aside from commitments to liturgical integrity, it should not be copied by other churches without thought as to its fit with local conditions.

12. Frances FitzGerald (1986) vividly portrays several such processes in her survey of 1970s and 1980s subcultures.

13. Immanuel Lutheran Church (ELCA) of Evanston, Illinois, is one of some 300 "excellent Protestant congregations" in the U.S. identified by Paul Wilkes (2001, 220) in his Parish/Congregation Study.

14. Note that neither of these hypothetical processes involves the old paradigm's "plausibility" dynamic in either direction.

15. Wuthnow's analysis is situated within the discussion of "social capital" that was set off by the work of Robert Putnam (1995) and Sidney Verba et al. (1995); see Wuthnow 1998: 2–3, 239. See also Putnam 2000.

16. Mark Chaves's (1997) analysis of the movements for and against women's ordination is admirably balanced in this regard, with the claims of neither side being religiously valorized.

17. In this regard, I regret the unjustified assumption on the part of my colleagues Rodney Stark and Roger Finke that serving the religious needs of gays and lesbians *ipso facto* represents "low tension" (highly secularized) religion, as if, for example, only the opponents of gay marriage are religiously motivated (cf. Stark and Finke 2000: 209–210, 269–270).

18. This is not the place to discuss Putnam's causal theory—he blames the advent of television and a generation raised without a sense of common peril for the decline of civic associations—nor his remedies, for his interest is the renewal of American civic life, not the fate of religion. Yet at least in one respect his prognosis deserves special scrutiny from scholars of religion. He is not sanguine about the fact that conservative Protestant institutions have been less subject to decline than liberal or mainline ones because he thinks the conservatives devote too much energy to "bonding" rather than "bridging" social capital; this is very much an arguable proposition (Putnam 2000: 22–24, 77–79, 161–162).

REFERENCES

Ammerman, Nancy T. 1997a. "Religious Choice and Religious Vitality: The Market and Beyond." In *Rational Choice Theory and Religion: Summary and Assessment*, edited by Lawrence A. Young. New York: Routledge, 119–132.

———. 1997b. "Organized Religion in a Voluntaristic Society," *Sociology of Religion* 58 (Fall): 203–216.

———. 2000. "New Life for Denominationalism," *Christian Century* 117 (March 15): 302–307.

———, Jackson Carroll, Carl Dudley, and William McKinney, eds. 1998. *Studying Congregations: A New Handbook*. Nashville: Abingdon.

Armstrong, Karen. 1993. *A History of God: The 4000–Year Quest of Judaism, Christianity, and Islam*. New York: Alfred A. Knopf.

Bankston, Carl L., III, and Min Zhou. 2000. "De Facto Congregationalism and Socioeconomic Mobility in Laotian and Vietnamese Immigrant Communities: A Study of Religious Institutions and Economic Change," *Review of Religious Research* 41 (June): 453–470.

Bellah, Robert N., Richard Madsen, William M. Sullivan, Ann Swidler, and Steven M. Tipton. 1985. *Habits of the Heart: Individualism and Commitment in American Life*. Berkeley and Los Angeles: University of California Press.

Berger, Peter L. 1969. *The Sacred Canopy: Elements of a Sociological Theory of Religion*. Garden City, N.Y.: Anchor.

Carpenter, Joel A. 1997. *Revive Us Again: The Reawakening of American Fundamentalism*. New York: Oxford University Press.

Cavendish, James C. 2000. "Church-Based Community Activism: A Comparison of Black and White Catholic Churches," *Journal for the Scientific Study of Religion* 39 (September): 371–384.

———. 2001. "To March or Not." In *Christian Clergy in American Politics*. Sue E. S. Crawford and Laura R. Olson, eds. Baltimore: Johns Hopkins University Press, 203–223.

Chai, Karen. 1998. "Competing for the Second Generation: English-Language Ministry in a Korean Protestant Church." In *Gatherings in Diaspora: Religious Communities and the New Immigration*. R. Stephen Warner and Judith G. Wittner, eds. Philadelphia: Temple University Press, 295–331.

———. 2001. "Beyond 'Strictness' to Distinctiveness: Generational Transition in Korean Protestant Churches." In *Korean Americans and Their Religions: Pilgrims and Missionaries from a Different Shore*. Ho-Youn Kwon, Kwang Chung Kim, and R. Stephen Warner, eds. University Park: Penn State University Press, 157–180.

Chaves, Mark. 1997. *Ordaining Women: Culture and Conflict in Religious Organizations*. Cambridge, Mass.: Harvard University Press.

———. 2000. "Are We 'Bowling Alone'—And Does It Matter?" *Christian Century* 117 (July 19–26): 754–756.

Chaves, Mark and Philip S. Gorski. 2001. "Religious Pluralism and Religious Participation," *Annual Review of Sociology* 27.

Chiswick, Carmel U. 1995. "The Economics of American Judaism," *Shofar* 13 (Summer): 1–19

Davidman, Lynn. 1991. *Tradition in a Rootless World: Women Turn to Orthodox Judaism*. Berkeley and Los Angeles: University of California Press.

Eiesland, Nancy L. 2000. *A Particular Place: Urban Restructuring and Religious Ecology in a Southern Exurb*. New Brunswick, N.J.: Rutgers University Press.

Finke, Roger. 1997. "The Consequences of Religious Competition: Supply-side Explanations for Religious Change." In *Rational Choice Theory and Religion: Summary and Assessment*. Lawrence A. Young, ed. New York: Routledge, 46–65.

Finke, Roger and Rodney Stark. 1992. *The Churching of America, 1776–1990: Winners and Losers in Our Religious Economy*. New Brunswick, NJ: Rutgers University Press.

———. 1998. "Religious Choice and Competition (Reply to Olson)," *American Sociological Review* 63 (December): 761–766.

FitzGerald, Frances. 1986. *Cities on a Hill: A Journey Through Contemporary American Cultures*. New York: Simon and Schuster.

Fitzgerald, Paul J. 2001. "Faithful Sociology: Peter Berger's Religious Project," *Religious Studies Review* 27 (January): 10–16.

Fletcher, Richard. 1997. *The Barbarian Conversion: From Paganism to Christianity*. New York: Henry Holt.

Goette, Robert D. 2001. "The Transformation of a First-Generation Church into a Bilingual Second-Generation Church." In *Korean Americans and Their Religions: Pilgrims and Missionaries from a Different Shore*. Ho-Youn Kwon, Kwang Chung Kim, and R. Stephen Warner, eds. University Park: Penn State University Press, 125–140.

Greeley, Andrew M. 1989. *Religious Change in America*. Cambridge, Mass.: Harvard University Press.

Harris, Frederick C. 1999. *Something Within: Religion in African-American Political Activism*. New York: Oxford University Press.

Hatch, Nathan O. 1989. *The Democratization of American Christianity*. New Haven: Yale University Press.

Hernández, Edwin. 1995. "The Browning of Adventism," *Spectrum* 25 (December): 29–50.

Herberg, Will. 1960. *Protestant, Catholic, Jew: An Essay in American Religious Sociology*. Second ed. Garden City, N.Y.: Doubleday.

Heyrman, Christine Leigh. 1998. *Southern Cross: The Beginnings of the Bible Belt*. Chapel Hill: University of North Carolina Press.

Hutchison, William R., ed. 1989. *Between the Times: The Travail of the Protestant Establishment in America, 1900–1960*. Cambridge, England: Cambridge University Press.

Iannaccone, Laurence R. 1991. "The Consequences of Religious Market Structure: Adam Smith and the Economics of Religion," *Rationality and Society* 3 (April): 156–177.

———. 1994. "Why Strict Churches Are Strong," *American Journal of Sociology* 99 (March): 1180–1211.

Kuhn, Thomas S. 1970. *The Structure of Scientific Revolutions*. Second edition. Chicago: University of Chicago Press.

Lawson, Ronald. 1998. "From American Church to Immigrant Church: The Changing Face of Seventh-day Adventism in Metropolitan New York," *Sociology of Religion* 59 (Winter): 329–351.

McRoberts, Omar M. 1999. "Understanding the 'New' Black Pentecostal Acticism: Lessons from Ecumenical Urban Ministries in Boston," *Sociology of Religion* 60 (Spring): 47–70.

———. 2000. *Saving Four Corners: Religion and Revitalization in a Depressed Neighborhood*. Ph.D. dissertation, Harvard University Department of Sociology.

Mead, Sidney E. 1963. *The Lively Experiment*. New York: Harper and Row.

Miller, Donald E. 1997. *Reinventing American Protestantism: Christianity in the New Millennium*. Berkeley: University of California Press.

Molokotos-Liederman, Lina. 2001. "Identity Crisis: Greece, the European Union, and Religious Nationalism." Paper presented at annual meetings of the Association for the Sociology of Religion, Anaheim.

Morris, Aldon D. 1984. *The Origins of the Civil Rights Movement: Black Communities Organizing for Change*. New York: The Free Press.

Neitz, Mary Jo. 1990. "Studying Religion in the Eighties." In *Symbolic Interaction and Cultural Studies*. Howard S. Becker and Michal M. McCall, eds. Chicago: University of Chicago Press, 90–118.

Neitz, Mary Jo and Peter R. Mueser. 1997. "Economic Man and the Sociology of Religion: A Critique of the Rational Choice Approach," In *Rational Choice Theory and Religion: Summary and Assessment*, Lawrence A. Young, ed. New York: Routledge, 105–118.

Niebuhr, H. Richard. 1929. *The Social Sources of Denominationalism*. New York: Henry Holt.

Olson, Daniel. 2000. "Religious Pluralism and Church Involvement: Steps in the Exploration of a Changing Relationship." Paper presented at the spring meeting of the Chicago-Area Group for the Study of Religious Communities.

Pattillo-McCoy, Mary. 1998. "Church Culture as a Strategy of Action in the Black Community," *American Sociological Review* 63 (December): 767–784.

Perry, Troy D. 1972. *The Lord Is My Shepherd and He Knows I'm Gay*. Los Angeles: Nash.

Perry, Troy D. and Thomas L. P. Swicegood. 1990. *Don't Be Afraid Anymore: The Story of Reverend Troy Perry and the Metropolitan Community Churches*. New York: St. Martin's Press.

Princeton Religion Research Center. 1988. *The Unchurched American—Ten Years Later*. Princeton, N.J.: Princeton Religion Research Center.

Putnam, Robert D. 1995. "Bowling Alone: America's Declining Social Capital," *Journal of Democracy* 6 (1): 65–78.

———. 2000. *Bowling Alone: The Collapse and Revival of American Community*. New York: Simon and Schuster.

Roof, Wade Clark. 1978. *Community and Commitment: Religious Plausibility in a Liberal Protestant Church*. New York: Elsevier.

———. 1999. *Spiritual Marketplace: Baby Boomers and the Remaking of American Religion*. Princeton, N.J.: Princeton University Press.

Roof, Wade Clark and William McKinney. 1987. *American Mainline Religion: Its Changing Shape and Future*. New Brunswick, N.J.: Rutgers University Press.

Sherkat, Darren E. 2001. "Tracking the Restructuring of American Religion: Religious Affiliation and Patterns of Religious Mobility, 1973–1998," *Social Forces* 79 (June): 1459–1493.

Smith, Christian, with Michael Emerson, Sally Gallagher, Paul Kennedy, and David Sikkink. 1998. *American Evangelicalism: Embattled and Thriving*. Chicago: University of Chicago Press.

Stark, Rodney. 1996. *The Rise of Christianity: How the Obscure, Marginal Jesus Movement Became the Dominant Religious Force in the Western World in a Few Centuries*. Princeton, N.J.: Princeton University Press.

Stark, Rodney and Roger Finke. 2000. *Acts of Faith: Explaining the Human Side of Religion*. Berkeley: University of California Press.

Voas, David, Daniel V. A. Olson, and Alasdair Crockett. 2001. "Studies of Religious Pluralism and Participation: Was Everybody Wrong?" Paper to be presented at annual meetings of the Society for the Scientific Study of Religion, Columbus, Ohio.

Verba, Sidney, Kay Lehman Schlozman, and Henry E. Brady. 1995. *Voice and Equality: Civic Voluntarism in American Politics*. Cambridge, Mass.: Harvard University Press.

———. 1972. *The Methodology of Max Weber's Comparative Studies*. Unpublished Ph.D. dissertation; University of California at Berkeley.

———. 1988. *New Wine in Old Wineskins: Evangelicals and Liberals in a Small-Town Church*. Berkeley and Los Angeles: University of California Press.

———. 1993. "Work In Progress Toward a New Paradigm for the Sociological Study of Religion in the United States," *American Journal of Sociology* 98 (March): 1044–1093.

———. 1994. "The Place of the Congregation in the American Religious Configuration." In *New Perspectives in the Study of Congregations* (vol. 2 of *American Congregations*), James P. Wind and James W. Lewis, eds. Chicago: University of Chicago Press, 54–99.

———. 1995. "The Metropolitan Community Churches and the Gay Agenda: The Power of Pentecostalism and Essentialism." In *Sex, Lies, and Sanctity: Religion and Deviance in Contemporary North America*. Mary Jo Neitz and Marion S. Goldman, eds. Greenwich, Conn.: JAI Press, 81–108.

———. 1997a. "Convergence Toward the New Paradigm: A Case of Induction." In *Rational Choice Theory and Religion: Summary and Assessment*. Lawrence A. Young, ed. New York: Routledge, 87–101.

———. 1997b "A Paradigm Is Not a Theory: Reply to Lechner," *American Journal of Sociology* 103 (July): 192–198.

———. 1998a. "Immigration and Religious Communities in the United States." Introduction to *Gatherings in Diaspora: Religious Communities and the New Immigration*. R. Stephen Warner and Judith G. Wittne, eds. Philadelphia: Temple University Press, 3–34.

———. 1998b. "Approaching Religious Diversity: Barriers, Byways, and Beginnings" (1997 Presidential Address to the Association for the Sociology of Religion), *Sociology of Religion* 59 (Fall): 193–215.

———. 2000. "Religion and New (Post-1965) Immigrants: Some Principles Drawn from Field Research," *American Studies* 41 (Summer/Fall): 267–286.

———. 2001a. "The Korean Immigrant Church as Case and Model." In *Korean Americans and Their Religions: Pilgrims and Missionaries From a Different Shore*. Ho-Youn Kwon, Kwang Chung Kim, and R. Stephen Warner, eds. University Park: Penn State University Press, 25–52.

———. 2001b. "Ambiguity and Ambivalence in Discourse over the 'Generation Gap' in Religion." Paper prepared for the annual meeting of the Society for the Scientific Study of Religion, Columbus, Ohio.

Warner, R. Stephen, Elise Martel, and Rhonda Dugan. 2001. "Catholicism Is to Islam as Velcro Is to Teflon: Religion and Ethnic Culture Among Second Generation Latina and Muslim Women College Students." Unpublished paper; Youth and Religion Project, University of Illinois at Chicago.

Wilcox, Melissa M. 2000. "When Sheila's a Lesbian: Religious Individualism among Lesbian, Gay, Bisexual, and Transgendered Christians." Paper presented at annual meetings of the Society for the Scientific Study of Religion, Houston.

Wilkes, Paul. 2001. *Excellent Protestant Congregations: The Guide to Best Places and Practices*. Louisville, Ky.: Westminster John Knox.

Williams, Rhys H. and Gira Vashi. 2001. "Hijab and American Muslim Women: Creating the Space for Autonomous Selves." Paper presented at annual meetings of the Midwest Sociological Society, St. Louis, Mo., April.

Wuthnow, Robert. 1988. *The Restructuring of American Religion: Society and Faith Since World War II*. Princeton, N.J.: Princeton University Press.

———. 1998. *Loose Connections: Joining Together in America's Fragmented Communities*. Cambridge, Mass.: Harvard University Press.

2

Beyond Church and Sect: Dynamics and Stability in Religious Economics

Rodney Stark and Roger Finke

The rapidly growing literature on religious economies suffers from too narrow a focus on several of our key propositions and pays far too little attention to the more complex theoretical structure within which they are embedded. Not only does this lead to misunderstanding, it also fails to reveal the truly immense array of research findings made coherent by the full theory and which, in turn, give it substantial credibility. Consequently, we shall not limit this essay to the several propositions concerning pluralism, but will spell out the entire theoretical model of religious economies.

What follows is not simply excerpts from earlier publications. The model presented here is significantly more refined even than the version in *Acts of Faith* (Stark and Finke 2000) and, of course, the pertinent evidence continues to grow rapidly.

During the past few years a great deal of effort had been devoted by many social scientists to constructing dynamic models of religious economies (Warner 1993). Taking Niebuhr's (1929) theory of the transformation of sects into churches as one of its primary starting points, this work emphasizes *change* and is focussed on the *supply*-side of religious economies—on the behavior of religious organizations. Consequently, too little attention has been given to the *demand*-side, to the preferences of religious "consumers" and thus to the basis of *stability* in religious economies and how this relates to the church-sect dynamic—an omission to be found in our early work on this topic. More recent versions of our model address these omissions by attending to the demand-side of the religious marketplace as a source of stability while continuing the emphasis on the supply-side as the principal engine of change. We propose that the demand-side of the market consists of a quite stable and distinctive set of market niches, while on the supply-side we observe the shift of religious bodies from niche to niche with the consequence that groups rise and fall in terms of their market shares.

To illustrate just how fundamental is the shift of emphasis we propose, consider that when confronted with major shifts in the religious composition of societies—as when Buddhism swept China or when the Methodists churched America—proponents of the older paradigm usually pose the basic question as: *Why did people's religious preferences change?* Why did they abandon one religious institution (or set of institutions) for another? That seems an entirely reasonable question. Yet, when posed this way we are directed to seek our answer in shifting demand—to conclude such changes occur because people suddenly develop new, unmet religious needs and turn to or produce new religious institutions able to meet these needs.

Not only do we think this is the wrong answer, we think it answers the wrong question. We suggest that religious demand is very stable over time and that religious change is largely the product of supply-side transformations. Hence, we would pose the fundamental question this way: *Why do religious organizations change so that they no longer enjoy mass appeal?*

To begin, three basic concepts must be defined:

Religion: any system of beliefs and practices concerned with ultimate meaning that assumes the existence of the supernatural.

Religious Organizations or *Firms*: social enterprises whose primary purpose is to create, maintain, and supply religion to some set of individuals.

Religious Economy: consists of all the religious activity going on in any society. Religious economies are like commercial economies in that they consist of a market of current and potential customers, a set of organizations or firms seeking to serve that market, and the religion offered by the various organizations (Stark 1985a).

For reasons we shall never fully understand, a number of critics have chosen to misrepresent our use of the term "religious economy" as a descent into vulgar materialism with utter disregard for the sacred aspects of faith (Bruce 1999; Demerath 1995; Marty 1993: 88).[1] In this essay, as in all our previous work, faith and doctrine are central to our efforts to construct a model of the behavior of religious firms within a religious economy. To begin, we will anchor the model in demand and pursue the implications of the principle that, other things being equal, the inherent diversity of demand requires a diversity in supply. Having developed a set of eleven propositions, we then review evidence relevant to the key hypotheses that derive from these propositions. The second major theoretical section of the chapter develops eighteen propositions devoted primarily to the supply-side and which greatly expand church-sect theory to encompass the whole range of options facing religious firms. We then review the evidence pertinent to this portion of our model.

IMPLICATIONS OF THE DIVERSITY OF RELIGIOUS DEMAND

All religious economies are anchored in generic patterns of demand:

1. *All religious economies include a set of relatively stable market niches.*

Niches are market segments of potential adherents sharing particular religious preferences (needs, tastes, and expectations).

We postulate the existence of *stable* preferences as an antidote to the temptation to account for every shift in religious life by postulating a corresponding shift in public preferences. The result of such ad hoc explanations is to beg all of the important issues, as is so frequently illustrated by studies of American religious history. An immense literature, by sociologists and political scientists as well as historians, is written almost entirely from the point of view of a public constantly shifting its religious preferences in response to all manner of social crises and natural disasters. For example, the American "Great Awakenings" that are claimed to have taken place during the middle eighteenth and early nineteenth centuries are credited to a sudden, generalized need for more intense religion because people were subject to "grave personal stress" (McLoughlin 1978: 2) due to such things as floods, epidemics, crop failures, financial panics, financial booms, the incursions of a market economy, industrialization, rapid immigration, and so on (Barkun 1986; Gordon-McCutchan 1983; Thomas 1989). But, a far more plausible interpretation of these "awakenings" makes no mention of any changes in preferences or of the impact of social or natural crises (Butler 1982, 1990; Finke and Stark 1992; Lambert 1990; Smith 1983). Instead, these scholars trace the revivals in question to supply-side innovations. Religious organizations led by George Whitefield in the eighteenth century and Charles Finney in the nineteenth used vigorous and effective marketing techniques to sustain revival campaigns, which later historians have classified as "awakenings." In contrast to scholars who explain that "the times" were right for huge crowds to "materialize" to hear Whitefield, for example, the new interpretation stresses that Whitefield's very elaborate marketing efforts caused the crowds to materialize. Indeed, as we introduce additional propositions, it will become evident that what Whitefield accomplished was not to change preferences, but to appeal successfully to preferences going essentially unserved in the highly regulated American religious economy of his time—something which he fully recognized, remarking during his visit to Boston in 1740, "I am persuaded, the generality of preachers [in New England] talk of an unknown and unfelt Christ. The reason why congregations have been so dead, is because they have had dead men preach to them" (Whitefield 1969: 471).

Thus, while we propose to pay much closer attention to the demand-side of religious economies, we assume that religious preferences are quite stable and form distinctive and durable niches.

The growing literature on niches and voluntary associations (Blau 1977, 1994; McPherson 1981; McPherson and Smith-Lovin 1987; McPherson, Popielarz and McPherson 1995) stresses the "homophily principle"—that people tend to associate with people similar to themselves and that voluntary organizations are rooted in specific homophilous niches. This literature stresses "sociodemographic characteristics" as the basis for niche homophily. As will be seen, to some extent religious niche homophily does involve such characteristics, but these are much less significant than a *homophily of preferences*.

To the degree that a religious economy is unregulated and market forces prevail, these niches will be quite visible and, as we shall see, each will sustain a set of specialized religious bodies. However, even in highly regulated religious economies limited to a single monopoly faith these niches will exist, if less distinctly. Under these conditions some major niches will lack suitable religious options and thus will serve as a current basis for religious apathy and resentment and as a future basis of potential change.

Recently, Popielarz and McPherson (1995) proposed that voluntary organizations remain relatively fixed in social space because they "lose members at the edge of the niche faster than in the center. This differential loss of members at the edge of the niche keeps groups from spreading unchecked in social space." But, that "rule" has very limited application to religious organizations, precisely because they *do not* remain fixed in social space. It is not church-switching that is the primary dynamic in religious economies. Rather, it is *the shifting of religious firms from niche to niche* that has the greatest impact on the overall economy with the consequence that the primary religious suppliers change over time. Thus, rather than ask why so many people abandoned Congregationalism (and did so long before it changed its name to the United Church of Christ), we suggest that we ask why did the Congregational Church abandon a relatively large market niche, progressively shifting to smaller niches notable for the lukewarm commitment of their consumers (Finke and Stark 1992)?

We also shall attempt to explain that the stability and dynamics of religious economies are interdependent. Stability consists of the durability of niches in terms of their relative size and the character of their demand. Within free-market religious economies, the dynamic of niche-switching by firms ensures that each niche is effectively supplied.

All discussion of niches and niche-switching presupposes the fundamental notion of church-sect theory: that there is a clear axis of variation. The most useful and parsimonious conceptualization of the church-sect axis was provided by Benton Johnson (1963):

2. *All religious groups can be located along an axis of tension between the group and its socio-cultural environment.*

Churches are religious bodies in relatively lower tension with their surroundings while *sects* are religious bodies in relatively higher tension (see Iannaccone 1988 for a formal derivation of this proposition). *Tension* consists of differences in norms and values and refers to the degree of distinctiveness, separation, and antagonism in the relationship between a religious group and the "outside" world (Stark and Bainbridge 1980, 1985). Put another way, the higher the tension between a religious group and its surroundings *the more costly it is to belong*. As Laurence Iannaccone (1992) pointed out, these costs can be separated into stigmas and sacrifices. *Stigmas* are costs imposed on members by outsiders as reflected in nouns such as "cultists," "heretics," or "fanatics." *Sacrifices* consist of the things that members must do (contribute funds, shave their heads, or burn incense), or refrain from doing (thou shalt not . . .), in order to remain in good standing. It is far less costly to belong to a church than to a sect.

Note that in this essay we ignore the distinction between cults and sects, which classifies groups on the basis of whether their religion is rooted in the dominant religious traditions of the society in which they are being observed (sects), or whether they represent a novel or alien religious tradition (cults). Although this distinction is crucial for some purposes (cf. Stark 1996b), here it suffices to distinguish groups only according to their tension with their socio-cultural environment.

The tension dimension not only provides a clear axis for analyzing the supply-side of religious economies, it also serves to organize the demand-side efficiently. Suppose we ranked people according to their preference for intense religion. The result would approximate a bell-shaped curve in that people would cluster towards the center of the axis in the area of medium tension, as shown in Figure 1. Of course, the real world is probably somewhat lumpier than this, but it seems reasonable to assume that to the extent that people prefer levels of intensity that are higher or the lower than medium, the less numerous they will be.

In every known society, people have differed in how much religious intensity they prefer. Weber recognized this sort of variation, but explained it in terms of personal abilities or charisma (1993: 162), "That people differ greatly in their religious capacities was found to be true in every religion . . . not everyone possesses the charisma that makes possible the continuous maintenance in everyday life of the distinctive religious mood." We can avoid the implicit circularity which often mars Weber's use of the term "charisma" if we distinguish people on the basis of their preferences rather than in terms of some imputed semi-magical or psychic power. That is, rather than focus on religious capacities, it seems far more efficient to settle for the observation that some people always want the religious rewards available only from high tension (strict) religion (Iannaccone 1988, 1994) and are willing to pay high costs to obtain them, others want very low intensity and inexpensive faith, while most people want religion that maintains some moral reservations vis-à-vis secular life, but not too many.

This variation in demand is obvious in an unregulated religious economy with highly developed competition and specialization. It is less obvious in highly regulated and monopolized religious economies where the preferences of many niches go unmet. But, even in these societies, the existence of niches wishing higher and lower tension options shows up as the never-ending line of heretical challengers to the monopoly, some offering higher-tension faith and some proposing more worldly faiths. Put another way, in monopoly situations religious deviants seem to have little trouble finding receptive consumers.

It is far easier to describe the array of market niches than it is to explain why they exist. Sociologists mostly have been content to attribute diversity in religious taste to social class, despite the fact that empirical studies have found only very weak class effects on religious preferences (Demerath 1965; Stark 1965, 1971). Indeed, the received wisdom that the lower classes prefer higher-tension faith is offset by the fact that the lower classes are least active in any form of religion, while historically it has been the upper classes that have been most prone to adopt extremely ascetic forms of faith (Stark, forthcoming a). Unfortunately, the misplaced emphasis on class has deflected our attention from factors that do have strong and consistent impact on religious preferences, many of which cross-cut social class. Indeed, socialization effects tower above everything else: Most people resemble their parents in terms of their religious preferences and participation (Cornwall 1988; Sherkat and Wilson 1995; Sherkat 1996; Wallace 1975). In addition, women seem more inclined than men to favor higher-tension faiths (Miller and Hoffman 1995; Stark in press). A similar preference for higher tension is typical of disadvantaged racial and ethnic minorities (Argyle and Beit-Hallahmi 1975; Ellison and Sherkat 1995; Yinger 1957). Nor should one overlook existential factors stemming from particular life events (Ellison 1991, 1993; Wallace 1975; Yinger 1957, 1970). For example, some people have their religious tastes intensified by crises and subsequently attribute many positive benefits to their faith (Iannaccone 1988). Others develop a preference for a particular niche on the basis of experiences such as participating in secular social movements (Sherkat 1998).

In any event, we shall assume the existence of a stable distribution of diversity of religious demand and will identify clusters of persons with shared preferences as market niches. The importance of these niches for the overall religious economy lies in the fact that they make it impossible for one religious organization to satisfy demand. We now explain why this is so.

3. *To the degree that a religious economy is unregulated, it will tend to be very pluralistic (limited by redundancy).*

Pluralistic refers *to the number of firms active in the economy; the more firms having a significant market-share, the greater the degree of pluralism.*

Degree of pluralism must be assessed from the point-of-view of the individual and thus is a local phenomenon, limited to an easily travelled area. Thus, a large area may have many religious firms, but any locale within that area may offer few choices, and hence be lacking in pluralism.

Redundancy refers *to an excess of firms beyond the number needed to fully serve all market niches.*

In unregulated economies redundancy often imposes severe pressures on religious firms located at both the highest and lowest tension ends of the religious spectrum. At the high end, redundancy causes intense competition which emphasizes theological differences, and because there are far more firms than the market can sustain, the vast majority of sects never amount to much. At the low tension end, redundancy encourages mergers (Nauta 1994).

4. *The capacity of a single religious firm to monopolize a religious economy depends upon the degree to which the state uses coercive force to regulate the religious economy.*

Variations in *demand* result in the inherent inability of a single religious product line to satisfy divergent tastes. More specifically, pluralism arises in unregulated markets because of the inability of a single religious firm to be at once worldly and otherworldly, strict and permissive, exclusive and inclusive, expressive and reserved, while market niches will exist with strong preferences on each of these aspects of religion. Other things being equal, diversity of demand will result in diversity of supply. Thus, no single religious organization can achieve monopoly through voluntary assent—religious monopolies rest upon coercion.

By the same logic, it becomes clear that religious economies never can be fully monopolized, even when backed by the full coercive powers of the state. Indeed, even at the height of its temporal power, the medieval church was surrounded by heresy and dissent (Lambert 1990; Stark 2001). Of course, when the repressive efforts of the state are sufficiently intense, religious firms competing with the state-sponsored monopoly will be forced to operate underground. But, whenever and wherever repression eases, pluralism will begin to develop. And this pluralism will be sustained by specialized religious firms, each anchored in a specific niche or a complementary set of niches.

5. *To the degree that a religious firm achieves a monopoly, it will seek to exert its influence over other institutions and thus the society will be sacralized.*

Sacralized means *that there will be little differentiation between religious and secular institutions and that the primary aspects of life, from family to politics, will be suffused with religious symbols, rhetoric, and ritual.*

Sacralization is precisely the social phenomenon that so often is mistaken for universal piety. The "Age of Faith" attributed to medieval Europe, for example, is based on the fact that religion was intertwined with other institutions, especially politics and education, and because the presence of religion was so impressively visible. Travelling across Europe today, one's attention constantly is drawn to the magnificent churches and cathedrals that dominate local landscapes. Because all these buildings were built many centuries ago, they seem to offer undeniable proof that once-upon-a-time faith was so universal and robust as to erect these marvelous structures. The truth is quite different. These structures were, in effect, extracted from an unwilling and sullen populace who seldom crossed their thresholds—at least not for religious purposes (Stark 1999). It was because of the piety and self-interest of the medieval ruling classes that religion was so omnipresent and visible on all public occasions. For example, all ceremonies were religious in character, especially political ceremonies such as coronations. Indeed, in sacralized societies political leadership per se typically has a vivid religious hue, as in the "divine right" of kings and emperors. Close ties between religious and political elites are inherent in religious monopolies since without such ties religious monopolies are impossible. Sacralization of the political sphere is the *quid pro quo* by which a religious firm enlists the coercive powers of the state against its competitors (Smith [1776] 1981).

6. *To the degree that deregulation of the religious economy occurs in a previously highly regulated economy, the society will be desacralized.*

When the state, for whatever reasons, no longer ensures claims of exclusive legitimacy by the monopoly faith, desacralization must ensue. Where there are a plurality of religious firms, no one of them is sufficiently potent to sustain sacralization.[2] Nor can sacralization be sustained by some coalition of competing religious firms, for any statements emitted by such a group must be limited to vague generalizations to which all can assent. Perhaps such is the stuff of "civil religion" (Bellah 1967), but it is not the stuff of sacralization. But then, neither is it necessarily a symptom of religious decline.

Desacralization, as we define it, is identical to what many scholars have referred to as the macro form of *secularization*. So long as this definition of secularization is limited to the differentiation of religious and other primary social institutions, we accept it. However, few who apply the term secularization to institutional differentiation are able to resist linking desacralization to a general decline in individual religious commitment (the micro version of secularization), because they are convinced that only religious monopolies can sustain belief. We take the entirely opposite position. Our model of religious economies holds that the demise of religious monopolies and the deregulation of religious economies will result in a general *increase* in individual religious commitment, as more firms (and more motivated firms) gain free access to the market.

Keep in mind that there will be a lag between the onset of desacralization and the rise of a vigorous religious pluralism. Thus, although the Roman Catholic Church, for example, has been stripped of its monopoly standing and much of its temporal power in many parts of Europe and Latin America, this did not *immediately* create unregulated religious economies filled with eager firms competing for souls. Considerable desacralization will tend to occur before there is sufficient pluralism to greatly increase religious participation. Thus, over the short term, desacralization can give the *appearance* of secularization. We must emphasize, however, that this sort of "secularization" is temporary and largely limited to a decline in religious participation—it never is the "extinction" of religion proposed by the standard theories of secularization.

Many factors can slow the development of vigorous pluralism. For one thing, deregulation of a religious economy often is more apparent than real (Stark and Finke 2000). The government may announce a policy of religious freedom, or at least of religious toleration, but continue to grant special privileges and financial aid to the traditional monopoly firm, while imposing many hindrances upon new firms. Fully developed pluralism can thus be distorted and delayed by de facto establishment.

In addition, cultural inertia (tradition) will delay the acceptance of new firms as normal and legitimate. The stigmas attached to its competitors by the old monopoly faith will linger, sustaining various forms of prejudice and discrimination against new firms (Stark and Finke 2000).

Another cause of delay in the development of pluralism is that, to the extent that new firms are branches of outside firms, their success must await the development of social ties between missionaries and locals because network ties must exist or be created in order for religious firms to attract members. Thus, for example, American Evangelical Protestant missionaries have been active in Latin America for decades, but growth was extremely slow until after World War II when the primary missionary work was progressively taken over by local converts. Subsequently, growth has been so rapid that by now Evangelical Protestant bodies claim very substantial followings in most of the continent—in many nations Protestants now make up the majority of those actually in church on Sunday (Gill 1998; Stoll 1990; Martin 1990).

Finally, it must be recognized that much of the "decline" in commitment that accompanies desacralization is illusory. Monopoly churches always manage to appear vastly more popular and pervasive than they actually are. A major effect of desacralization in Europe and Latin America may have been to *reveal* widespread apathy, rather than to reflect a decline in piety. Keep in mind too that monopolists always claim that should they be dislodged, religious life will suffer (and social scientists have been too quick to believe them).

7. *To the degree that religious economies are unregulated and competitive, overall levels of religious participation will be high.* (Conversely,

lacking competition, the dominant firm(s) will be too inefficient to sustain vigorous marketing efforts and the result will be a low overall level of religious participation.)

Notice our theoretical emphasis on *competition*. Religious pluralism (the presence of multiple suppliers) is important *only* insofar as it increases choices and competition, offering consumers a wider range of religious rewards and forcing suppliers to be more responsive and efficient. A society whose religious economy consists of a dozen rigid castes, each served by its own independent, distinctive religious firm, would be highly pluralistic, but utterly lacking in religious competition. Functionally, the situation of any given individual in such a society would be identical with the situation of an individual in a society having only one, monopoly religious firm. And our prediction would be the same: that within each caste there would be the same low levels of religious commitment as are expected in monopolized religious economies. Pluralism and competition usually are linked, but when they are not, it is competition that is the energizing force. Misunderstanding of this point seems to have arisen because, lacking direct measures of competition, measures of pluralism often have been used as proxy measures of competition.

It also is important to recognize that sometimes *conflict can substitute for competition* as the basis for creating aggressive religious firms able to generate high overall levels of religious commitment.

8. *Even where competition is limited, religious firms can generate high levels of participation to the extent that the firms serve as the primary organizational vehicles for social conflict.* (Conversely, if religious firms become significantly less important as vehicles for social conflict, they will be correspondingly less able to generate commitment.)

Consider the example of the society noted above in which a dozen rigid castes each has its own religious firm. Now suppose there is a high level of conflict among these castes and that the religious firms serve as the organizational basis for these conflicts. Perhaps the temples serve as the gathering place for planning all political action, that protest demonstrations begin at the temples, and religious symbols are used to identify caste solidarity. In these situations religious commitment would be inseparable from group loyalty, just as high levels of Catholic commitment in Ireland and Quebec symbolized and sustained opposition to the English ruling elites in both societies. For generations, Catholic piety was inseparable from Irish and French-Canadian nationalism. The same principle applies to Islamic "fundamentalism." Opposition to political, economic, and cultural colonialism has found its firmest institutional basis in the mosque.

Three additional propositions conclude this portion of the theory:

9. *Societies having low levels of religious participation will be lacking in effective religious socialization.*

Effective religious socialization is sustained not by what parents may believe, but by the exposure of children to organized religion—even "primitive" societies utilize elaborate religious initiations to instill faith and doctrine. Where parents seldom or never take part in organized religion, religious socialization lags and this is exacerbated where the dominant religious firm(s) are inefficient and lack vigor. That Europe's medieval upper classes were far more pious than the peasantry can be explained almost entirely by the fact that only upper-class children regularly participated in organized religion and received formal religious education (Stark forthcoming b).

10. *Where large numbers of people receive ineffective religious socialization, subjective religiousness will tend to be idiosyncratic and heterodox, but will be far more widespread than will organized religious participation.*

Most medieval peasants worshipped a jumble of supernatural beings, only some of them Christian, but belief in such supernatural beings was far more widespread than was mass attendance (Stark and Finke 2000). In similar fashion, Grace Davie (1994) perceptively described contemporary Europeans as "believing non-belongers."

11. *The capacity of new religious firms to successfully enter relatively unregulated markets is inverse to the efficiency and variety of existing religious firms.*

Other things being equal, new firms may enter any market only to the extent that opportunity exists either because of weak competition from firms already in place or because of unserved or underserved niches in the market. Anything that results in inefficiency among existing religious firms, or in an unserved market niche, will ease the entry of new firms. The reference to relatively unregulated markets is to call attention to the fact that start-up costs for new religious firms will be high when the state represses challengers to an established faith. But, the larger point is that entry also will be difficult (albeit usually less dangerous) when the market is saturated with efficient firms. Thus, the relationship between the degree of regulation of a religious economy and start-up costs for new religious firms is curvilinear, declining as the state exerts less coercion on behalf of a monopoly firm, but rising again as fully developed pluralism results in a crowded marketplace of effective and competitive firms.

This completes the first portion of the theory.

EVIDENCE

This summary of pertinent evidence is organized by a series of hypotheses that derive from the above propositions.

H1. The more intense the competition among firms within any religious economy, the higher the overall level of individual religious participation.

It is this claim about the effects of competition that has generated so much research and provoked such heated antagonism—as will be clear in some of the following chapters. But for all of the controversy, the fact is that few current theoretical propositions in the sociology of religion enjoy nearly so extensive an empirical basis.

The degree of competition has been inferred from the extent of pluralism (using multiple indicators) and the amount of state regulation of a religious economy. The pertinent studies are remarkable for their cross-cultural and temporal diversity, having confirmed the hypothesis in: the 942 towns and villages of New York in 1855 and 1865 (Finke, Guest, and Stark 1996); American cities in 1890, 1906, and 1926 (Finke 1992; Finke and Stark 1988); a sample of small American towns and villages in the 1920s (Brunner 1927); the developed Protestant nations (Iannaccone 1991; Chaves and Cann 1992); the 284 municipalities of Sweden (Hamberg and Pettersson 1994, 1997; Petterson and Hamberg 1997); the counties of England and Wales and the 48 registration districts of Wales in 1851 (Stark, Finke, and Iannaccone 1995); in contrasts between Germans and German-Americans (Stark 1997); in nations where religious regulations have been lifted (Finke 1990; Finke and Iannaccone 1993; Gill 1994 and 1998; Greeley 1994; Iannaccone, Finke, and Stark 1998; Stark and Iannaccone 1994); in nations having appreciable Muslim communities (Chaves, Schraeder, and Sprindys 1994); in the nations of the world (Duke, Johnson, and Duke 1993).

A recent communication from Massimo Introvigne (2001) seems worth specific note. Italy thoroughly deregulated its religious economy in the early 1980s. This not only facilitated Protestant groups, but, when faced with a credible competitive threat, there was an eruption of renewal efforts among Roman Catholics, especially by unofficial Catholic associations. As a result, attendance rates have risen quite substantially in Italy, especially among Catholics.

The source of controversy surrounding this hypothesis has been over the relationship between religious involvement and a single measure of religious pluralism called the diversity or Herfindahl index. Several studies using the index, especially those analyzing contemporary North American data where religious pluralism is uniformly high or those failing to control for Catholics, have reported results contrary to the hypothesis (Blau, Land, and Redding 1992; Breault 1989; Land, Deane, and Blau 1991; Olson 1998, 1999; Olson and Hadaway 1999). Olson's cross-sectional research on pluralism and involvement was been described by Chaves and Gorski (2001) as "decisively" refuting the hypothesis.

But Olson and co-authors David Voas and Alasdair Crockett recently concluded: "results from previous cross-sectional studies on pluralism and religious involvement must now be abandoned" due to a "mathematical relationship between measures of religious participation and the index of pluralism (Voas, Olson, and Crockett forthcoming). Regardless of the outcome of this most recent debate, however, the hypothesis has been supported using multiple measures of competition. And, as we have pointed out in the past, the diversity index has many limitations in measuring competition. One of the most serious is the ceiling effect of religious pluralism.

H2. Redundancy creates a ceiling effect: above a certain level, increased pluralism does not increase the overall level of individual commitment.

As with any market, there is a saturation point beyond which additional choices do not increase the level of consumption. This was a key finding in our study of New York towns and villages (Finke, Guest, and Stark 1996). Pettersson and Hamberg (1997) found a ceiling effect in their longitudinal study of pluralism and commitment in Sweden. This is a matter of great importance for all attempts to test the hypothesis on contemporary American data: *most American communities would seem to offer sufficient pluralism to satisfy diverse demand and produce effective competition*, hence pluralism is effectively a constant, and correlations between the number of churches per capita and commitment probably will be zero.

H3. Individual religious groups will be more energetic and produce higher levels of commitment to the degree that they have a marginal market position (e.g., lack market share).

That is, other things being equal, small religious minorities will be more vigorous than will religious groups with a large local following. Catholics display higher levels of commitment in places where Catholics are few, be it American dioceses (Stark 1998; Stark and McCann 1993), all nations having a significant number of Catholics (Stark 1992), or European nations (Jelen and Wilcox 1998). Canadian Catholics are more active, the lower the percentage of Catholics in their province (Bibby 1987; Stark and Iannaccone 1996) and the same holds for the major regions of Italy (Pisati 1998). Indeed, Catholics in Northern Ireland are substantially more religious than are Catholics in noncompetitive Ireland.

The hypothesis also is sustained for European and American Protestants. European Protestants are more active in Catholic than in Protestant nations (Iannaccone 1991), and a study of five major American denominations, including Assemblies of God, Southern Baptist Convention, Evangelical Lutheran Church of America, Roman Catholic, and the Presbyterian Church, USA, reports that membership commitment increases as the denomination's market share declines (Perl and Olson 2000). Likewise, American Jews give more generously to Jewish charities in American cities having few Jews (Silberstein et al. 1987).

A recent study of Mormons seems inconsistent with the hypothesis—Mormons outside Utah are a bit less religious than those living in Utah where they are the majority (Phillips 1998). We could suggest several plausible reasons for this exception. Perhaps it is the less-committed Mormons who are more likely to leave Utah, and highly committed converts who move there. Or, in Utah the social costs of being seen as a less-committed or uncommitted member may be far higher than in a community where Mormons are few. Whatever the case, we find it extremely significant that major Protestant bodies respond to their minority status in Utah with elevated levels of commitment. In forthcoming work we will show that groups such as the Southern Baptists and United Methodists have substantially higher levels of commitment in Utah, where they are faced with competition from an intensely conversionist Mormon Church, than do their co-religionists elsewhere in the nation.

Finally, Fenggang Yang and Helen Rose Ebaugh (2001) have documented how new immigrant religions have been energized by being immersed in the competitive American religious economy, in particular by adopting American religious organizational forms and outreach tactics.

H4. Social conflict can substitute for competition in generating high levels of commitment.

This not only is supported by the high levels of Catholic commitment displayed in Poland, Ireland, and Quebec, but by the corresponding declines in commitment as the pertinent conflicts have waned (Stark and Iannaccone 1996). It is plausible too that the high levels of Mormon commitment in Utah (noted above) is due a greater sense of historic conflicts and persecutions.

H5. The success of new religious movements will be inverse to the efficiency and diversity of existing competitors.

This was one of the earliest predictions from the theory and was confirmed in a series of studies finding that new religious movements did far better in those areas of the United States and Canada where the "conventional" churches were weaker (Bainbridge and Stark 1982; Nock 1987; Stark and Bainbridge 1980, 1981b; Stark and Finke 2000). Indeed, Reginald Bibby (2000) has found that even immigrant non-Christian religions face very hard going in the face of energetic Canadian Christian firms—intermarriage usually results in the Christianization of the non-Christian spouse.

Objections that if the hypothesis were true, then Europe ought to have more new religious movements than the United States have been swamped by studies showing that such movements are *far more prevalent in Europe* (Stark 1985b, 1993; Stark and Finke 2000). When we suggested that the only reason it was not well known that Europe abounded in new religions was because European intellectuals preferred not to see them, only James Beckford (1988) agreed, and we were showered with considerable antagonism and ridicule by other European scholars (Campiche 1987; Dobbelaere 1987; Hervieu-Léger 1986; Wallis 1986a, 1986b, 1987; Wallis and Bruce 1984). Consequently, we take considerable satisfaction in the remarkable new *Enciclopedia Delle Religioni in Italia* (Introvigne et al. 2001). Applying methods pioneered by J. Gordon Melton, and using Melton's conceptual scheme, this work includes sections on more than 700 new religious movements operating in Italy! In contrast, we could document only 66 such movements in Italy and 1,317 for all of Europe in previous publications, which nevertheless showed that Europe was more hospitable to new religions than was the United States (Stark 1993; Stark and Finke 2000).

In addition, the hypothesis is supported by data from Mexico (Stark and Finke 2000) and by the rapid growth and success of new religious movements in Eastern Europe and the former Soviet Union (Borenstein 1997; Borowik 1999; Borowik and Babinski 1997; Rosenthal 1997).

SUPPLY-SIDE PROCESSES

H. Richard Niebuhr (1929) gave theoretical life to the terms "sect" and "church" by linking them in a process. According to Niebuhr, sects arise to meet the religious needs of the "masses." However, over time the more successful sects tend to be taken over by the privileged and transformed into churches that no longer adequately serve the needs and tastes of the proletariat. Consequently, dissidents break away to found a new sect. This gives rise to an endless cycle of birth, transformation, and rebirth of sect movements.

As a convinced Marxist, Niebuhr saw no need to look beyond class interests to explain shifts from sect to church. But, as noted in the earlier discussion of niches, class effects on religious orientations are modest and inconsistent. In fact, through the centuries, the great sect movements were not based on the proletariat—not the Essenes (Baumgarten 1997), not the early Christians (Stark 1996a), not the Cathars or the Waldensians (Lambert 1998; Stark forthcoming a). All were movements based primarily on persons of privilege. We must turn elsewhere to understand the rise and transformation of sects.

Keep in mind that the vast majority of sects never significantly reduce their initial level of tension and never amount to much (Stark and Bainbridge 1981a). As for sects that do begin to grow, that factor, in and of itself, can initiate their transformation from sects into churches.

12. As sects grow, the intensity of the average member's commitment will decline.

For over 200 years social scientists have commented on the relationship between the small fellowships and high membership demands of Protestant sects. Adam Smith reported that "in little religious sects, . . . the morals of the common people have been almost always remarkably regular and orderly" ([1776] 1981: 317). Weber (1946: 316) argued that "in principle, only relatively small congregations" can enforce strict standards for membership. Troeltsch wrote that because the sects "aspire after personal inward perfection, and they aim at direct personal fellowship between the members of each group . . . they are forced to organize themselves in small groups" (Troeltsch 1911 [1960], I: 331). This relationship is not unique to religious organizations. Mancur Olson (1965) has argued that "unless the number of individuals in a group is quite small, or unless there is coercion or some other special device to make individuals act in their common interest" (2) there will be substantial free-riding and that "the larger the group, the farther it will fall short of providing an optimal amount of a collective good" (34). At least initially, the loss of fervor as groups grow is not a function of recruiting from lower-tension niches, but is due to the dilution of the density of social networks and the ability to monitor behavior. Elsewhere we have spelled this process out in detail (Stark and Finke 2000).

A second important factor transforming sects involves intergenerational regression to the mean. Sects are founded by persons having unusually strong preferences for intense religion. Their children will tend towards the mean in this regard, thereby reducing the average level of intensity preference in the group. If we must note a specific mechanism for regression, it is simply that socialization is imperfect in all human groups. As Bryan Wilson (1966: 207) noted, "there is certainly a difference between those who are converted to a revolutionist sect, and those who accept adventist teachings at their mother's knee." Consequently, persons of privilege can take the lead in founding sects *and* their offspring can take the lead in moving them into lower tension.

That strictness is more costly for the privileged seems obvious. At the turn of the twentieth century it was rich Methodists who bore the heaviest burden of rules such as those against drinking, gambling, dancing, card-playing, and theater-going (Finke and Stark 1992)—for these rules hindered their association with others of their class. In similar fashion the emancipation of Jews in most of Europe during the middle of the nineteenth century presented wealthy Jews with intolerable temptations to shed the very distinctive appearance of Orthodoxy (yarmulkes, side curls, and shawls) and to abandon kosher dietary restrictions, as these greatly limited their ability to associate with non-Jews—Reform Judaism was the organizational result (Stark 2001; Steinberg 1965).

It doesn't require a large proportion of privileged members to transform a sect into a lower state of tension. Studies repeatedly have found that church contributions are extremely skewed—most of the funds come from a few large donors (Hoge 1994; Hoge and Yang 1994; Hoge et al. 1996). Laurence Iannaccone (1997) has shown that this is *necessarily* the case in all instances when members of a religious body vary substantially in terms of both commitment and wealth, and when commitment and wealth are little correlated. The wishes of the few who provide the funds are bound to matter and this will be especially the case when a new generation of seminary-trained clergy have their own motives for wishing to make the sect more "respectable"

(Finke and Stark 1992; Stark and Bainbridge 1985). But it also should be noted that it is not only (or always) the sons and daughters of the privileged who may prefer a lower-tension faith. Regression to the mean occurs at all class levels for those initially selected for an extreme value on some characteristic.

It also is important to realize that sect transformation is *gradual*—religious groups don't jump from one niche to another, rather they slowly proceed down the tension dimension. Internal conflicts arise as they begin to pass out of range of a higher-tension niche causing people in that niche to begin to display sectarian discontents.

To sum up this discussion more formally:

13. *Religious organizations mainly originate through sect formation.*

Note that this proposition does not mention schisms, leaving open the possibility for sects to form to serve high-tension niches without having actually broken away from a lower-tension religious organization. Thus, in addition to Niebuhr's mechanism whereby new sects are created via schisms as sects are transformed into churches, this proposition can be derived otherwise as will be shown in proposition 24.

14. *Sect movements that endure and grow will tend to reduce their tension with the socio-cultural environment, thereby moving away from the market niche(s) on which they originally were based (a process referred to as the sect-to-church transformation).*

This is the central proposition in Niebuhr's theory. At the beginning of this process, reduction in tension will be reinforced by results:

15. *As sects initially lower their tension they become more appealing to larger niches and therefore will grow.*

The recent history of the Seventh-Day Adventists offers an instructive example (Lawson 1995). Not only will growth confirm the wisdom of modest reductions in tension, it will begin to draw members with a preference for less tension.

16. *As religious groups move into range of the largest niches and abandon their original market niche(s), they tend to suffer schisms as sect movements break away to serve members having higher tension preferences.*

This helps explain why larger religious groups are substantially more subject to schisms (Liebman, Sutton, and Wuthnow 1988).

Propositions 13 through 16 can be found in Niebuhr, at least implicitly. However, if this line of theorizing is pursued, additional results come to light.

17. *Where free market conditions prevail, given the relative size of niches, at any given moment religious bodies based on medium-tension niches will enroll the larger portion of the population.*

This is obviously true in the United States where free market conditions prevail, but may be distorted in societies where the religious economy is highly regulated and where there may be no religious options for the largest preference niches. Thus, in European nations with state churches, in terms of actual participation the higher-tension niches claim a larger membership, while apathy characterizes most of those in the medium niches.

18. *As moderate religious bodies continue to reduce their tension, they move away from the larger niches and cease to grow.*

Propositions 13 through 18 explain the rise and subsequent decline of many American religious bodies.

19. *Therefore, at any given moment religious growth will be limited primarily to somewhat higher-tension bodies.*

20. *Because of the transformation of sects into churches, there will tend to be an oversupply of lower-tension religious bodies.*

As bodies move from higher- to lower-tension niches, they will tend to accumulate at the liberal end of the spectrum, and thus growing numbers of organizations will attempt to serve a relatively static number of potential members (Finke 1997a). Consequently:

21. *Low-tension bodies typically will have a declining membership and will tend to disappear via mergers.*

From examination of many church mergers, André Nauta (1994: 46) concluded that "mergers seem to be primarily related to supply. In particular, there is a recognition on the part of adherents in two (or more) denominations that their organizations are serving the same type of consumers, that they are offering essentially the same product." This principle applies mainly to the oversupply of low-tension bodies, high-tension groups being dedicated to the belief that their product is unique.

22. *Because of the transformation of sects into churches, there will tend to be an undersupply of religious bodies serving the medium-tension niches, creating an opportunity for new bodies, most of which will migrate from stricter niches.*

This adds to the opportunity for growth noted in proposition 15. Now let's see more clearly where the seeming abundance of sects comes from.

23. *Religious organizations are easier to form to the extent that they can be sustained by a small number of members.*

There are two reasons why this is the case. First, the smaller the number needed, the easier it will be for a founder or founders to attract the necessary number—to attract 20 followers rather than, say, 2,000. Second, small groups can much more easily reduce free-riding by better monitoring of members' contributions and by being better able to motivate these contributions, hence the smaller the group the greater the proportional per capita contributions. Consequently, it takes amazingly few people to sustain a sect, *if* they are sufficiently committed. In the late 1970s, of 417 American-born sects, about thirty percent had fewer than 500 members and more than half had fewer than 2,000 (Stark and Bainbridge 1981a). There are many sects able to own a church building despite having fewer than two dozen members. Such groups can exist only if each member makes a substantial contribution of both time and money. Therefore:

24. *Most religious groups will begin in a relatively high state of tension.*

Thus we have re-derived proposition 13. Strict groups are strong because only they can inspire very high levels of commitment in their followers. However, people who can be motivated to the extent required to sustain the birth of a sect make up a relatively small market niche. Thus, as noted, the subsequent success of a sect will require eventual relaxation of tension, thus enabling the group to appeal to a larger niche. But, despite the small size of the highest-tension niche, it seems fairly easy to recruit a founding nucleus of members from within this niche if a group displays sufficient intensity of purpose, particularly a group that is just forming and aspires to great accomplishments. Perhaps this is because some people are especially receptive to what might strike others as minor differences in theology or worship style. That surely is consistent with the immense amount of diversity to be found among the very strict sects and the emphasis each gives to these differences.

25. *Most sects do not reduce their initial level of tension and do not grow and, therefore, the high-tension end of the church-sect spectrum will abound in small, unsuccessful religious organizations.*

That most sects are *not* transformed into lower-tension religious groups has been derived formally (Iannaccone 1988) and this necessarily will result in the existence of a large number of sects. Here we depart from Niebuhr's classic thesis that sects naturally evolve into mainstream denominations, for the evidence is overwhelming that most sects never evolve. Most are dead ends. They start small, remain small, and slowly wither away.

There are many reasons why most sects fail. As with all organizations that must face the marketplace, sects often fail for want of a sufficiently attractive or distinctive product. Others fail because of ineffective marketing. Still others fail because of internal faction fights and/or lack of effective leadership. Sometimes sects begin with a level of tension that virtually precludes much recruitment. Many sects are created by the efforts of one person—they form around a leader having exceptional interpersonal skills (some call this charisma). In many such instances, initial growth ceases as the leader becomes smothered in intragroup relationships and no longer has the capacity to form new attachments with outsiders (Stark and Roberts 1982). Finally, the success or failure of many sects stems from lack of a sufficient market opening. As a result of the overproduction of sects, they face fierce competition.

Thus, for every sect movement that achieves great things, there are scores that amount to very little. Only one of the many Bible student groups that formed in response to the teachings of Charles Taze Russell went on to become the Jehovah's Witnesses. The others were (and some remain) small and obscure. In our judgment, Niebuhr was fully aware of this, but focussed his theorizing on the fate of "successful" sects since these are the ones that change religious history. Yet, because sect formation occurs so frequently, especially in an unregulated religious economy, it is important to include the failures as well as the rare successes in any general model.

While it is true that some people do move from religious niche to niche in response to various factors, most do not. Most Americans who switch churches select a new church that is very similar to their old one in terms of the church-sect continuum (Sherkat and Wilson 1995). That is, most church-switching occurs *within* niches and what switching across niches that does occur tends to be intergenerational. Since, as already noted, higher-tension religion is more costly for the more privileged, niche-switching is mildly related to status attainment. Some people who have achieved higher status will shift to a lower-tension faith and some who are downwardly mobile will switch towards higher tension. But, keep in mind that these are *not strong effects*. Socialization is many times more important than class in determining religious tastes, which is why niches are so stable and why so few people switch. But, even socialization effects are far from being determinative and there remains substantial latitude for people to formulate religious preferences on the basis of quite idiosyncratic life experiences and influences (Sherkat 1991, 1996; Sherkat and Wilson 1995; Stark and Glock 1968; Stolzenberg, Blair-Loy, and Waite 1994).

It also should be noted that a major mode of demand-side niche-cycling does not show up in church-switcher statistics, because the people don't switch. Instead, they move to a lower-tension niche along with their religious body—indeed they propel that body into lower tension. Thus did genteel Congregationalists shift niches without shifting affiliation.

Niebuhr denied that it was possible for churches to shift in the direction of higher tension. And, although Benton Johnson (1963: 543) did point out in a footnote that a shift in this direction "is at least conceivable," such a possibility has been ignored by most.[3] Probably because so many social scientists have such a pronounced preference for low-tension religion (or for none at all), it has been all but unthinkable that once a denomination was well along the road to liberalism that anything could cause it to move back up the tension dimension. Yet, as the Counter-Reformation demonstrated, this is entirely possible.

26. *If the secular rewards of religious vocations decline, then religious rewards must play an increasing part in the motivation of those who pursue such vocations.*

27. *To the extent that religious rewards motivate religious leaders, they will prefer a relatively higher level of tension for the group.*

Many such church-to-sect movements are taking place in the United States and elsewhere.

28. *As a religious body in a low state of tension moves to a higher state of tension, it moves from smaller to larger niches and has an increased opportunity for growth.*

29. *In an unregulated religious economy, where the survival of all religious groups rests on market processes, growth will facilitate the efforts of clergy to move the group into lower or higher tension.*

Thus the circle is closed. If growth tempts sects to reduce their strictness, growth also may tempt declining liberal groups to increase their tension with society. The implication of both kinds of shifts occurring simultaneously greatly complicates the model. That is, the onset of church-to-sect movement by firms that have found the liberal niche too small and too uncommitted may cause an oversupply of firms appealing to the medium-tension niches. What then? It may be that if religious firms begin to enter the medium-tension niches from the left, this will reduce the opportunities for groups entering from the right. Will this eventually lead former liberal groups to be transformed back into lower tension as they had been previously? Could offsetting tendencies to move towards the center stabilize the religious marketplace with firms coming to rest within specific niches and thereby conforming to the "rule" whereby voluntary organizations become fixed in social space, as proposed by Popielarz and McPherson (1995)? If so, then the dynamic forces would be found on the demand-side, as *church-switching became the primary basis of change*. Because America has the first fully unregulated religious economy, and it has not been functioning very long, we may have yet to see the full range of processes inherent in it. That fact also should remind us that church-to-sect shifting is likely to occur only to the extent that the religious economy is unregulated and therefore that individual firms are fully market-dependent. In regulated economies, although the state-supported churches draw their members only from the moderate to liberal niches, they will not benefit from growth as they are not at the mercy of the market. To the contrary, when clergy are civil servants (as they are in Germany and parts of Scandinavia), they have more to gain from empty churches (which make no demands on their time) than from full ones.

EVIDENCE

H6. *As congregations become larger, the average level of member commitment will decline.*

Contemporary research on American Protestant denominations supports these views (Alston and Aguirre 1970; Wilken 1971; Pinto and Crow 1982; Hougland and Wood 1980; Finke 1994; Zalenski and Zech 1995). For example, Hoge, Zech, McNamara, and Donahue (1996) identified small congregational size as one of the "Big Five Factors" in explaining congregational giving (also see Bahr and Finke forthcoming). Elsewhere we demonstrated the negative effects of congregational size among the Southern Baptists, Methodists, and Nazarenes (Stark and Finke 2000).

Fully aware of the negative impact of size on commitment, two of the world's fastest-growing religious movements, the Jehovah's Witnesses and the Mormons, intentionally limit the size of local congregations. The Jehovah's Witnesses tend to split when the group exceeds two hundred (Alston and Aguirre 1970), and the Mormon stake president can choose to split a ward once it exceeds three hundred.[4] The leadership of each movement is so committed to small local fellowships that they will split the local group into two fellowships even when only one building is available. In areas where land prices are high and membership growth is rapid, it is common practice for two or more fellowships to share the same building. Until recent decades, the Southern Baptists have tended to have smaller congregations, not due to official policy, but to the intense competition among pastors for a church of their own. This is caused by an oversupply of pastors because local congregations retain the right to ordain anyone who seeks it and whom the local members deem fit (Finke and Stark 1992). This same factor is at work in many small sects.

At first glance the new megachurches would seem to defy the small group thesis. But, this is an illusion. What outsiders see are the huge gatherings for worship services—the highly publicized Willow Creek Community Church (Illinois) averages over 14,000 in attendance for weekend worship services, and is best known for its "seeker" services offering contemporary music, drama, and anonymity for all who attend. Yet, church leaders describe their small cell groups (approximately ten members) as the "basic unit of church life" (Trueheart 1996: 54) and explain that these groups provide "accountability, instruction, encouragement, and support for each of its members" (Mellado 1991: 12). Likewise, the largest church in the world, the Yoido Full Gospel Church in Seoul, Korea, reports that its small groups provide fellowship, instruction, and discipline for church members. A former staff member of the church described small groups as the "fabric of the church," where the church changes from "an event to attend" to a "community to belong to" (Hurston 1994:99).[5]

H7. *As religious bodies move from medium to low tension, their membership will decline.*

By now it is obvious that Dean Kelley (1972) was right, the liberal churches have been in serious decline. In fact, we devoted much of *The Churching of America* to demonstrating that these declines are not new, but began at least two centuries ago when the Congregationalists, Presbyterians, and Episcopalians moved towards the low-tension end of the religious spectrum (Finke and Stark 1992). This process is not limited to the United States. The same trend has been taking place in Canada (Bibby 1987). As for Europe, the state churches fail to generate participation, although higher-tension bodies can—despite the many hindrances imposed on them by state regulation. Indeed, the market weakness of liberal religious bodies underlay more than a millennium of efforts to reform the Roman Catholic Church, culminating in the Reformation (Stark forthcoming b).

H8. *As the lowest-tension bodies decline in membership, those entering the clergy will increasingly be motivated by religious concerns and will attempt to move the body into a higher level of tension.*

The many new studies of clergy are unanimous in reporting a "return" to traditional theology and to evangelical attitudes. This holds in America for Methodists, Presbyterians, Episcopalians, Unitarians, and Reform Jews (Stark and Finke 2000; McKinney 2001). Younger Catholic priests both in the United States and Brazil are far more traditional and conservative in their views than are their older colleagues (Hoge, Shields, and Griffin 1995; Cimino 1996). The same shifts can be observed in those entering Catholic religious orders (Stark and Finke 2000). The hypothesis also is supported by data on Anglicans: The 1997 class of Ordinands in the Church of England was dominated by "evangelicals" (Gilliat-Ray 2001).

H9. *In the lowest-tension denominations, congregations led by more conservative, "evangelical" clergy will be more successful than the others.*

It is the traditional Catholic religious orders (many of them founded recently) that are growing and it is primarily the more traditional Catholic dioceses that are attracting seminarians (Finke 1997b; Stark and Finke 2000; Yuengert 2001). Among Methodists, a still-declining denomination, the congregations headed by young evangelical pastors are thriving and the same is true among Presbyterians (Stark and Finke 2000; Finke and Stark 2001). In Sweden it is the more evangelical pastors who attract the laity to the state church (Hamberg and Pettersson 1994). Meanwhile, in Latin America the rapid growth of Pentecostalism is being confronted by a new generation of energetic, evangelical Catholic priests (Gill 1998; Clarke 1999).

CONCLUSION

Niebuhr wrote *The Social Sources of Denominationalism* in order to explain the "evils of denominationalism" (1929: 21). In recognizing the existence of a cyclical process by which sects are born, transformed, and born again he made a most important (if grudging and often vituperative) contribution to social theory. Here we have attempted to take Niebuhr's parsimonious little model and embed it in a larger system wherein many additional processes and relationships can be seen and explained. Our expanded model reveals the "whys" of many things we already knew as facts, such as why most religious movements begin as sects; why liberal churches have been prone to mergers as well as to declining membership; why growth is concentrated in the higher-tension sector. The model also prompts awareness of things not previously obvious: for example, that clergy of liberal denominations may turn conservative and that religious organizations may move from lower to higher tension.

Underlying the entire model are two very simple assumptions. First, effort is productive. Other things being equal, the harder a religious group works to achieve success, the more successful it will be. Second, people will only work as hard as they must to achieve their goals. Thus, competition creates and rewards eager and efficient religious firms and they, collectively, sustain high levels of public religious commitment. These points seem so self-evident that only trained social scientists could doubt them.

NOTES

1. In his review of *The Churching of America*, Martin E. Marty (1993: 88) proclaimed that we had reduced religious life to mere "winning and losing," presenting a "world [that] contains no God or religion or spirituality, no issue of truth or beauty or goodness. . . ." Provided that he even read the dust jacket summary, it is inconceivable that Marty could have failed to grasp that our central argument is that doctrine holds the key to organizational health. On the first page of that book we wrote "to the degree that denominations rejected traditional doctrines and ceased to make serious demands on their followers, they ceased to prosper. The churching of America was accomplished by aggressive churches committed to vivid otherworldliness." As with the first page, so with the last and with most pages in between, our message was that it is *vague* and *permissive doctrines* that turn religious groups into "losers." In our judgment it is precisely our focus on doctrine, not the word economy, that really upsets our ultra-liberal and anti-religious opponents and motivates their misleading claims.

2. This may well be the reason that sociologists regard religious monopolies as the basis for strong faith and pluralism as inevitably eroding faith. If Peter Berger's notion of the "sacred canopy" is equated with the sacralization of societies, then it is true that a single canopy is necessary, and that multiple canopies don't suffice. But, when the sacred canopy line of thought is construed to mean that personal piety is more abundant under monopoly faith, that is clearly wrong.

3. Nancy T. Ammerman's (1990) study of Southern Baptists and Armand L. Mauss's (1994) examination of Mormons each review the struggle of a conservative denomination attempting to return to a higher level of tension. R. Stephen Warner (1988) has also provided a detailed case study of a congregation's switch away from liberalism.

4. We would like to thank the Public Affairs Office of the Latter-day Saints, Salt Lake City, Utah for providing this information.

5. The Yoido Full Gospel Church uses small groups as a powerful tool for evangelism, encouraging "each cell group to win at least one person to the Lord every six months (Hurston 1994: 99)."

REFERENCES

Alston, Jon P. and B. E. Aguirre. 1970. "Congregational Size and the Decline of Sectarian Commitment: The Case of the Jehovah's Witnesses in South and North America," *Sociological Analysis* 40: 63–70.

Ammerman, Nancy Tatom. 1990. *Baptist Battles: Social Change and Religious Conflict in the Southern Baptist Convention*. New Brunswick, N.J.: Rutgers University Press.

Argyle, Michael and Benjamin Beit-Hallahmi. 1975. *The Social Psychology of Religion*. London: Routledge & Kegan Paul.

Bahr, Matthew and Roger Finke. Forthcoming. "Toward Explaining Congregational Giving."

Bainbridge, William Sims and Rodney Stark. 1982. "Church and Cult in Canada," *Canadian Journal of Sociology* 7: 351–366.

Barkun, Michael. 1986. *Crucible of the Millennium*. Syracuse, N.Y.: Syracuse University Press.

Baumgarten, Albert I. 1997. *The Flourishing of Jewish Sects in the Maccabean Era: An Interpretation*. Leiden: Brill.

Beckford, James. 1988. "Introduction." In *Cults, Converts and Charisma*. Thomas Robbins, ed. Beverly Hills, Calif.: Sage, 1–23.

Bellah, Robert N. 1967. "Civil Religion in America." *Daedalus* 96: 1–21.

Bibby, Reginald W. 1987. *Fragmented Gods: The Poverty and Potential of Religion in Canada*. Toronto: Irwin Publishing.

———. 2000. "Canada's Mythical Religious Mosaic: Some Census Findings," *Journal for the Scientific Study of Religion* 39: 235–239.

Blau, Judith R., Kenneth C. Land, and Kent Redding. 1992. "The Expansion of Religious Affiliation," *Social Science Research* 21: 329–52.

Blau, Peter M. 1977. *Inequality and Heterogeneity: A Primitive Theory of Social Structure*. New York: Free Press.

———. 1994. *Structural Contexts of Opportunities*. Chicago: University of Chicago Press.

Borenstein, Eliot. 1997. "Indigenous and Eclectic Religious Faiths Find Following in Russia," *Religion Watch* 12 (Sept.): 1–2.

Borowik, Irena and Grzegorz Babinski (editors). 1997. *New Religious Phenomena in Eastern and Central Europe*. Krakow: Nomos.

Breault, Kevin D. 1989. "New Evidence on Religious Pluralism, Urbanism, and Religious Participation," *American Sociological Review* 54: 1048–53.

Bruce, Steve. 1999. *Choice and Religion: A Critique of Rational Choice*. Oxford: Oxford University Press.

Brunner, Edmund de S. 1927. *Village Communities*. New York: George H. Doran Company.

Butler, Jon. 1982. "Enthusiasm Described and Decried: The Great Awakenings as Interpretative Fiction," *Journal of American History* 69: 305–325.

———. 1990. *Awash in a Sea of Faith: Christianizing the American People*. Cambridge, Mass.: Harvard University Press.

Campiche, Roland J. 1987. "Sects et nouveaux mouvements religieux: divergences and convergences." Paper presented to the First Latin American Conference on Popular Religion, Identity, and Ethnology, Mexico City.

Chaves, Mark and David E. Cann. 1992. "Regulation, Pluralism, and Religious Market Structure: Explaining Religion's Vitality," *Rationality and Society* 4 (3): 272–290.

Chaves, Mark and Philip E. Gorski. 2001. "Religious Pluralism and Religious Participation," *Annual Review of Sociology* 27: 261–281.

Chaves, Mark, Peter J. Schraeder, and Mario Sprindys. 1994. "State Regulation of Religion and Muslim Religious Vitality in the Industrialized West," *The Journal of Politics* 56: 1087–1097.

Cimino, Richard P. 1996. "Brazilian Seminarians Indifferent to Liberationist Concerns," *Religion Watch* 11 (#4): 5.

Clarke, Peter B. 1999. "'Pop-Star' Priests and the Catholic Response to the 'Explosion' of Evangelical Protestantism in Brazil: The Beginning of the End of the 'Walkout'?" *Journal of Contemporary Religion* 2: 203–216.

Cornwall, Marie. 1988. "The Influence of Three Agents of Socialization." In *The Religion and Family Connection*. Darwin Thomas, ed. Provo, Utah: Religious Studies Center, Brigham Young University, 207–231.

Davie, Grace. 1994. *Religion in Britain since 1945: Believing Without Belonging*. Oxford: Blackwell.

Demerath, Nicholas J., III. 1965. *Social Class in American Protestantism*. Chicago: Rand McNally.

———. 1995. "Rational Paradigms, A-Rational Religion and the Debate Over Secularization," *Journal for the Scientific Study of Religion* 34: 105–112.

Dobbelaere, Karel. 1987. "Some Trends in European Sociology of Religion: The Secularization Debate," *Sociological Analysis* 48: 107–137.

Duke, James T., Barry L. Johnson, and James B. Duke. 1993. "Rate of Religious Conversion: A Macrosociological Study," *Research in the Sociology of Religion* 5 89–121. Greenwich, Conn.: JAI Press.

Ellison, Christopher G. and Darren E. Sherkat. 1990. "Patterns of Religious Mobility Among Black Americans," *The Sociological Quarterly* 31: 551–568.

———. 1995. "The 'Semi-Involuntary Institution' Revisited: Regional Differences in Church Participation Among Black Americans," *Social Forces* 73: 1415–1437.

Finke, Roger. 1990. "Religious Deregulation: Origins and Consequences," *Journal of Church and State* 32: 609–626.

———. 1992. "An Unsecular America." In *Religion and Modernization: Sociologists and Historians Debate the Secularization Thesis*. Steve Bruce, ed. Oxford: Clarendon Press.

———. 1994. "The Quiet Transformation: Changes in Size and Leadership of Southern Baptist Churches," *Review of Religious Research* 36: 3–22.

———. 1997a. "The Consequences of Religious Competition: Supply-Side Explanations for Religious Change." In *Assessing Rational Choice Theories of Religion*. Lawrence A. Young, ed. New York: Routledge.

———. 1997b. "An Orderly Return to Tradition: Explaining Membership Recruitment to Catholic Religious Orders," *Journal for the Scientific Study of Religion* 36: 218–230.

Finke, Roger, Avery M. Guest, and Rodney Stark. 1996. "Pluralism and Religious Participation: New York, 1855–1865," *American Sociological Review* 61: 203–218.

Finke, Roger and Laurence R. Iannaccone. 1993. "Supply-Side Explanations for Religious Change in America," *The Annals* 527: 27–29.

Finke, Roger and Rodney Stark. 1988. "Religious Economies and Sacred Canopies: Religious Mobilization in American Cities, 1906," *American Sociological Review* 53: 41–49.

———. 1992. *The Churching of America, 1776–1990*. New Brunswick, N.J.: Rutgers University Press.

———. 1998. "Religious Choice and Competition," *American Sociological Review* 63: 761–766.

———. 2001. "The New Holy Clubs: Testing Church-to-Sect Propositions," *Sociology of Religion* 62: 175–189.

Gill, Anthony J. 1994. "Rendering Unto Caesar?: Religious Competition and Catholic Political Strategy in Latin America, 1962–1979," *American Journal of Political Science* 38: 403–425.

———. 1998. *Rendering Unto Caesar*. Chicago: University of Chicago Press.

Gilliat-Ray, Sophie. 2001. "The Fate of the Anglican Clergy and the Class of '97: Some Implications of the Changing Sociological Profile or Ordinands," *Journal of Contemporary Religion* 16: 209–225.

Gordon-McCutchan, R. C. 1983. "Great Awakenings," *Sociological Analysis* 44: 83–95.

Greeley, Andrew M. 1994. "A Religious Revival in Russia?" *Journal for the Scientific Study of Religion* 33: 253–272.

Hamberg, Eva M. and Thorleif Pettersson. 1994. "The Religious Market: Denominational Competition and Religious Participation in Contemporary Sweden," *Journal for the Scientific Study of Religion* 33: 205–216.

———. 1997. "Short-Term Changes in Religious Supply and Church Attendance in Contemporary Sweden," *Research in the Social Scientific Study of Religion* 8: 35–51.

Hervieu-Léger, Danièle. 1986. *Vers un nouveau Christianisme?* Paris: Cerf.

Hoge, Dean R. 1994. "Introduction: The Problem of Church Giving," *Review of Religious Research* 36: 101–110.

Hoge, Dean R., Joseph J. Shields, and Douglas L. Griffin. 1995. "Changes in Satisfaction and Institutional Attitudes of Catholic Priests, 1970–1993," *Sociology of Religion* 56: 195–213.

Hoge, Dean R. and Fenggang Yang. 1994. "Determinants of Religious Giving in American Denominations: Data from Two Nationwide Surveys," *Review of Religious Research* 36: 123–148.

Hoge, Dean R., Charles Zech, Patrick McNamara, and Michael J. Donahue. 1996. *Money Matters: Personal Giving in American Churches*. Louisville, Ky.: Westminster Jon Knox Press.

Hougland, James G. and James R. Wood. 1980. "Control in Organizations and the Commitment of Members," *Social Forces* 59: 85–105.

Hurston, Karen. 1994. *Growing the World's Largest Church*. Springfield, Mo.: Gospel Publishing House.

Iannaccone, Laurence R. 1988. "A Formal Model of Church and Sect," *American Journal of Sociology* 94 (supplement): S241–S268.

———. 1991. "The Consequence of Religious Market Structure," *Rationality and Society* 3: 156–177.

———. 1992. "Sacrifice and Stigma: Reducing Free-riding in Cults, Communes, and Other Collectives," *Journal of Political Economy* 100 (2): 271–291.

———. 1994. "Why Strict Churches Are Strong," *American Journal of Sociology* 99: 1180–1211.

———. 1997. "Skewness Explained: A Rational Choice Model of Religious Giving," *Journal for the Scientific Study of Religion* 36: 141–157.

Iannaccone, Laurence R., Roger Finke, and Rodney Stark. 1998. "Deregulating Religion: The Economics of Church and State," *Economic Inquiry* 36: 373–389.

Introvigne, Massimo. 2001. Personal Communication to Stark.

Introvigne, Massimo, with the assistance of Pierluigi Zoccatelli, Nelly Ippolito Macrina, and Veronica Roldan. 2001. *Enciclopedia Delle Religioni in Italia*. Torino: Elledici.

Jelen, Ted G. and Clyde Wilcox. 1998. "Context and Conscience: The Catholic Church as an Agent of Political Socialization in Western Europe," *Journal for the Social Scientific Study of Religion* 37: 28–40.

Johnson, Benton. 1963. "On Church and Sect," *American Sociological Review* 28: 539–549.

Kelley, Dean M. 1972. *Why Conservative Churches Are Growing*. New York: Harper and Row.

Lambert, Frank. 1990. "'Peddlar in Divinity': George Whitefield and the Great Awakening, 1737–1745," *Journal of American History* 77: 812–837.

Lambert, Malcolm. 1992. *Medieval Heresy: Popular Movements from the Gregorian Reform to the Reformation* (second edition). Oxford: Basil Blackwell.

———. 1998. *The Cathars*. Oxford: Basil Blackwell.

Land, Kenneth C., Glenn Deane, and Judith Blau. 1991. "Religious Pluralism and Church Membership: A Spatial Diffusion Model," *American Sociological Review* 56: 237–249.

Lawson, Ronald. 1995. "Sect-State Relations: Accounting for the Differing Trajectories of the Seventh-Day Adventists and Jehovah's Witnesses," *Sociology of Religion* 56: 351–377.

Liebman, Robert C., John R. Sutton, and Robert Wuthnow. 1988. "Exploring the Social Sources of Denominationalism: Schisms in American Protestant Denominations, 1890–1980," *American Sociological Review* 53: 343–352.

McKinney, Jennifer. 2001. *Clergy Connections*. Unpublished Dissertation.

McLoughlin, William G. 1978. *Revivals, Awakenings, and Reform*. Chicago: University of Chicago Press.

McPherson, J. Miller. 1981. "A Dynamic Model of Voluntary Affiliation," *Social Forces* 59: 705–728.

McPherson, J. Miller, Pamela A. Popielarz, and Sonja Drobnic. 1992. "Social Networks and Organizational Dynamics," *American Sociological Review* 57: 153–170.

McPherson, J. Miller and Lynn Smith-Lovin. 1987. "Homophily in Voluntary Organization: Status Distance and the Composition of Face to Face Groups," *American Sociological Review* 52: 370–79.

Martin, David. 1990. *Tongues of Fire: The Explosion of Protestantism in Latin America*. Oxford: Basil Blackwell.

Marty, Martin E. 1993. "Churches as Winners, Losers," *Christian Century*, January 27: 88–89.

Mauss, Armand L. 1994. *The Angel and the Beehive: The Mormon Struggle with Assimilation*. Evanston: University of Illinois Press.

Mellado, James. 1991. *Willow Creek Community Church*. Cambridge, Mass.: Harvard Business School.

Miller, Alan S. and John P. Hoffman. 1995. "Risk and Religion: An Explanation of Gender Differences in Religiosity," *Journal for the Scientific Study of Religion* 34: 63–75.

Nauta, André. 1994. "'That They All May Be One:' Can Denominationalism Die?" *Research in the Social Scientific Study of Religion* (JAI Press) 6: 35–51.

Niebuhr, H. Richard. 1929. *The Social Sources of Denominationalism*. New York: Henry Holt.

Olson, Daniel V. A. 1998. "Comment: Religious Pluralism in Contemporary U.S. Counties," *American Sociological Review* 63: 759–761.

———. 1999. "Religious Pluralism and U.S. Church Membership: A Reassessment," *Sociology of Religion* 60: 149–174.

Olson, Daniel V. A., C. Kirk Hadaway, and Penny Long Marler. 1999. "Religious Pluralism and Church Involvement in Modern Britain." Paper presented at the annual meeting of the Society for the Scientific Study of Religion, November, Houston.

Olson, Mancur. 1965. *The Logic of Collective Action*. Cambridge, Mass.: Harvard University Press.

Perl, Paul and Daniel V. A. Olson. 2000. "Religious Market Share and Intensity of Church Involvement in Five Denominations," *Journal for the Scientific Study of Religion* 39: 12–31.

Pettersson, Thorleif and Eva Hamberg. 1997. "Denominational Pluralism and Church Membership in Contemporary Sweden: A Longitudinal Study of the Period, 1974–1995," *Journal of Empirical Theology* 10: 61–78.

Phillips, Rick. 1998. "Religious Market Share and Mormon Church Activity," *Sociology of Religion* 59: 117–130.

Pinto, Leonard J. and Kenneth E. Crow. 1982. "The Effects of Size on Other Structural Attributes of Congregations within the Same Denomination," *Journal for the Scientific Study of Religion* 21: 304–316.

Pisati, Maurizio. 1998. "Non di Solo Cattolicesimo: Elementi per un'Analaisi Dell'Offerta Religiosa in Italia," *Polis* 12: 53–73.

Popielarz, Pamela A. and J. Miller McPherson. 1995. "On the Edge or In Between: Niche Position, Niche Overlap, and the Duration of Voluntary Association Memberships," *American Journal of Sociology* 3: 698–720.

Rosenthal, Bernice Glatzer, ed. 1997. *The Occult in Russian and Soviet Culture*. Ithaca, N.Y.: Cornell University Press.

Sherkat, Darren E. 1991. "Leaving the Faith: Testing Theories of Religious Switching Using Survival Models," *Social Science Research* 20: 171–187.

———. 1996. "Embedding Religious Choices: Integrating Preferences and Constraints into Rational Choice Theories of Religious Behavior." In *Assessing Rational Choice Theories of Religion*. Lawrence Young, ed. New York: Routledge.

———. 1998. "Counterculture or Continuity? Competing Influences on Baby Boomers' Religious Orientation and Participation," *Social Forces* 76: 1087–1115.

Sherkat, Darren E. and John Wilson. 1995. "Preferences, Constraints, and Choices in Religious Markets: An Examination of Religious Switching and Apostasy," *Social Forces* 73: 993–1026.

Silberstein, Richard, Jonathan Rabinowitz, Paul Ritterband, and Barry Kosmin. 1987. "Giving to Jewish Philanthropic Causes: A Preliminary Reconnaissance." *Spring Research Forum Working Papers*. New York: United Way Institute, 1–8.

Smith, Adam. [1776] 1981. *An Inquiry into the Nature and Causes of the Wealth of Nations*, 2 vols. Indianapolis: Liberty Fund.
———. 1982. *The Theory of Moral Sentiments*. Indianapolis: Liberty Fund.
Smith, Timothy L. 1983. "My Rejection of the Cyclical View 'Great Awakenings' in American Religious History," *Sociological Analysis* 44: 97–101.
Stark, Rodney. 1965. "A Taxonomy of Religious Experience," *Journal for the Scientific Study of Religion* 5: 97–100.
———. 1971. "The Economics of Piety: Religion and Social Class." In *Issues in Social Inequality*. Gerald W. Theilbar and Saul D. Feldman, eds. Boston: Little, Brown and Co., 483–503.
———. 1985a. "From Church-Sect to Religious Economies." In *The Sacred in a Post-Secular Age*. Phillip E. Hammond, ed. Berkeley: University of California Press, 139–149.
———. 1985b. "Europe's Receptivity to Religious Movements." In *New Religious Movements: Genesis, Exodus, and Numbers*. Rodney Stark, ed. New York: Paragon, 301–343.
———. 1992. "Do Catholic Societies Really Exist?" *Rationality and Society* 4: 261–271.
———. 1993. "Europe's Receptivity to New Religious Movements: Round Two," *Journal for the Scientific Study of Religion* 32: 389–397.
———. 1996a. *The Rise of Christianity: A Sociologist Reconsiders History*. Princeton, N.J.: Princeton University Press.
———. 1996b. "Why Religious Movements Succeed or Fail: A Revised General Model," *Journal of Contemporary Religion* 11: 133–146.
———. 1997. "German and German-American Religion: Approximating a Crucial Experiment." *Journal for the Scientific Study of Religion* 36: 182–103.
———. 1998. "Catholic Contexts: Competition, Commitment, and Innovation," *Review of Religious Research* 39: 197–208.
———. 1999. "Secularization, R.I.P.," *Sociology of Religion*, 60: 249–273.
———. 2001. *One True God: Historical Consequences of Monotheism*. Princeton, N.J.: Princeton University Press.
———. In Press. "Physiology and Faith: Addressing the 'Universal' Gender Difference in Religious Commitment," *Journal for the Scientific Study of Religion*.
———. Forthcoming a. "Upperclass Asceticism."
———. Forthcoming b. *Gods and Culture: Revelations, Reformations, Science, Witchcraft, Slavery, and Morality*.
Stark, Rodney and W. S. Bainbridge. 1980. "Secularization, Revival, and Cult Formation," *The Annual Review of the Social Sciences of Religion* 4: 85–119.
———. 1981a "American-Born Sects: Initial Findings," *Journal for the Scientific Study of Religion* 20: 130–149.
———. 1981b. "Secularization and Cult Formation in the Jazz Age," *Journal for the Scientific Study of Religion* 20: 360–373.
———. 1985. *The Future of Religion: Secularization, Revival, and Cult Formation*. Berkeley: University of California Press.
Stark, Rodney and Roger Finke. 2000. *Acts of Faith: Explaining the Human Side of Religion*. Berkeley: University of California Press.
Stark, Rodney Roger Finke, and Laurence R. Iannaccone. 1995. "Pluralism and Piety: England and Wales, 1851," *Journal for the Scientific Study of Religion* 34: 431–444.

3

A Prophet's Reward: Dynamics of Religious Exchange

William Sims Bainbridge

"A squirrel turning in a cage —
Can he escape? At least the forces
That led him to such desperate courses
Are known as in no earlier age."

From "Fundamentals of Sociology"
by George C. Homans

"He that receiveth a prophet
in the name of a prophet
shall receive a prophet's reward."

Matthew 10:41

In his presidential address to the American Sociological Association, my mentor George Homans (1964) condemned Durkheim's idea that social facts existed independently from the actions of individuals. Homans named his famous presidential speech, "Bringing Men Back In," meaning that he intended to restore living, acting human beings to the center of sociological analysis. However, he explicitly drew his psychological insights from the narrow behaviorist school led by his friend B. F. Skinner (1938; Homans 1974, 1984). The Stark–Bainbridge theory of religion, through its emphasis on the exchange of *explanations*, gives far greater emphasis to both cognition and communication. We bring back the factor that Homans explicitly exiled from his doctrinaire behaviorism, namely the *mind*.

As Stark and I defined it (Stark and Bainbridge 1987: 29), "The *mind* is the set of human functions that directs the action of a person." It is "a complex but finite information-processing system that functions to identify problems and attempt solutions to them." And, "Human *problems* are recurrent situations that require investments (costs) to obtain rewards." The mind is the combination of hardware (brain) plus software (culture) that develops and acts on more-or-less general strategies to gain rewards and avoid costs. Here I will consider some of the strategies humans may employ to obtain rewards in the context of religious exchange.

I will do so not through abstract analysis of philosophical principles, nor through surveying the growing literature on the connection between brain and mind coming from cognitive neuroscience (Gazzaniga 1995). Rather, I will employ a method that is not usually applied in behaviorism or the rational choice perspective, namely *psychohistory* (Asimov 1951; Erikson 1958; Elms 1981). This will be a social psychohistory of an entire family, not of an isolated individual, and it will employ a slightly expanded version of the principles of the new exchange paradigm in social science of religion, not the dubious psychoanalytic paradigm.

EXCHANGE

Social science has recently emphasized the ways that religions compete with each other for adherents in a marketplace for the *exchange* of supernatural rewards, as individual consumers select the denominations or sects that best meet their needs (Stark, Iannaccone, and Finke 1996; Stark and Finke 2000; cf. Bainbridge 1995c). More than forty years ago, Karl Polanyi (1957) argued that *exchange* is only one of three processes that can provide unity and stability to an economic system, the other two being *reciprocity* and *redistribution*. According to Polanyi, exchange generates competitive markets, but the other two economic processes do not. Reciprocity typically takes place in or around a kinship system, and it should be very significant for religion, because religious observance is typically family-based and religious organizations are often constructed on the model of a family. Redistribution takes resources from those who have them, whether by custom or physical force, and it delivers them to the state or to organizations in alliance with the state, such as established churches. Because this essay focuses on a family in its dealings with individuals and voluntary organizations, both exchange and reciprocity will loom large here, but redistribution will not.

Under the heading of exchange, there are at least two competing theoretical paradigms, *rational choice theory* and *learning theory*. With only slight simplification, we can say that learning theory was introduced to sociology from behavioral psychology by George Homans, whereas his rival James Coleman was responsible for bringing rational choice theory in from economics (Coleman 1990; Baron and Hannan 1994; cf. Homans 1967: 38). As early as

1985, Gartrell and Shannon were writing about religion from an avowed rational choice perspective and suggesting that work by Stark and myself (1979, 1980) belonged to the same tradition. When Collins (1993) called *A Theory of Religion* "a leading accomplishment of the rational choice school," my only qualm was that I thought it belonged instead to learning theory.

In a sense, rational choice theory is forward-looking, modeling individual action as the result of calculations about future costs and rewards. In contrast, learning theory is backward-looking, explaining current behavior in terms of past schedules of reinforcement. The first axiom of the Stark–Bainbridge (1987: 27) theory states: "Human perception and action take place through time, from the past into the future." The theory defines these anchoring concepts in terms of human action and cognition: "The *past* consists of the universe of conditions which can be known but not influenced." "The *future* consists of the universe of conditions which can be influenced but not known."

Paradoxically, humans imagine the future as a kind of subjective past, contemplating the results of future actions as if they had already occurred (Schutz 1945, 1972). Thorough-going behaviorism, of the sort Homans admired, excluded imagination from consideration, whereas rational choice theory at least postulates that humans engage in mental calculations of the possible benefits and costs that would be entailed in some future action. Thus, rational choice theory seems to give greater scope for "mind" than does behaviorism-based learning theory.

Learning theory incorporates a theory of mind, however, as soon as it begins to model the learning process. For example, Michael Macy (1990, 1991) has employed computer simulations akin to neural networks to show that learning theory can handle the classic problem of the evolution of cooperation (cf. Miller and Dollard 1941; Sidowski et al. 1956; Kelley et al. 1962). Homans himself admired the computer simulation work of Robert Axelrod (1984) on the evolution of cooperation. In the early 1980s I undertook a research program to explore how abstract conceptualization might be modeled mechanistically in learning theory, ultimately leading to a neural network program that simulated faith in God (Bainbridge 1995b).

Computer simulation links to the theory of religion in two ways through the fundamental computing concept: *algorithm*. First, the term *algorithm* is synonymous with *explanation*, as it is used in the theory of religion. Standard dictionaries define *algorithm* as a procedure for solving a problem in a finite number of steps, and the theory defines an *explanation* as a "statement about how and why rewards may be obtained and costs are incurred" (Stark and Bainbridge 1987: 57). That is, explanations are algorithms that provide humans with instructions on how to solve their problems.

Second, a formal scientific theory is a deductive series of statements, that lead from a set of well-established principles to the proposition that the theory seeks to explain (Homans 1967; Stark and Bainbridge 1987: 13–14). That is, a formal, deductive theory is itself composed of algorithms, each of which reaches the solution of an intellectual problem in a finite number of steps. But a computer program is also a system of algorithms. Thus, a properly designed computer simulation of social behavior may be structurally isomorphic with and functionally equivalent to a theoretical argument. Given certain initial conditions and proper design, both the computer program and the theoretical argument will grind out the desired result. Or, one may say that a properly designed computer program can be an effective dynamic way of representing a theoretical argument that can test its coherence and increase its rigor.

My simplest learning theory computer simulation modeled the behavior of a single mouse in a T-maze (Bainbridge 1986: 22–29). Then, in a simulation of three human beings interacting with each other, I began exploring the consequences of algorithms that included but discounted events in the distant past, thus giving the people rather exploratory personalities exhibiting lack of commitment (Bainbridge 1987: 69–77).

Two more complex neural network simulations employing hierarchical neural nets modeled individual human beings interacting with each other in pursuit of various rewards, developing the mechanistic equivalent of conceptual categorization schemes to guide them in accepting or rejecting trades with other people having various combinations of traits. One of these studies simulated Gordon Allport's (1954) cognitive effort theory of ethnic prejudice (Bainbridge 1995a), and the other explored the logic of the Stark–Bainbridge (1987) exchange theory of religion (Bainbridge 1987: 88–101; 1995b).

These studies were thoroughly reductionist, using utterly mechanistic processes to model two modes of human thought that might seem very subtle: ethnic prejudice and religious faith. Although they violate the behaviorist ban on looking inside the human mind, the computer programs are totally transparent, and it is easy at any point to inspect the contents of all the memory registers. In both studies, the simulated humans develop categorization schemes for describing exchange partners, and in both it is possible for the simulated people to postulate beings that do not actually exist within the rules of the game. That is, they can develop not only false stereotypes of fellow simulated people but also belief in supernatural beings. Perhaps this study proves there is nothing sacred when it comes to computer simulations, but I think instead it shows one does not need a soul to believe in God. However, faith does require emotions (Thoits 1989).

EMOTIONS AND RELATIONSHIPS

When Homans first read the Stark–Bainbridge theory, he reminded me of the famous statement by the first-century satirical writer, Petronius: "Fear first brought gods into the world." William James (1902: 89) contended: "The ancient saying that the first maker of the Gods was fear receives voluminous corroboration from every age of religious history; but none the less does religious history show the part which joy has evermore tended to play. Sometimes the joy has been primary; sometimes secondary, being the gladness of deliverance from the fear." Either way, religion seems rooted in emotion, and the primary dimension is our feeling about costs and rewards.

Sacred discourse frequently concerns feelings, from guilt to bliss, terror to awe, and longing to ecstasy. The Bible is eloquent in its depiction of human emotion, across the entire spectrum: Job 4:14: "Fear came upon me, and trembling, which made all my bones to shake." Job 38:7: "When the morning stars sang together, and all the sons of God shouted for joy." John 16:21: "A woman when she is in travail hath sorrow, because her hour is come: but as soon as she is delivered of the child, she remembereth no more the anguish, for joy that a man is born into the world." 2 Corinthians 4:8: "We are troubled on every side, yet not distressed; we are perplexed, but not in despair." Luke 13:28: "There shall be weeping and gnashing of teeth, when ye shall see Abraham, and Isaac, and Jacob, and all the prophets, in the kingdom of God, and you yourselves thrust out." And who could forget the comforting words of John 3:16, which testify that even the Lord has emotions: "For God so loved the world, that he gave his only begotten Son, that whosoever believeth in him should not perish, but have everlasting life."

If religion elicits and shapes the meaning of emotions, surely the fundamental human feelings are shared by the higher animals, who are apparently incapable of religion. A purring cat must be experiencing bliss, and it can inspire fear in pigeons and mice. The tender care lavished upon their babies by birds and mammals is behaviorally indistinguishable from human love. Thus, emotion is deeply rooted in our animal biology, even if our recently evolved cognitive abilities are required for religious belief. In addition, as Homans said, ". . . the laws of human learning have themselves evolved and maintained themselves genetically as one mechanism for helping humans to survive in their environment" (Homans 1987: 139–141; cf. Wilson 1975: 551).

Robert H. Frank (1988) has alerted rational choice researchers to the idea that emotions, whether in humans or higher animals, may partly have evolved to signal intentions to other individuals, and to force them to behave in desired ways. Thus with the human capacity for role playing, emotional expressions become moves in a game. This insight is as old as history, and Porter Abbott has analyzed the strategic use of emotion in *The Portuguese Letters*, a work of fiction published in 1669. From her bare room in a convent, a nun writes five letters to her former lover. Abbott (1984: 74) argues that she expresses her feelings in accordance with a syllogism that she thinks will logically force him to love her again: "(1) All great love is greatly to be loved,

(2) I love greatly, (3) therefore I am greatly to be loved." Jay Haley (1963, 1969) analyzed psychotherapy as a strategic interaction in which the therapist maneuvers the patient to take his or her emotional assumptions to their illogical extreme, and he said the crucifixion was the masterful sacrifice move made by Jesus Christ in a game where the human soul was the prize.

The strategic use of emotion featured in my own analysis of how Scientologists appear to believe they can attain a higher state of being called *clear*, and I have briefly considered the comparable states of *sanctification* in the Holiness tradition and *satori* in Zen Buddhism (Bainbridge and Stark 1980; Bainbridge 1997). Like many birds and mammals, humans cry for parental attention, shriek in fear, and shout for help. Clearly, communication intended to cause another person to help us is deeply rooted in our biological inheritance, as well as in the psychology of childhood.

Humans sometimes become trapped in a pattern of emotionally intense help-seeking behavior when no help is in fact available, and this condition may be called neurosis, dependency, or depression. Perhaps this is most common for people with insoluble practical problems of ill health, poverty, lovelessness, or powerlessness. But the human capacity to imagine a better life, and the social demands that so often inspire shame and guilt, could force anyone into this vicious circle. The person invests so much energy in self-defeating obsessions to get help, that his or her life becomes significantly worse than it would otherwise be, and sometimes the person is even prevented from finding a real solution to the problems. *Clear*, *sanctification*, and *satori* are spiritualized conceptions of the psychological state of being free of such help-demanding and self-blaming obsessions.

Homans's classic, *The Human Group*, makes much of *sentiment*, a term that was meant to cover such murky concepts as: "sentiments of affection, affective content of sympathy and indulgence, intimate sympathy, respect, pride, antagonism, affective history, scorn, sentimental nostalgia" (Homans 1950: 37). Homans restricted *sentiments* to the feelings of one human being toward another. Much later work by Homans and others in his tradition conceptualizes social relationships as concrete *bonds* that are studied as structural elements in networks, or as stable patterns of interaction that readily can be observed. Yet we should recognize that social relationships are fundamentally based in emotions and images that exist only within human minds. Thus, many of the same challenges and opportunities associated with the sociology of emotions apply also to research on social relationships.

In this essay, emboldened by the essays Homans (e.g., 1981) published about his ancestors, I shall use data on my own ancestral family to develop a model of how religious emotions are embedded in social exchange. Fundamentally, reciprocity is the principle of obligation that links members of a family into an enduring relationship. Rooted in biological bonds, reciprocity at times resembles exchange, and of course nothing prevents members of a family from also being exchange partners. Alternatively, one could say that market exchange is merely a highly rationalized form of reciprocity that has outgrown the boundaries of the biological family.

Homans wrote about the exchange between two abstract individuals, Person and Other. Let us give them more human names, Lucy and George. Whether from biology, habits acquired in family-based reciprocity, or a history of mutually profitable exchanges, let us say that Lucy has developed a powerful relationship with George. Then she realizes that he is dying.

The Stark–Bainbridge theory immediately suggests that Lucy will be open to supernaturally based compensators to comfort her in her loss. But what does it say about her obligations to George? What does she have to offer him in his greatest time of need? In fact, Lucy was George's sister, and he lay dying slowly and painfully of typhoid fever in the early 1860s, when medicine had not yet discovered a cure. There is considerable doubt how much religion can really compensate an individual for his or her own most severe losses. Because Lucy and George shared the same religious assumptions, however, she could feel that the prayers she gave him really did fulfill some of her obligation to help him.

At a first approximation, we can distinguish two kinds of religious compensation, primary and secondary.

- *Primary compensation* substitutes a compensator for a reward that people desire for themselves.
- *Secondary compensation* substitutes a compensator for a reward that a person is obligated to provide to another person.

Secondary compensation may be a major factor in the creation and maintenance of religious organizations, even though the literature on the subject has concentrated on primary compensation. If religious compensators actually do not satisfy sufferers' needs very well, they might still satisfy their exchange partners' obligations to provide assistance. I am not here asserting that religious primary compensation is ineffective, merely raising the theoretical point that it might be and suggesting we should examine scientifically how much of the success of religious organizations is due to secondary compensation.

If religious compensators can satisfy existing obligations, they may also make a person attractive as a prospective exchange partner. In other words, secondary compensation is an issue prior to the formation of exchange relationships, as well as afterward. Two of the propositions in the Stark–Bainbridge theory are relevant here: "Religious specialists promulgate norms, said to come from the gods, that increase the rewards flowing to the religious specialists" (Stark and Bainbridge 1987: 99). "Religious specialists share in the psychic rewards offered to the gods, for example: deference, honor, and adoration" (Stark and Bainbridge 1987: 101).

To appear to be a valuable exchange partner is beneficial to any individual. A person is attractive to the extent that other people will give rewards to that person without requiring the person immediately to reciprocate by giving them a reward of equal or greater value. People invest in someone they find attractive, in hopes that they will receive great rewards in the future, perhaps in the distant future or in some undefined context. Another way of looking at this is to say that an attractive person receives rewards from others but can satisfy them in the immediate exchanges by providing compensators. Thus, a religious specialist may invest in activities to increase the apparent value of the compensators he or she has to offer.

In some societies, the individual may undergo costly spiritual ordeals, perhaps to forge a publicly acknowledged exchange relationship with a supernatural being. In a society with a highly professionalized clergy, the individual may invest in extensive formal training and attempt to create masterworks of the spirit (such as ritual performances, religious art, or sacred scholarship) that demonstrate that he or she has the requisite spiritual skill, sacred knowledge, or divine talent.

There are many different strategies for becoming an attractive exchange partner, and no cosmopolitan culture restricts itself to just one or two, even in the limited realm of religion. However, strategies are simply general explanations about how to attain certain goals, so they tend to be learned from other people as are most other valuable algorithms. Members of a family or other intimate social group will tend to share a particular strategy. To the extent that being a religious specialist is an inherited profession, therefore, supernatural strategies will tend to run in families. Members of such families who enter professions that are functionally similar to the clergy will tend to carry over the family's religious strategy, with only such modifications as are required to make the strategy appear to fit the secular occupation.

General explanations about how to obtain highly desired rewards are difficult to evaluate. In a competitive cultural specialty, individuals and groups will often become committed to the wrong strategy, or at least to one that is suboptimal and can be defeated by other, more effective strategies. If an individual has invested heavily in one strategy, he is unlikely to be able to switch to a different one quickly and easily. Therefore, a person who has wholeheartedly adopted one particular strategy for becoming an attractive exchange partner will be relatively committed to it. Especially if the strategy is supernatural (which means that explanations are especially difficult to evaluate), he or she may respond to failure by exerting even more effort, rather than by backtracking and looking for a different strategy. Sometimes this can lead to success, if the person can innovate in strategy-specific ways that are attractive to other people, and if the person's amplified emotions are of a kind to arouse positive feelings in others. Arguably, this is the source of much religious charisma. In many cases, however, exaggeration of a poor strategy will lead to catastrophic failure, and what the individual considers to be religious inspiration will appear to other people as madness.

Becoming an attractive exchange partner through increasing the potency of the compensators one offers is a strategy that aggressively employs secondary compensation. If other people accept the compensators, it can be successful. But if other people ignore or reject the compensators, the individual may become trapped in isolated primary compensation. The dreams that one wished to sell to others may become a costly liability that prevent the individual from investing elsewhere, until the person's social capital has been exhausted. The cases described below illustrate how primary and secondary compensation may lead to extremely successful or unsuccessful social outcomes.

BIOGRAPHICAL OUTLINE

The father of Lucy and George, John Seaman, was born in 1804, and their mother, Cleora Augusta Stevens, in 1814. John and Cleora married in 1831 and settled in Cleveland, Ohio, which was then only a modest village of a thousand souls. John established a small shoe-and-boot factory, and after some difficult years the business prospered, providing footwear for such diverse customers as the miners on Lake Superior and the North Union Shaker community. In 1833, John and six other men formally established the First Baptist Church of Cleveland (Rouse 1883).

When Cleora was a small child, she fell from a roof into the hot ashes of an open fire, suffering terrible burns to her back. For months, her mother tended her on a pillow, and for the rest of her life she carried deep scars from her neck to the base of her spine. Chronic physical complaints and this close brush with an early death may explain her lasting interest in experimental medical treatments, from water cures and food fads to electrified baths and color therapy, and she became a doctor of homeopathic medicine in 1860 (Ingham 1893; L. Bainbridge 1921).

John and Cleora had eight children: a baby who died before being named, Frances, George, Solomon ("Sollie"), Lucy Elizabeth, Charles, Cleora Augusta ("Cora Gussie"), and Walter. The custom was to give children the names of relatives, both living and dead, and name inheritance is one method by which people attempt to limit death's triumph. Frances was named after Cleora's deceased sister. Lucy carried the first names of both of her grandmothers. Brother Sollie was stuck with the imposing name Solomon because he had been born during a visit by his mother's brother, Presbyterian minister Solomon Stevens. In an attempt to cure his pathological shyness during his teens, his too-demanding name was changed to that of his father's brother, Henry. Cora Gussie was named after her mother.

Lucy attended Cleveland Female Seminary, a highly progressive school, then followed the advice of one of her teachers and went to Ipswich Female Seminary just north of Boston (cf. Guilford 1890: 74–75). Historically connected to Mount Holyoke College, Ipswich enjoyed a sterling reputation as a teachers college and finishing school that combined evangelical Christianity with high intellectual standards (Anonymous 1839; Cole 1940; Green 1979).

Shortly after graduation, in May 1864, Lucy and her mother visited Washington, where they were recruited to Ohio Relief, one of many voluntary organizations operating under the aegis of the United States Sanitary Commission that were providing medical care along the battlefront in Virginia. Even this late in the war the government was still not fulfilling this duty adequately (L. Bainbridge 1919; Maxwell 1956). The Battle of the Wilderness had begun on the fifth of the month, and Union losses were running at ten thousand a week, so there was ample work tending shattered and dying men (Catton 1965). Lucy served as a war nurse for a few weeks, at Aquia Creek, Port Royal, White House Landing, and City Point, enduring horrifying experiences and writing some of her observations for a newspaper.

At this time she met her future husband, William Folwell Bainbridge, who was a student minister attached to the Christian Commission, which was distributing tracts and providing spiritual comfort to the soldiers (Shattuck 1987). Nominally, the Sanitary Commission and the Christian Commission were partners with a well-defined division of labor between them, the former seeking to save men's lives, and the latter saving their souls. But often the two groups were rivals, as each competed for the resources to carry out its mission with less than total appreciation for the other's goals. This difference of approach was to remain between Lucy and William throughout their lives, with Lucy somewhat more ready to give people material and emotional rewards, while William offered them supernatural compensators.

William had graduated from Rochester University two years earlier, having worked his way through college, and was on summer break from Rochester Theological Seminary. This graduate school was open to students from all Protestant denominations, but the Baptist influence was strong, and candidates for admission were required to present certificates of membership in an evangelical church. Senior students served as "supplies" (temporary clergy) throughout the region, and graduates were much sought after by churches in need of educated but fundamentalist ministers. The teachings stressed the divine authority of the Bible, but the training was highly intellectual. Students were instructed in the most convincing arguments for the existence of God and the best refutations for skeptical assaults on their tradition. Official doctrines included original sin, the second coming of Christ, and judgment after death of the righteous and the wicked (Anonymous 1863). William's clergyman father, Samuel McMath Bainbridge, did not live to see his son ordained, nor to celebrate the Union victory, dying on the first day of 1865 and leaving his wife and several children in poverty (De Forest 1950).

In July, William became the pastor of the First Baptist Church in Erie, Pennsylvania. He began taking the hundred-mile railroad to Cleveland to court Lucy, and in September 1866 they were married. The following year her father financed a grand tour that took them through England, France, Egypt, Palestine, Germany, and Russia. Extensive travel in biblical lands provided William with invaluable material for sermons, and Lucy wrote a book-length account that was serialized in a newspaper.

In 1869, William took over the second-largest Baptist church in New England, Central Baptist in Providence. Lucy, being a woman, was never permitted to join the clergy formally, but the centennial history of the church called her "nevertheless a most efficient minister" who operated extensive programs for working girls from the nearby factories and other humanitarian efforts (Anderson 1906: 76–77), while her husband achieved some success recruiting new members. A daughter, named Cleora (the first name of Lucy's mother and of her dead sister), was born soon after. Dr. Cleora Seaman came from Cleveland to help Lucy with her namesake, but contracted "intermittent fever" and died. In February 1870 Lucy gave birth to her son, William Seaman Bainbridge (named after his father and Lucy's father), but baby Cleora died two months afterward of water on the brain. Lucy dealt with her grief partly by adopting a girl and naming her Helen Augusta (combining a dead cousin's first name with her dead mother's middle name). During a successful ten-year pastorate, both Lucy and William published magazine and newspaper essays, and she became the first president of the state chapter of the Woman's Christian Temperance Union.

After Lucy's father died, her inheritance permitted William to resign his pastorate and embark on a two-year world tour of Christian missions to develop what he called "a science of missions." They took nine-year-old "Willie" with them but left little Helen in Cleveland with William's mother Mary, who had escaped her poverty by marrying Lucy's father. The three traveled extensively through Japan, China, Burma, and India as William gathered data by visiting hundreds of mission outposts including the Chinese station of his influential cousin John Nevius (J. Nevius 1869; H. Nevius 1869, 1895). At Bombay the family split up, Lucy taking Willie by boat through Egypt to Lebanon, and William reaching Lebanon by horseback after an extensive tour of the archeological ruins of Mesopotamia. A stop in Germany allowed them to attend the 1880 performance of the Oberammergau Passion Play.

In a wisteria-wreathed cottage on Narragansett Bay, William wrote two books about their trip around the world, Lucy produced one, and the family hoped to live on their royalties and on speakers' fees from lecture tours

(W. F. Bainbridge 1882a, 1882b; L. Bainbridge 1882). Although filled with noble thoughts and keen observations in the sociology of missions, William's books were rather dry, and audiences preferred Lucy's lively lecturing style that employed clothing and props from exotic lands. William's third book, *Self Giving*, was an angry novel about overseas mission work that was based on the thinly disguised stories of real people, many of whom must have been exceedingly displeased to see themselves parodied in print. The hero and heroine were grossly idealized versions of William and Lucy themselves, and the arrogant book undoubtedly hurt William's standing in the missionary movement. He began work on a fourth book, *From Eden to Patmos*, that would be a travelogue of Bible lands, but a publisher did not quickly materialize and the family was running out of money.

Half-heartedly, William accepted the directorship of the Brooklyn City Mission Society, where Lucy soon created a women's branch, but his chief energies continued to go into his manuscript. Amid terrible family arguments, William lost his job. His wife and children had to confront the growing suspicion that he was descending into madness. Briefly William took the pastorate of the financially strapped Delaware Avenue Baptist Church in Wilmington, able to draw upon personal connections because the first pastor had been a member of his mother's family. Lucy staged exotic tableaux to boost her husband's ministry, but he continued to sink into his scholarly project, and he was soon unemployed again. Their son was a student of medicine at Columbia University, but he could not finish his training without financial help. The family disintegrated, and intermittent separations between William and the others eventually became permanent.

In abject despair, on January 2, 1891, Lucy knelt to pray. How her husband's compounded failures served God's plan, she could not imagine. Nearing her forty-ninth birthday, it was hard to see how she could start life anew. From her lonely vigil in Wilmington she cried to the Lord, and at the very depths of her agony, she sensed someone standing over her.

A reporter for the *New York Times* later heard her describe this moment to a Christian audience: "'I was in great perplexity what the Lord wanted me to do. One day I was alone on my knees, and I fancied—strange fancy, you may think—I saw our personal Savior standing before me. 'Wait,' he said to me, 'wait and you shall know what to do.'

"'At the very moment I was on my knees,' continued Mrs. Bainbridge, while the room was hushed in silence, 'Mrs. Brown, Superintendent of the Women's Branch of the New York City Mission, died suddenly. Next day her place was offered to me!'" (Anonymous 1895).

Lucy had no doubts of the reality of this Epiphany, as she later told the Mission ladies: "It was not a dream that came to me in a distant city, on the very afternoon of Mrs. Brown's translation, when, kneeling and alone, pleading for light upon perplexity, the Savior stood for a moment visibly at hand

and spoke the needed words of comfort. But such experiences are not for the world, and can only be hinted at for the encouragement of our sisters, who sit with us around the same hearthstone of the household of faith, and to whom we repeat the text" (L. Bainbridge 1892).

For the next sixteen years she directed a full-time staff of fifty women doing religious social work with immigrants in lower Manhattan. Her son, now called Will, became a spectacularly successful surgeon with a world-spanning career, and he devoted much of his energy to showering love and honor upon his mother. Over the next few years Lucy wrote three books, including an autobiography, with the help of a secretary provided by Will (L. Bainbridge 1917, 1920, 1924). As a young bride in 1867, she had visited Bethel in the Holy Land, and for years the family used to express its hopes for the future by quoting Genesis 35:3: "And let us arise, and go up to Bethel." In response to Lucy's urging that she wanted to go to Bethel, Will obtained a beautiful country farm for her in the town of Bethel, Connecticut, where she enjoyed the summer of 1928, before returning to New York City where the flu epidemic of that winter carried her off.

COPING WITH DEATH

In the original statement of the Stark–Bainbridge theory, religious comfort for death is the principal example of primary compensation. Death cast its shadow across Lucy's childhood, in a way that few modern American children experience so acutely. Sister Frances tumbled down the stairs to her death before Lucy was born. Lucy's darling sister, Cora Gussie, died at age five, and brother Walter, at age two. She greatly admired her older brother, George, who was ready to become a partner in the family business after a tour of Europe in 1860. But he contacted typhoid fever, an often lingering disease marked by high fever, pain, and intestinal bleeding. George begged his sister to stay with him and tend him in his illness (L. Bainbridge ca. 1920). George eventually died, and they buried him in Woodland Cemetery, sixty new acres of graveyard with a fine grove of trees and an ancient, sixty-foot Indian mound (Rose 1950: 262). Then they transferred the other Seaman corpses to lie beside him in this soothing paradise.

Always a reticent man, John Seaman became even more reluctant to express his feelings after the death of George. For many years, he would not show love to anyone. Cleora by now had lost four of her seven children, and she wondered which of the remaining three might be taken from her next. Lucy fell into deep despondency, not only because she had lost her beloved brother, but also because she was convinced that she herself would soon die. She thought of Cora Gussie, Uncle Solomon who had simply dropped dead one day, her favorite cousin Helen who had died about the same time, and of George—all gone within the space of two years. Lucy lost heart and waited to die. It was at this point that the family decided to send Lucy to school back East, in what proved a successful attempt to cure her profound depression.

At Ipswich Female Seminary, Lucy did several things that handled her grief. They can be described as strategies for getting control over her fate, ways of expressing personal competency, or fundamental algorithms for success. With great diligence she studied Alexander's (1851) *Evidences of Christianity*, a collection of pious essays by various scholars that sought to prove the truth of faith intellectually. Many of her free hours were spent in melancholic reverie, and one result was a tender six-stanza poem in which she imagined her dead loved ones waiting for her in the afterlife: "Loving arms are round me twining, heavenly music fills the air—Brother, friend and sister singing, sad but sweet to have you there." When a Boston newspaper published these verses, her friends in Cleveland hailed her as a poetess, but she was never again able to express serious thoughts in poetry.

Soon after her daughter died in 1870, Lucy published a sentimental story about grief and charity, featuring the death of a small child: "The Christian parents could in submission say, 'It is well, since God wills it so,' but the mother's heart was aching still for the earthly presence. She longed for a sight of the sunny face and the sound of the prattling lips so still. Heaven seemed too far away, and a long weary way ere she should reach it. How apt the sorrowing Christian heart is to forget the daily toil for Jesus, and 'look too eagerly beyond'" (L. Bainbridge ca. 1870). This passage raises the question of how effective primary compensation can be. Although compensators are treated by humans as if they were rewards, humans prefer rewards to compensators (Stark and Bainbridge 1987: 36–37). The fact that very few people have chosen religious martyrdom suggests that most people would vastly prefer to live than to die with the promise of afterlife. All the religious compensators of her devout Baptist faith could not fully comfort Lucy at the loss of George and the others.

In each of these episodes, Lucy used structured forms of social communication to deal with her own grief, and to give herself confidence that she was competent to live her own life in the face of personal death. One interpretation, from the exchange perspective, is that she was obtaining social support for the religious algorithms that told her she would still benefit from her investments in her departed loved ones, in Heaven if not on Earth.

However, Lucy had some responsibility to protect several of the people who died near her, so secondary compensation was at work as well. At the time there were no easy medical cures for typhoid, intermittent fever, and hydrocephalus, but Lucy's brother, mother, and daughter were in her care when they died. Faith in the Christian afterlife would allow Lucy to feel less guilt, because her loved ones had presumably not lost all at death, but had "gone to their reward." Through sharing her religion publicly, in literature or everyday life, she forced her living associates to agree that the family deaths were acceptable or even rewarding, thereby socially legitimating her lack of responsibility for their loss. Thus, she could be free from shame as well as guilt.

Lucy's few weeks as a nurse in the Civil War were an intense initiation into adulthood that established an identity she would cherish for the rest of her life. She wore a red silk badge with gold lettering: "OHIO Relief Committee." Once when she was improvising a tent over a desperately wounded man whose face was blackened by dirt, gunpowder, and sunburn, a passing doctor called out to her, "Bully for you, Miss Ohio." Later she was feeding another man, shot in both arms, who asked, "Say, please, Ohio Relief, what's your name?" Whether from fatigue, or reluctance to let the men become too attached to her, Lucy declined to give her name and instead pointed at her badge, so he called her "Sister Ohio." Lucy gave him bread and milk, learned that he was an Ohio boy, and tended him for several days until he was transported to a hospital in Washington. After the war he showed up in Cleveland, one arm healed but the other gone, and proposed marriage to her. She declined, but ever afterward she would proudly think of herself as "Sister Ohio" (L. Bainbridge 1919, 1924).

Given the lack of sanitary conditions and the impotence of medical technology to deal with loss of blood or the ubiquitous infections, death often followed wounding. Lucy's letters home from the battlefront and her published reminiscences contain sentimental stories of how she provided soldiers with religious compensators as she watched them die. Lucy was especially fond of Franky, a Michigan boy. He had been shot in both arms and one leg, and the wounds had become gangrenous and infested with maggots. "He said he was not afraid to die; he knew his mother had been praying for him a long time, and he thought Jesus would help him to die if he had to, but he would rather live."

Over the following days of Franky's final agony, Lucy fed him tea, soft bread, apple jelly, and oranges, singing sentimental songs like *Homeward Bound* and assisting Reverend Prugh with prayers and reading the Twenty-third Psalm. "Little Franky will not probably live many hours. I have been with him a good deal. I have written to his mother, and by and by shall write of his death. I have a lock of his hair and two little rings to send her. Poor little fellow he does suffer terribly." He had carved one of the rings from a nutshell, and his pathetic possessions included skeins of green and yellow sewing silk he had picked up at Fairfax Court House.

On June 10, 1864, after the wounded men in best condition had been sent to Washington hospitals, she wrote her family, "I have only Franky left and he can't live long. After seeing 'my boys' safely on board the steamer, I went up and sat with Franky until nearly bed time. The terrible pain he had suffered was nearly gone; he was very weak and hiccoughed badly, and I sat with him on the grass and fanned him and hummed *There Is a Light in the Window Brother*. I told him he could not get any better—that he was almost home. I told him of Jesus, and that if he would ask him to be with him when he went through the dark valley, he would lead him safely through, for he had promised to. I asked him if he was afraid to die. He said, 'Oh, no, Jesus will be with me,' and the tears ran down his face while I spoke of Jesus, of home and Heaven." She sang *Jesus Loves Me*, *Rock of Ages*, and *I Have a Father in the Promised Land*. Franky tried to sing with her, in a broken voice that strengthened briefly in the last verse: "I hope to meet you in the promised land."

Fortified by the explanation that death is always part of God's plan, Lucy frequently saw positive benefit in the deaths of people for whom she had some responsibility. At the end of summer, in about 1886, the family was preparing to close the cottage in Rhode Island, as Willie and his adopted sister Helen readied to attend boarding schools and their parents headed back to Brooklyn, but there was a problem of how to provide for their faithful servant, Maggie the Irish girl, and her frail baby. Maggie would have to find work in Providence, but she could not do so with the infant. Lucy hunted high and low for a willing orphanage or nursery, to no success. At the last possible moment, during a terrible thunderstorm, Lucy and Maggie knelt on the cottage floor and prayed for divine aid. Suddenly there was a terrible flash of lightning! Maggie ran terrified to her baby and found him lifeless. When a physician had finished his examination, he said, "The little fellow has gone away on the storm" (L. Bainbridge 1924: 101).

At the New York City Mission Society, assisting the dying was considered to be a noble success, as the case of poor Fanny illustrates. For twenty years, Fanny had lived in one corner of her mother's room, seldom going outdoors and judged too "idiotic" for work or education. The only alternative was to send her to the snake-pit institutions of Blackwell's Island, when the phrase "the island" struck terror into the hearts of poor New Yorkers. Lucy used to visit forty-year-old Fanny and marvel at this wretched loss of a life: "Do you wonder at the wasted form and wild stare of the poor creature housed year after year amidst such dreadful surroundings?" Her aged mother's only comfort was the missionary's visits. "The old, wrinkled face would light up as she talked about Christ, and the future life. 'I could die if only Fanny was cared for. I am getting so old and tired I'd be glad to be at rest.'"

Then, "the old woman dropped dead in the hallway, and no one could understand the sorrow of the poor, half-witted daughter as the coffin that contained her best earthly friend was carried out. Since then she has been dreadfully neglected; her drunken stepfather did not want any one to do anything for her. 'She'll have to get out now,' he said." Fanny begged Lucy to find her a job so she would not have to go to the Island. Lucy told her to trust Jesus, as her mother had, and when they came to take her away, they found that Fanny, too, had died. "Suddenly she exchanged the dark hovel for a glorious mansion of the Father's house" (Bainbridge 1997: 322).

Many times during Lucy's long career of service, someone whom she was trying to help out of a desperate situation died, and at least publicly she always interpreted the death as a blessing and a perfect solution to the person's problems. However, given his intellectual training and critical temperament, her husband may not have possessed the most comforting brand of faith, as the following missionary story he liked to tell suggests: "That sudden death of Rev. J. Thomas in 1837, when, just in sight of his expected lifework, a tree fell over on his boat from the bank of the Brahmaputra, killing him instantly—what could God have meant by this?" (W. F. Bainbridge 1882a: 187).

When Lucy herself died in 1928, her son Will sat for days in her darkened apartment, brooding, until his son John reminded him that his religious beliefs asserted that there was no need for sorrow because she had gone to a better life. By giving free medical care to the family of the leading clergyman of the Mission Society, Will arranged for publication of a rather unctuous biography of his mother (McKinney 1932). For his remaining nineteen years, he constantly distributed his mother's books around the world and badgered influential people with her story, apparently continuing to feel unfulfilled obligations to her despite a plenitude of religious compensators. His own death in 1947 was described by Norman Vince Peale as the ideal Christian passing, sustained by absolute confidence in the life hereafter (Peale and Blanton 1950).

QUEST FOR GLORY

William Folwell Bainbridge inherited from his father Samuel the career strategy that education and scholarship would make one an attractive religious specialist. Samuel McMath Bainbridge was born in Romulus, New York, in 1816, a generation after members of his family had helped found the first Baptist church in that town (Centennial Executive Committee 1894: 104–105; cf. Folwell 1933). His father was a printer in Philadelphia for a few years, but came to Romulus to farm in 1793. Two of his uncles were part-time clergy and a third had graduated from medical college. In 1836 Samuel entered Hamilton Theological Seminary, and was ordained pastor of a church in Stockbridge, New York, in 1841. He married Romulus neighbor Mary Price Folwell, whose father had graduated from Brown College in the class of 1796. Until his death at the age of 49, he constantly moved from one small congregation in central New York to another (Slocum 1908; Root 1940; Schmidt 1953).

Samuel took a leading role on the modernist side in the Baptist "Removal Controversy," which wanted to transform Hamilton into a nonsectarian university, an effort that failed but led to the founding of Rochester University (Anonymous 1872; Rosenberger 1925; Williams 1969), and Hamilton later evolved into Colgate University without Samuel's help. One of his sermons survives, a fiery but scholarly essay on the revolutionary social and religious transformations of the decade before the Civil War (S. M. Bainbridge 1856).

In taking this intellectual path, Samuel ignored the successful strategy followed by most preachers of his denomination. Finke and Stark (1988, 1992; Stark and Finke 2000) have argued that the Baptists gained market share in the American religious economy during the nineteenth century because they resisted the Methodists' trend toward increasingly educated clergy and remained culturally and emotionally close to their parishioners. Samuel's family was highly educated, and the career strategy of becoming highly educated worked for members of the younger generations who entered secular careers of public service, notably William Watts Folwell (1933), president of the University of Wisconsin, and Bainbridge Colby (Spargo 1963; Smith 1970), U.S. Secretary of State and law partner of President Wilson. But for Samuel's son, William Folwell Bainbridge, the strategy ultimately failed.

William attended the highly intellectual graduate theology school that his father had helped create, and even joined the same fraternity to which his father had belonged (Delta Upsilon 1934). The curriculum of Rochester Theological Seminary was extremely demanding. Sacred Philology required instruction and daily recitations in the languages of the Holy Scriptures: Hebrew, Greek, Aramaic, and Latin. Biblical Criticism and Exegesis stressed analysis in the original tongues of the texts, while Homiletics prepared students to compose and deliver sermons in English or German. Ecclesiastical History traced the growth and transformation of the Christian church, with special attention to the struggle between state-established churches and nonconforming resistance movements and to "the corruptions and reformations of the Christian life and worship in medieval and modern times" (Anonymous 1863).

Immediately after Lucy married William, she discovered that he discretely shaved the hair back on his forehead, in the belief this made him appear more intelligent. Like his father before him he had ambitions to be an influential writer, and pastoral care did not interest him greatly. The two books he published in 1882 offered a "science of missions," and his 1883 novel overflowed with advice for missionaries, but the response was disappointing. He hoped to win literary glory through his travelogue, *From Eden to Patmos*, but no publisher was willing to take it. Unfortunately there was little fresh about it. On his first trip to the Holy Land, he had been personally helped by William McClure Thomson, who had then already published a popular travelogue (Thomson 1859) which by the early 1880s was expanding into a three-volume set. Other competitors abounded (e.g., Tristram 1866). The story of William's trek through Babylon would merely duplicate the book by John Newman (1876), who had ridden the identical route, and it could not be half so exciting as Layard's (1854) classic. Rather than give up his project, William became obsessed with it, eventually transforming it into a linguistic and geographic study of all the names of places and tribes mentioned in the Bible.

This gave the project a supernatural dimension. As John 1:1 explains, "In the beginning was the Word, and the Word was with God, and the Word was God." But many words in the Bible are obscure, so William could serve God by clarifying them. This would make him a valued exchange partner, playing the profoundly important role of intellectual mediator with the deity. Furthermore, his great project was scientific, like his earlier world tour books combining the power of religion and science. In China in 1879, William had convinced John Nevius to turn his long interest in spirit possession into a scientific study. Immediately after William departed, Nevius sent a questionnaire on the subject to all the Protestant missionaries in China (J. Nevius 1896). Given Nevius's great prestige in the missionary community, William could feel he had an ally in believing that science could strengthen religion.

When Lucy and her children expressed doubts about William's all-consuming project, he could argue that it served the Lord, that it employed the best scientific methods, and that success would bring fame and prosperity to his family. In a sense this was the familiar problem in economics that people fail to realize that investing more money in a questionable scheme to recover sunk costs is usually a mistake. But it was more than that, because admitting failure would attack the basis of his subjective value as an exchange partner, which was based on shaky assertions of intellectual grandeur (cf. Lemert 1967).

William's publications in the early 1880s, his few surviving letters, newspaper reports of his activities in Delaware, and the committee meeting minutes of a church he served in 1906 at Allston, Massachusetts, reveal a mind that was lucid and logical but convinced of its own brilliance and severely critical of other people. It is hard to say whether he fully exhibited the grandiosity and conspiratorial delusions of classical paranoia, but his personality certainly leaned in that direction, and we know of no other symptoms that would have caused his family to doubt his sanity. In 1915, William Folwell Bainbridge died, in a fine apartment at Harvard University where his son was supporting his fruitless scholarship. Lucy and her son rushed to Boston, and Will made a remarkable attempt to redeem his father's honor by personally dissecting his father's brain in a vain search for a physiological excuse for the obsessions.

William Seaman Bainbridge ("Will") inherited from his father the same career strategy of gaining great glory through "scientific" intellectual activity, but he became a surgeon not a clergyman. One influence was Lucy's admiration for her physician mother and for the successful physician who lived next door when she was a child and who left a large inheritance for his family when he died young. Another was her friend Dr. Eliza Mosher, who taught Will how to dissect cats in Brooklyn when he was a boy and first took him to Chautauqua (Vincent 1885), the famous religious resort, where he later established a summer medical clinic. A third influence was Lucy's relative, Dr. Louis Livingston Seaman, older than Will and prominent in New York social circles, who had toured the hospitals of China and India in 1886 to study contagious and epidemic diseases and later observed medical practices in the Russo-Japanese War (Seaman 1905, 1906).

In the summer of 1896, Will began practicing medicine at Chautauqua and faced the difficult decision of how to launch his career among the prosperous classes of New York City. Unexpectedly, a telegram came, asking Will to become the personal physician of John Sinclair, a wealthy patient connected with Lucy's Mission Society, who had gone violently insane. Will had to answer immediately, but his mother was vacationing in the Catskills and could not be reached. That night, Lucy awoke suddenly, with the terrible feeling that her son needed her. She anxiously told her surprised host she must leave instantly, and traveling all night, she reached Will late the next day. His astonishment was so great that he became absolutely convinced that he and his mother had been in telepathic communication. Together they prayed, and the answer came to them. Will would accept a roving commission to adjust Sinclair through travel, especially a walking tour through Switzerland and visits to the leading medical centers of Europe where Will could study with the best surgeons and develop valuable international contacts. For two years Will tended Sinclair, at one point barely escaping death when Sinclair tried to stab him in his sleep, and their extensive medical odyssey provided a great boost for his general practice, which he established at Manhattan's fashionable Gramercy Park.

Although surgery is a secular profession, Will relied upon religion to provide many of his clients: from Chautauqua, from the Mission Society, and from teaching a huge Bible class for women at the Fifth Avenue Baptist Church, where John D. Rockefeller, Jr., was teaching one for men. Like his father, Will believed that publishing authoritative intellectual books would confer valuable charisma upon him, so he wrote a surgical textbook on gynecology based on a course in which he and his medical students dissected female cadavers (Bainbridge and Meeker 1906). He did not marry until the age of 41 in 1911, when he wed June Ellen Wheeler, cultivated daughter of a beef tycoon.

Like his father, around 1906 he began a massive book project, collecting all kinds of information about cancer, anthropological as well as medical. But unlike his father, he finished the project, publishing *The Cancer Problem* in 1914. Intended as a comprehensive guide for medical professionals, this was a scholarly as well as clinical book, and the bibliography ran to fifty-three pages. His surgical expertise was sorely tested, however, when his first child, named Elizabeth (after Lucy's middle name), was born without an esophagus. At that point, Will held the world record for operating on the youngest child using spinal analgesia, in successful surgery of a three-month-old. But for Elizabeth, he could do nothing, and she died after four days.

Years later, Will would tell a Baptist men's club that Elizabeth had been a bud from his June rose, saying she "has been transplanted and is now in the Garden of the King." Like him, June and Lucy had religious rhetoric ready to cloak feelings of loss and failure, but how well faith actually comforts the bereaved is an open question. Will always prayed before operating, and he considered Jesus to be the "Good Physician" who could cure any ailment. But when his technical competence was challenged by the death of Elizabeth, like Festinger's (1957; Festinger et al. 1956) disappointed millenarians he began to proselytize all the more vigorously. Will became the leading American advocate for the now-discredited theories of the King's surgeon, Dr. William Arbuthnot Lane, who believed that many ills were caused by intestinal blockages that could be cured by surgically straightening out kinks and separating adhesions (Barnes 1977). Not only did Will perform numerous unnecessary abdominal operations, but he stormed the country convincing provincial surgeons to do the same. His most publicized case was an operation on the humorist Irvin S. Cobb (1915), and he also operated on this author's wife for "chronic intestinal stasis." He refused to recant even when the New York surgical establishment threatened to have him disbarred from medical practice.

During the World War I, he followed the example of his father and of his cousin Louis Seaman in exploiting the opportunities for career advancement through foreign travel to write fame-enhancing reports. In 1915 he toured medical facilities on both sides of the western front, and after the United States entered the war he did an extensive survey of treatment of the wounded in France and Britain (W. Seaman Bainbridge 1919). With a Belgian friend, he organized the first Congrès International de Médecine et de Pharmacie Militaires in 1922, and he became permanent American co-president of the important international organization that resulted (W. Seaman Bainbridge 1922; Voncken 1939; Anonymous 1971: 404). Will published eight book-length reports of these meetings, and he mercilessly exploited his international fame to boost his New York practice. At the height of his career, he employed a man full-time to arrange publicity and distribute his more than 100 publications.

CONCLUSION

The biographical stories told in this paper are very specific, but they illustrate general principles. Some of the deepest human emotions are roused by the twin issues of *death* and *glory*. How can humans deal both personally and professionally with the crushing awareness of mortality? How can individuals win the competition to become valued exchange partners? If the people described here responded to those challenges in their own way, fundamentally they employed secondary compensators, which other people also regularly employ, each in accordance with his or her life's strategies.

It is not easy in all cases to distinguish when religion compensated Lucy's personal loss when someone close to her died (primary compensation), from when religion chiefly allowed her to fulfill her social obligations to others despite their deaths (secondary compensation). But in a number of her professional dealings with death, it is clear that religion was of great value to her as a secondary compensator, allowing defeat to be declared victory. Thus, through secondary compensation, religion can be a tactic for sustaining one's reputation as a valuable exchange partner, despite manifest failure to provide rewards to an exchange partner when one is obligated to do so.

Lucy shared with her husband and son the larger strategy of combining publications with foreign contacts to publicize herself as a potentially valuable exchange partner in the general field of religion and related professions, such as her own social work and her son's medicine. To some extent, glory is a primary compensator which gives the person self-esteem (the belief that one is a valuable exchange partner) and possibly a sense of immortality. But most obviously, glory associated with intellectual and professional accomplishments advertises one's value as an exchange partner to potential customers.

Stark and I have criticized the traditional sociological concept of charisma (Stark and Bainbridge 1987: 195), and we have also noted that it might be conceptualized as an unusual ability of religious leaders to build effective social bonds (Stark and Bainbridge 1985: 356). Now I suggest that secondary compensation is another way of conceptualizing charisma.

Charisma means the possession of spiritual gifts. I Corinthians 12:8–11 lists the gifts that different individuals may have: "For to one is given by the Spirit the word of wisdom; to another the word of knowledge by the same Spirit; to another faith by the same Spirit; to another the gifts of healing by the same Spirit; to another the working of miracles; to another prophecy; to another discerning of spirits; to another diverse kinds of tongues; to another the interpretations of tongues; but all these worketh that one and the selfsame Spirit, dividing to every man severally as he will." Wisdom, knowledge, healing, and the interpretations of tongues are the professional goals Lucy, William, and Will set for themselves, and in so doing they harnessed secondary compensation to the service of their personal charisma, energized by the emotions communicated in social exchange.

NOTE

The views expressed in this essay do not necessarily represent the views of the National Science Foundation or the United States.

REFERENCES

Abbott, H. Porter. 1984. *Diary Fiction: Writing as Action*. Ithaca, N.Y.: Cornell University Press.

Alexander, Archibald (ed.). 1851. *The Evidences of Christianity*. Philadelphia: Hayes and Zell.

Allport, Gordon W. 1954. *The Nature of Prejudice*. Cambridge, Mass.: Addison-Wesley.

Anderson, Thomas D. 1906. *The Centennial Services of the Central Baptist Church, Providence Rhode Island*. Providence, R.I.: Remington Printing Co.

Anonymous. 1839. *Catalogue of the Officers and Members of the Seminary for Female Teachers at Ipswich, Massachusetts for the Year Ending April 1839*. Salem, Mass.: Register Press.

———. 1863. *Twelfth Annual Catalogue of the Officers and Students of the Rochester Theological Seminary*. Rochester, N.Y.: A. Strong.

———. 1872. *The First Half Century of Madison University, 1819–1869*. New York: Sheldon.

———. 1895. "Work for the Downtown Poor," *New York Times* November 9: 5.

———. 1971. "Liège... and Military Medicine," *International Review of the Army, Navy and Air Force Medical Services* 5: 404.

Asimov, Isaac. 1951. *Foundation*. New York: Gnome.

Axelrod, Robert. 1984. *The Evolution of Cooperation*. New York: Basic Books.

Bainbridge, Lucy Seaman. ca. 1870. "Mrs. Dana's Christmas Day," published in an unidentified newspaper.

———. 1882. *Round the World Letters*. Boston: Lothrop.

———. 1892. No title. *New York City Mission Society Monthly* January: 61.

———. 1917. *Helping the Helpless in Lower New York*. New York: Fleming H. Revell.

———. 1919. "Sister Ohio," *The Outlook* 122, (4) May 28: 155.

———. 1920. *Jewels from the Orient*. New York: Fleming H. Revell.

———. ca. 1920. "A Remembrance of my Father and Mother, John Seaman and Cleora Augusta Stevens Seaman," typescript undated but no earlier than November 1915.

———. 1921. "One of the Pioneer Women in Medicine," *The Medical Woman's Journal* 28 March, 3: 75–79.

———. 1924. *Yesterdays*. New York: Fleming H. Revell.

Bainbridge, Samuel McMath. 1856. "The Last Great Shaking." Penn Yan, N.Y.: S. C. Cleveland.

Bainbridge, William Folwell. 1882a. *Along the Lines at the Front: A General Survey of Baptist Home and Foreign Missions*. Philadelphia: American Baptist Publication Society.

———. 1882b. *Around the World Tour of Christian Missions*. New York: Blackall.

———. 1919. *Report on Medical and Surgical Developments of the War*, special issue of *United States Naval Medical Bulletin*.

———. 1922. *Report on Congrès International de Médecine et de Pharmacie Militaires*, special issue of *United States Naval Medical Bulletin*.

Bainbridge, William Seaman and Harold D. Meeker. 1906. *A Compend of Operative Gynecology*. New York: Grafton.

Bainbridge, William Sims. 1986. *Experiments in Psychology*. Belmont, Calif.: Wadsworth.

———. 1987. *Sociology Laboratory*. Belmont, Calif.: Wadsworth.

———. 1995a. "Minimum Intelligent Neural Device: A Tool for Social Simulation," *Journal of Mathematical Sociology* 20: 179–192.

———. 1995b. "Neural Network Models of Religious Belief," *Sociological Perspectives* 38: 483–495.

———. 1995c. "Social Influence and Religious Pluralism," *Advances in Group Processes* 12: 1–18. Greenwich, Conn.: JAI Press.

———. 1997. *The Sociology of Religious Movements*. New York: Routledge.

Bainbridge, William Sims and Rodney Stark. 1980. "Scientology: To Be Perfectly Clear," *Sociological Analysis* 41: 128–136.

Barnes, Benjamin A. 1977. "Discarded Operations: Surgical Innovation by Trial and Error." In *Costs, Risks, and Benefits of Surgery*. John P. Bunker, Benjamin A. Barnes and Frederick Mosteller, eds. New York: Oxford University Press, 109–123.

Baron, James N. and Michael T. Hannan. 1994. "The Impact of Economics on Contemporary Sociology," *Journal of Economic Literature* 32: 1111–1146.

Catton, Bruce. 1965. *Never Call Retreat*. New York: Washington Square Press.

Centennial Executive Committee. 1894. *Centennial Celebration of the Official Organization of the Town of Romulus, Seneca County, New York*. Romulus, N.Y.: Centennial Executive Committee.

Cobb, Irvin S. 1915. "Speaking of Operations." In *Irvin Cobb At His Best*. Garden City, N.Y. [1923]: Sun Dial Press.

Cole, Arthur C. 1940. *A Hundred Years of Mount Holyoke College: The Evolution of an Educational Ideal*. New Haven, Conn.: Yale University Press.

Coleman, James S. 1990. *Foundations of Social Theory*. Cambridge, Mass.: Harvard University Press.

Collins, Randall. 1993. "A Theory of Religion," *Journal for the Scientific Study of Religion* 32: 402–406.

De Forest, Louis Effingham. 1950. *Ancestry of William Seaman Bainbridge*. Oxford: The Scrivener Press.

Delta Upsilon. 1934. *Delta Upsilon: One Hundred Years*. No place of publication, Delta Upsilon Fraternity.

Elms, Alan C. 1981. "Skinner's Dark Year and *Walden Two*," *American Psychologist* 36: 470–479.

Erikson, Erik H. 1958. *Young Man Luther*. New York: Norton.

Festinger, Leon. 1957. *A Theory of Cognitive Dissonance*. Stanford, Calif.: Stanford University Press.

Festinger, Leon, Henry W. Riecken, and Stanley Schachter. 1956. *When Prophecy Fails*. New York: Harper and Row.

Finke, Roger and Rodney Stark. 1988. "Religious Economies and Sacred Canopies: Religious Mobilization in American Cities," *American Sociological Review* 53: 41–49.

———. 1992. *The Churching of America: 1776–1990*. New Brunswick, N.J.: Rutgers University Press.

Folwell, William Watts. 1933. *The Autobiography and Letters of a Pioneer of Culture*. Minneapolis: University of Minnesota Press.

Frank, Robert H. 1988. *Passions within Reason*. New York: Norton.

Gartrell, C. David and Zane K. Shannon. 1985. "Contacts, Cognitions, and Conversion: A Rational Choice Approach," *Review of Religious Research* 27: 32–48.

Gazzaniga, Michael S., ed. 1995. *The Cognitive Neurosciences*. Cambridge, Mass.: MIT Press.

Green, Elizabeth Alden. 1979. *Mary Lyon and Mount Holyoke: Opening the Gates*. Hanover, N.H.: University Press of New England.

Guilford, Linda T. 1890. *The Story of a Cleveland School*. Cambridge, England: John Wilson and Son.

Haley, Jay. 1963. *Strategies of Psychotherapy*. New York: Grune and Stratton.

———. 1969. *The Power Tactics of Jesus Christ*. New York: Avon.

Homans, George C. 1950. *The Human Group*. New York: Harcourt, Brace and World.

———. 1964. "Bringing Men Back In," *American Sociological Review* 29: 809–818.

———. 1967. *The Nature of Social Science*. New York: Harcourt, Brace and World.

———. 1974. *Social Behavior: Its Elementary Forms*. New York: Harcourt Brace Jovanovich.

———. 1981. "John Adams and the Constitution of Massachusetts," *Proceedings of the American Philosophical Society* 125 (4): 286–291.

———. 1984. *Coming to My Senses*. New Brunswick, N.J.: Transaction.

———. 1987. *Certainties and Doubts*. New Brunswick, N.J.: Transaction.

Ingham, Mrs. W. A. 1893. *Women of Cleveland and Their Work*. Cleveland: W. A. Ingham.

James, William. 1902. *The Varieties of Religious Experience*. London: Fontana (1960).

Kelley, Harold H., John W. Thibaut, Roland Radloff, and David Mundy. 1962. "The Development of Cooperation in the 'Minimal Social Situation,'" *Psychological Monographs* 76.

Layard, Austen Henry. 1854. *Nineveh and Its Remains*. London: John Murray.

Lemert, Edwin. 1967. "Paranoia and the Dynamics of Exclusion." In *Human Deviance, Social Problems and Social Control*. Englewood Cliffs, N.J.: Prentice Hall, 246–264.

Macy, Michael W. 1990. "Learning Theory and the Logic of Critical Mass," *American Sociological Review* 55: 809–826.

———. 1991. "Chains of Cooperation: Threshold Effects in Collective Action," *American Sociological Review* 56: 730–747.

Maxwell, William Quentin. 1956. *Lincoln's Fifth Wheel: The Political History of the United States Sanitary Commission*. New York: Longmans, Green.

McKinney, A. H. 1932. *Triumphant Christianity: The Life and Work of Lucy Seaman Bainbridge*. New York: Fleming H. Revell.

Miller, Neil E. and John Dollard. 1941. *Social Learning and Imitation*. New Haven, Conn.: Yale University Press.

Nevius, Helen S. Coan. 1869. *Our Life in China*. New York: Robert Carter.
———. 1895. *The Life of John Livingston Nevius*. New York: Fleming H. Revell.
Nevius, John L. 1869. *China and the Chinese*. New York: Harper.
———. 1896. *Demon Possession and Allied Themes, Being an Inductive Study of Phenomena of Our Own Times*. New York: Fleming H. Revell.
Newman, John P. 1876. *The Thrones and Palaces of Babylon and Nineveh: From Sea to Sea, a Thousand Miles on Horseback*. New York: Harper and Brothers.
Peale, Norman Vincent and Smiley Blanton. 1950. *The Art of Real Happiness*. Englewood Cliffs, N.J.: Prentice-Hall.
Polanyi, Karl. 1957. "The Economy as Instituted Process." In *The Sociology of Economic Life*. Mark Granovetter and R. Swedberg, eds. Colorado: Westview Press [1992], 29–51.
Root, Mary R. 1940. *History of the Town of York, Livingston County, New York*. Caledonia, N.Y.: Big Springs Historical Society.
Rose, William Ganson. 1950. *Cleveland: The Making of a City*. Cleveland, OH: World.
Rosenberger, Hesse Leonard. 1925. *Rochester and Colgate: Historical Backgrounds of the Two Universities*. Chicago: University of Chicago Press.
Rouse, B. F. 1883. "The Early History of the First Baptist Church of Cleveland, O." In *History of the First Baptist Church of Cleveland, Ohio*. Cleveland, Ohio: J. B. Savange.
Schmidt, Carl F. 1953. *History of the Town of Wheatland*. Rochester, N.Y.: Schmidt.
Schutz, Alfred. 1945. "On Multiple Realities." In *Collected Papers*, Volume I. The Hague: Nijhoff [1971], 207–259.
———. 1972. *The Phenomenology of the Social World*. London: Heinemann Educational.
Seaman, Louis Livingston. 1905. *From Tokio through Manchuria with the Japanese*. New York: Appleton.
———. 1906. *The Real Triumph of Japan: The Conquest of the Silent Foe*. New York: Appleton.
Shattuck, Gardiner H., Jr. 1987. *A Shield and a Hiding Place: The Religious Life of the Civil War Armies*. Macon, Ga.: Mercer University Press.
Sidowski, Joseph B., L. Benjamin Wyckoff, and Leon Tabory. 1956. "The Influence of Reinforcement and Punishment in a Minimal Social Situation," *Journal of Abnormal and Social Psychology* 52: 115–119.
Skinner, B. F. 1938. *The Behavior of Organisms*. New York: Appleton-Century-Crofts.
Slocum, George E. 1908. *Wheatland, Monroe County, New York, a Brief Sketch of its History*. Scottsville, N.Y.: Isaac Van Hooser.
Smith, Daniel M. 1970. *Aftermath of War: Bainbridge Colby and Wilsonian Diplomacy 1920–1921*. Philadelphia: American Philosophical Society.
Spargo, John. 1963. "Bainbridge Colby." In *The American Secretaries of State and Their Diplomacy*, vol. 5. Samuel Flagg Bemis, ed. New York: Cooper Square, 179–218.
Stark, Rodney and William Sims Bainbridge. 1979. "Of Churches, Sects, and Cults: Preliminary Concepts for a Theory of Religious Movements," *Journal for the Scientific Study of Religion* 18: 117–131.
———. 1980. "Towards a Theory of Religion: Religious Commitment," *Journal for the Scientific Study of Religion* 19: 114–128.

———. 1985. *The Future of Religion*. Berkeley: University of California Press.
———. 1987. *A Theory of Religion*. New York: Toronto/Lang. Reprinted with new preface, New Brunswick, N.J.: Rutgers University Press, 1996.
Stark, Rodney and Roger Finke. 2000. *Acts of Faith*. Berkeley: University of California Press.
Stark, Rodney, Laurence R. Iannaccone, and Roger Finke. 1996. "Religion, Science, and Rationality," *AEA Papers and Proceedings* 86 (2): 433–437.
Thoits, Peggy A. 1989. "The Sociology of Emotions," *Annual Review of Sociology* 15: 317–342.
Thomson, William M. 1859. *The Land and the Book*. New York: Harper and Brothers.
Tristram, Henry B. 1866. *The Land of Israel: A Journal of Travels in Palestine*. London: Society for Promoting Christian Knowledge.
Vincent, John H. 1885. *The Chautauqua Movement*. Freeport, N.Y.: Books for Libraries Press [1971].
Voncken, Jules. 1939. "Address by the Secretary General of the International Committee." In *Proceedings of the Tenth International Congress of Military Medicine and Pharmacy*, volume 2. Washington: Government Printing Office, 51–54.
Williams, Howard D. 1969. *A History of Colgate University, 1819–1969*. New York: Van Nostrand.
Wilson, Edward O. 1975. *Sociobiology*. Cambridge, Mass.: Harvard University Press.

4

Religious Markets: Supply, Demand, and Rational Choices

Eva M. Hamberg and Thorleif Pettersson

In recent years, rational choice theory has been increasingly used to explain religious behavior. However, at the same time sociologists of religion have become sharply divided in their evaluations of rational choice theory as a tool for religious studies, and the use of it has stirred both a "storm of opposition" and a "spirited defense" (Beckford 2000: 491). One of the noticed discussants stated that he intended his negative evaluation as "the stake through the vampire's chest" that would demonstrate once and for all that rational choice theory is inadequate to the sociological study of religion (Bruce 1999: 2), while a principled review of the "Shifts in premises and paradigms underlying the scientific study of religion" stated that the sociology of religion has become less marginalized among the social sciences thanks to the inclusion of rational choice theory (Beckford 2000: 491). Such differing evaluations of rational choice theory seem at least partly to depend on different interpretations of the theory, which indeed is associated with differing basic premises and hypothetical assumptions, stemming from different traditions as, e.g., behavioralism, cost-benefit analysis, exchange theory, and game theory (e.g., Abell 1991; Beckford 2000). No wonder that the use of "rational choice theory" in religious studies can cause heated debates!

In earlier writings, we have demonstrated that, other things being equal, religious participation is highest among Swedish municipalities and parishes with the most pluralistic/diversified supply, both with regard to the types and numbers of churches and denominations, and the types of religious worship services offered (Hamberg and Pettersson 1994, 1997; Pettersson 2001; Pettersson and Hamberg 1997). This tendency was found in both cross-sectional and longitudinal analyses. We interpreted our findings in accordance with rational choice theory, and concluded that increased diversification of the religious supply led to increased religious participation. In this essay, we intend to extend our previous understanding, and suggest that the impact of increased diversification of the religious supply is moderated by the degree of diversity in religious demand: Other things being equal, we expect the positive impact of diversity in religious supply on religious participation to be higher where the diversity in religious demand is comparatively high. As will be discussed below, this may be an important reason why Sweden and the Nordic countries seem to be a particularly fruitful religio-cultural region for rational choice theory based on analyses of the impact of religious pluralism.

SOME CLARIFICATIONS AND DEFINITIONS OF CONCEPTS

Rational Choice Theory and Secularization

One of the heated debates concerns the relationship between rational choice theory and secularization theory. For instance, with regard to Europe, noticed proponents of rational choice theory have claimed that there is "*no demonstrable long-term decline in European religious participation*" (Stark and Finke 2000: 62, italics in the original), and the use of rational choice theory in the religious realm has come to be associated with the view that the secularization thesis is a myth that should be entombed "beneath a mountain of contrary fact" (Stark and Finke 2000: 33). Proponents of the opposite view on secularization have in turn argued that the dismissal of the secularization thesis is based on "a particular theory of human behaviour that is incompatible with the historical record" (Bruce 1999: 2). In this way, rational choice theory and secularization theory have been seen as incompatible. Without going into a detailed discussion of what is meant by a "long-term decline in European religious participation" and the secularization thesis, respectively, we find compelling evidence for declining church attendance during the last century/centuries in at least the European country we know comparatively well (Sweden). Hence, we wish to emphasize that we see no inherent incompatibility between rational choice theory and long-term declines in religious participation. Rather—as we will elaborate below—it can even be assumed that some rational choice theory assumptions on religious involvement do hold *because* the social context is affected by certain aspects of secularization processes.

The *Ceteris Paribus* Condition

To a certain degree, the heated discussions on whether rational choice theory is applicable or not to the religious field seem to be based on the assumption that the advocates of the theory propose it as a kind of full explanation of the degree of religious participation, that will exclude other ways of understanding religious processes. At least in our view, this is an unwarranted simplification. On the contrary, we assume that a complex social phenomenon as religious involvement *cannot* be "understood as the product of the unilinear extension of a single factor" (Salomon and Anheier 1998: 226). In a similar manner, a well-known treaty of the social psychology of religion concluded that "personal history, situational factors and personality dynamics all combine in determining why certain people will engage in religious activities" (Argyle and Beit-Hallahmi 1975: 179). As we see it, rational choice theory can explain part of the variations in religious involvement, no more and no less. Comparative multi-level analyses of the explanatory power of rational choice theory and other theoretical approaches might shed light on the relative explanatory power of different theoretical approaches to the understanding of religious participation. However, to the best of our knowledge, such comparative analyses are so far lacking. Such studies might therefore fill an important gap.

The assumption that religious activity is influenced by a number of different factors being is reflected in the use of the *ceteris paribus* (other things being equal) condition. However, the implications of this condition are sometimes misunderstood and hence a clarification may be in order. To say that a given change in a variable X will, other things being equal, lead to a certain change in variable Y, is sometimes misunderstood as implying that, unless all other things are equal, *nothing* can be said about the effect on Y of a change in X. As one of our colleagues once expressed it: "Other things never are equal"; this led our colleague to conclude that models based on the assumption that people act rationally *never* are applicable, since they include the *ceteris paribus* condition.

In order to illustrate what we do when we formulate theoretical models of this type, we may choose an example from economic studies of international migration, a field in which one of us has been doing research. Scholars who have studied migration processes often have worked with economic models, where theoretical hypotheses concerning the effects of so called push- and pull-factors on migration flows have been formulated and empirically tested. Many studies have found strong correlations between fluctuations in migration flows and economic conditions in the sending and receiving countries (see, e.g., Hamberg 1976). Thus, improvements in employment opportunities and wage levels in the receiving countries have led to increased immigration, while improved employment opportunities and wage levels in the sending countries have led to a decline in emigration, *ceteris paribus*.

The economic migration models assume that individuals tend to act rationally: Other things being equal, people will be more likely to emigrate if they can improve their economic position by doing so, and the results of many empirical studies are in accordance with this assumption. However, the economic migration models do *not* aim at giving a *total* explanation of migration processes. Many other factors may influence a person's decision to emigrate or not to emigrate. For instance, family ties and other personal networks, psychological factors, the access to information about conditions in an immigration country, legal restrictions on migration, and the ability to raise the money required for the journey are factors which may have a crucial impact on an individual's decision. Moreover, individuals have different preferences and place different emphasis on economic prosperity. Thus, what is (subjectively) rational behavior for an individual will depend on a number of factors, not only on the economic situation. The fact that even during periods of mass migration, only a relatively low proportion of a population tends to emigrate, is ample evidence that other factors apart from the possible improvement in economic status influence decisions whether or not to migrate. However, while other factors *also* influence migration, economic fluctuations can be shown to have an important impact on migration flows. Or in other words, other things being equal, people will be more likely to migrate, the more they can improve their economic position by doing so.

In a similar way, it may be assumed that, *other things being equal,* religious participation tends to be higher, the more pluralistic a religious market is. This does not imply, however, that the degree of pluralism is the *only* factor explaining the level of religious participation.

Human Rationality and Rational Choices

As differing definitions of "rational behavior" have been proposed, it is important to state how we use this concept. We do not define rational behaviour as equivalent with economic profit maximization. Rather, our understanding of rationality is similar to that of Rodney Stark and Roger Finke, who formulate their position as follows: "*Within the limits of their information and understanding, restricted by available options, guided by their preferences and tastes, humans attempt to make rational choices*" (Stark and Finke 2000: 38, italics in the original). Thus, we focus on subjective rationality and define subjectively rational behavior as behavior for which, from the actor's point of view, there appear to be good reasons. This kind of rationality can only be assessed from the "inside" of the actor, from the way he or she defines the situation. Rational choice theory is based on conceptions of actors as purposive and intentional, although it does not regard individual action as the product of intention only (Friedman and Hechter 1988: 202). Human behavior is also seen as subject to constraints from at least two independent sources. One set of constraints is due to scarcity of resources. "Differential possession of and access to resources make some ends easy for individuals to attain, some more difficult, and preclude the attainment of others altogether" (ibid.). Scarcity of desired forms of religious supply can be seen as one example of such constraints. Social institutions can be a second source of constraints. "The modal individual will find his or her action checked from birth to death by familial and school rules; laws and ordinances; firm polices; churches, synagogues, and mosques; and hospitals and funeral parlors" (ibid.). Social pressure to engage in or abstain from religious participation can be seen as an example of such constraints. Thus, we assume subjectively rational behavior to be governed by the actors' preferences and tastes, the availability of the necessary resources, and the constraints exercised by the various social institutions. According to this assumption, humans tend to evaluate the consequences of their actions; they try to avoid what they see as "bad" alternatives, and they strive for actions which are in accordance with their values and preferences. Thus, subjective rationality refers to the subjective reasonableness of a choice. And what is subjectively reasonable depends on the situation, the knowledge and information the actor has of the situation, and on the norms, beliefs, values, and goals of the actor.

Frankly speaking, we find it surprising that this understanding of human nature should be especially upsetting or alarming and we find a priori debates about "the right—or wrong-headedness of rational choice theory *in abstracto* somewhat of an irrelevance" (Abell 1991: xvii, italics in the original). The crucial issue would rather seem to be how rational choice theory understanding of human motivation can be used as the basis for fruitful research within the field of religious actions and choices. In this regard, it should be noted that "the rationality proposition is only *the starting assumption* of most modern social science. Thus, while of immense importance, it offers very little in the way of theory. . . . The real work is yet to be accomplished" (Stark and Finke 2000: 41, italics in the original). As we see it, the most challenging task is not to decide *in abstracto* and a priori whether a certain view on human subjective rationality is applicable or not to the religious realm, but to carefully investigate whether hypotheses deduced from the assumption of human subjective rationality get the necessary empirical support or not.

Religious Pluralism, Diversity, and Market Competition

Part of the debate on the effects of religious market structures seems to be based on different definitions and measurements of "pluralism" and "market competition." Hence, some comments on these questions may be in order.

With regard to *religious pluralism*, we need to make a distinction between several types of pluralism or diversity. The first type, that has usually been focused on in studies of religious market structures, concerns *the organizational level*, i.e., pluralism among churches, denominations, and other religious organizations. We will refer to this as *religious pluralism* or *pluralism at the organizational level*. It should be noted that analyses of the impact of this type of pluralism often combine two dimensions, namely (a) the number of churches and denominations on the religious market, and (b) the distribution of market shares among these (see below). The degree of pluralism at the organizational level is one of the factors that determine *the available options* of religious services and belief systems. We will refer to this as *diversity of the religious supply*. Another type of religious pluralism or diversity concerns *the individual level*, and refers to the degree of pluralism or diversity in people's religious outlooks. This type of pluralism/diversity, which may also be described as value pluralism, concerns the degree of heterogeneity in people's religious views and preferences. We will refer to this as *diversity of religious demand*. The two types of religious diversity that we have distinguished—*diversity of religious supply* and *diversity of religious demand*—each refer to a specific dimension of human rationality as this was defined above (the available religious options, and the religious tastes and preferences that determine how the available options are evaluated). Therefore, analyses of religious pluralism and rationality need to take both kinds of diversity into account.

Religious pluralism at the organizational level as we understand it refers to "the number of firms active in the economy: the more firms having a significant market share, the greater the degree of pluralism" (Stark and Iannaccone 1994: 232). Thus, we assume that the degree of religious pluralism depends on two related components: the number of religious firms, and the relative distribution of market shares among them. The more religious firms and the more evenly distributed market shares (i.e., more firms having a significant market share), the higher the degree of religious pluralism.

Religious pluralism thus defined can be measured by a market concentration index such as the Herfindahl index (Iannaccone 1991; Hamberg and Pettersson 1994). It is worth noting, however, that market concentration indices, while taking the number of firms and their respective market shares into account, do not measure the degree to which *the products* (the religious supply) actually differ from each other. To take an example, assume that we have two different regions, and that in both regions only three religious firms exist. Assume, further, that in both of these regions, the existing firms each have one-third of the market. In such a case, the Herfindahl index would be identical for the two regions. Assume, however, that in region A, the religious firms consist of a Presbyterian church, a Congregational church, and a Methodist church, while in region B they consist of a Pentecostal church, a Congregational church, and a Catholic church. From the point of view of differences in beliefs and in styles of worship, "consumers" would seem to have a choice between a wider range of options in region B than in region A, in spite of the fact that the Herfindahl index will be the same for both regions. Hence, *the extent to which "consumers" experience that they have a real choice between dif-*

ferent "religious goods" may be only partially captured by measures of market concentration like, e.g., the Herfindahl index.

As we understand it, the characterization of a religious market as *competitive* need not necessarily mean that the firms on the market consciously compete with other firms for market shares. They may do so, but a pluralistic religious market may have the characteristics of a competitive market, even if the "producers" should not see themselves as competing for "customers." The degree to which a market is competitive is related to the degree to which one firm (or a combination of firms) can dominate the market. Even if the producers in a competitive market should not consciously compete with each other, inefficiency will be punished and efficiency rewarded, as inefficient producers will lose market shares or be forced out of the market, while efficient producers will gain market shares. Hence, the market structure will create strong incentives for firms to produce efficiently the kind of goods which consumers demand. Thus, in our use of the term, *"competitive"* refers to the market structure, rather than to the psychological characteristics of the actors on such a market. Even if the producers in a pluralistic religious market should not see themselves as competing with other producers, the market may still function as a competitive market.

SUPPLY, DEMAND, AND RELIGIOUS PARTICIPATION

In this essay, we will discuss the relationship between religious supply, demand, and participation. As mentioned above, a number of studies have suggested that high levels of religious pluralism are associated with high levels of religious participation (see, e.g., Finke and Stark 1989, 1992; Finke et al. 1996; Iannaccone 1991, 1992; Stark and Iannaccone 1994; Stark and McCann 1993; Stark and Finke 2000; Hamberg and Pettersson 1994, 1997; Pettersson and Hamberg 1997). The existence of a positive relationship between religious pluralism and participation has also been questioned, both on theoretical and empirical grounds (Olson 1999, 2000; Bruce 1999).

Different theoretical explanations for a positive link between religious pluralism and religious participation have been offered (for a detailed discussion, see, e.g., Bruce 1999: 46f; Olson 1999, 2000; Stark and Finke 2000). Some relate the impact of religious pluralism to *competition* between "religious firms." The more competition "religious firms" face, the more likely they will be to adapt their products to the demands of the "consumers" in order to maintain or increase their market share. Such market adaptation can be expected to result in a rich and diversified supply of religious "goods" and thus to increase the likelihood that consumers can find religious goods well adapted to their individual tastes. Hence, "religious consumption" will, *other things being equal*, tend to be higher, the more pluralistic and competitive a religious market is. Associated with this line of thought is the assumption that religious participation will be lower the more *regulated* the religious sector is, since regulation limits competition and hence has a negative impact on the quality and diversity of religious supply.

Part of the debate concerning the effects of religious market structures on religious participation seems to be based on differing understandings of the relationship between religious pluralism, regulation of religious markets, and religious market competition. Some scholars have seen the degree of *regulation* as the crucial factor (e.g., Chaves and Cann 1992), while others have focussed on religious *pluralism* and its impact on *competition* between "religious firms." As we pointed out in an earlier study, religious pluralism and regulations of religious markets can be expected to have an impact on participation mainly *because of their impact on competition* and hence on *the quality and diversity of religious supply* (Hamberg and Pettersson 1994). Regulation of religious markets limits competition and diversity, while religious pluralism normally benefits the diversity and quality of supply. Hence, regulation of religious markets will have a negative impact on the quality and diversity of religious supply, while religious pluralism and competition will ensure the quality and diversity of religious supply and lead to high levels of religious participation (Hamberg and Pettersson 1994; Stark and Finke 2000: 218–219).

It is worth noting, however, that the relationship between religious participation on one hand, and religious pluralism, regulation, and competition on the other hand, may vary according to circumstances. For instance, religious participation may sometimes be high in a noncompetitive religious market. An obvious case occurs when regulations enable a state-supported monopoly church to enforce participation. Historically this has not been unusual in the European context. For instance, church attendance in Sweden was high during the period when the Church of Sweden enjoyed a full monopoly on the religious market. This can be attributed not only to conformity with the prevailing social norms, but also to state regulations, which enforced a certain level of attendance (Hamberg and Pettersson 1994).

Supply and Demand on Religious Markets

In discussing the effects of religious pluralism, it is necessary to distinguish between the effects on *supply* and the effects on *demand*. Obviously, a change in the degree of pluralism/market competition will have different impacts on producers and consumers, but often this distinction has not been clearly made in the debate on religious pluralism. We will therefore extend the discussion of religious market structures and explore the relationship between religious supply and participation, while taking *the relationship between supply and demand* on religious markets into account.

On a religious market without market imperfections, one would expect demand and supply to be in equilibrium: The supply of religious "goods" provided by religious organizations should match the demand of potential "customers." In a pluralistic religious market this can be expected to occur, at least in the long run. However, on a religious market characterized by, e.g., state regulations, a potential demand for religion may exist which is not met by the existing religious organizations (Stark and Iannaccone 1994), e.g., because the market structure may not provide enough incentives for other religious organizations to emerge. In such a market, although demand for the *existing* religious supply may be low, there may exist a *latent demand for other types of religion* not supplied by the existing organizations. Thus, what appears to be a low level of demand for religion may be a low level of demand for *the available forms* of religion. Although the level of latent demand may be very difficult to estimate, an attempt to understand changes in religious market structures needs to take both demand and supply factors into account. Moreover, as we will discuss in the following, we may assume both that the effect of changes in religious supply will vary depending on the religious demand structure in a society, and that the religious demand structure in a society will (at least in the long run) be affected by the religious supply structure.

Religious Supply

As for *the supply side*, we may have reason to consider which aspects of supply that are most likely to be affected by religious market competition. For a religious organization, there are limits to the extent to which a change is possible without endangering the identity and legitimacy of the organization as such. In addition, the nature of changes that are likely to occur needs to be specified. For instance, central parts of the religious doctrine will probably be quite resistant to change, while the liturgical form and style of worship services and the type of other religious activities that are offered are more likely to be changed if a church perceives a shift in demand. A church may for instance increase the number of worship services to make them more easily available, or it may increase the share of those worship services which are found to attract most participants. Thus, the changes in supply that are most likely to occur are such that are in accordance with central religious traditions and hence do not endanger the legitimacy of the church.

A special situation may occur if a church has a very heterogenous membership, such as is the case in, e.g., the Scandinavian Lutheran churches, to which a majority of the population belong. For instance, the Church of Sweden, although it has been formally separated from the state since 2000, still has more than 80 percent of the Swedish population as members. However, only a small minority of the members adhere to traditional Christian beliefs, while the majority of the members hold other types of religious beliefs, such as belief in a nonpersonal transcendent power, spirit, or life force, or express no religious beliefs at all. Hence, the Church of Sweden contains within itself members (as well as clergy and other employees) who belong to what Stark and Finke denote as different niches on the religious market (Stark and Finke 2000, chapter 8). Being separated from the state, the Church of Sweden is now for its economic survival dependent on those members who do not share the church's central beliefs, while those who still adhere to traditional Christian beliefs and practices constitute a minority too small to serve as an adequate economic basis for the church. In such a situation, it is conceivable that a church may choose to modify its religious doctrines so as not to offend those members who belong to the ultraliberal or liberal niches, and whose religious beliefs differ from those which have traditionally been held by the church.

Normally, however, we would expect religious pluralism to affect mainly such things as the form and style of worship services and the type of other religious activities that are offered, rather than doctrinal beliefs that are crucial for the churches' theological identity. Hence, the argument (based on sociology of knowledge theory) that religious pluralism will undermine religious plausibility structures and thus cause a decline in religious participation may need to be qualified. This argument often seems to be based on the assumption that the effect of pluralism mainly is to create a multitude of competing doctrines, i.e., a diversity in *beliefs* (see, e.g., Blau et al. 1992: 350). This assumption may be warranted in the case where different religions compete. In a situation where religious pluralism is created mainly by the existence of a number of churches or denominations *within* Christianity, however, differences in doctrinal beliefs may be less important and less evident (at least to those who are not theological experts) than are differences in, e.g., the forms for religious worship or the strictness in enforcing certain standards of behaviour. To the extent that this is the case, the possible negative impact on plausibility structures caused by differences in theological doctrines will probably be more than offset by the advantages to "consumers" of having a wide choice between different forms for worship or between more or less strict denominations.

It is worth noting that the diversity of religious supply depends not only on the degree of diversity *between* religious organizations, but also on the degree of diversity *within* organizations. Religious organizations may allow more or less freedom of internal variation with regard to beliefs, forms for religious worship, or degree of strictness. Hence, the diversity of supply on a religious market would be only partially measured by taking into account the number of religious firms, their market shares, and differences *between* firms with regard to the "products" they supply. In order to obtain a more accurate measure of the total diversity of religious supply, one would also need to measure the internal variation of supply *within* these firms. Needless to say, it would be very difficult to construct such an accurate measure of diversity of religious supply. In this instance, as in so many other instances in social scientific studies, the available measures have to serve as proxy variables for those theoretically optimal measures that are not available in empirical studies.

In empirical studies of the "religious market" in Sweden, we have studied the effects of diversity of supply, both with regard to organizational pluralism, and with regard to diversity of supply *within the dominant church*, the Church of Sweden (Hamberg and Pettersson 1994, 1997; Pettersson and Hamberg 1997). We have used both cross-sectional and longitudinal data. In all three studies, the unique Swedish church statistics enabled us to study local religious markets at the municipal/parish level, i.e., at the level where theoretically we can expect the effects of religious pluralism and diversity to be most evident (see Stark and Finke 2000: 219).

From a supply-side perspective, the religious situation in contemporary Sweden can be seen as the result of a long period of religious monopoly or near-monopoly, when almost the whole population have belonged to the Church of Sweden. With the exception for certain rites such as baptisms, weddings, and funerals, the religion supplied by the dominant church appears to be in low demand. However, although the overall degree of religious pluralism in Sweden is very low, our studies indicate that regional differences in religious pluralism, although small, do have an impact on participation. In two studies based on the Swedish church statistics, the hypothesis of a positive relationship between the degree of religious pluralism and the level of religious participation was tested (Hamberg and Pettersson 1994; Pettersson and Hamberg 1997). The results were consistent with the assumption that pluralism has an impact on participation: in those municipalities where the degree of religious pluralism was higher than average, religious participation also was higher. These studies indicate that the different degrees of pluralism in Swedish local religious economies may partially explain the regional differences in participation. However, the results do not indicate that the degree of pluralism should be regarded as the *only* factor influencing the level of religious participation. Rather, the degree of pluralism seems to be one among several factors that influence participation.

The effects of religious supply on religious participation have also been empirically studied from another perspective. In a study of changes in the supply of worship services and in church attendance within the Church of Sweden we were able to show that attendance had developed better in parishes which considerably had increased the diversity and/or availability of worship services than in parishes which had not (Hamberg and Pettersson 1997). Both increased availability of worship services and increased diversity between types of services were positively related to attendance. Thus, a rich supply of worship services within one church seems to lead to increased attendance. Hence, the very low levels of church attendance which generally prevail in Sweden may be due less to a general lack of demand for worship services than to a lack of demand for the types of worship services which are usually provided.

Religious Demand

As mentioned above, the hypothesis that an increase in pluralism at the organizational level and an associated increase in the diversity of religious supply will lead to an increase in participation, builds on the assumption that there exists a latent demand which is not met by the existing supply on the "religious market." Hence, an increased diversity of religious supply that gives consumers more choices may enable this potential demand to be realized. However, we assume the effects of changes in the diversity of the religious supply to depend on the situation.

It seems reasonable to assume that the effects on religious participation of an increase in religious pluralism will differ according to circumstances. An increase in religious pluralism may well have both negative and positive effects on overall levels of religious beliefs and participation, and the net result of such negative and positive effects will probably differ according to how pluralistic a society is. In a society that has previously been very homogenous with regard to religious beliefs and practices, the introduction of a new and different religious group will perhaps undermine plausibility structures for the dominant religion and thus undermine its status as taken for granted. In such cases, overall levels of religious participation may conceivably decline. Once religious pluralism has been introduced, however, it seems likely that a further increase in pluralism will no longer affect plausibility structures to the same extent. However, in a further development toward an even more pluralistic market, the effects of increasing pluralism need not be the same at all stages; when a certain level of religious diversity has been reached, a further increase in diversity may have little effect on participation. In other words, one can expect threshold effects to occur (Hamberg and Pettersson 1997).

Thus, one may need to take into account at which stage in a development from a religious monopoly situation to religious pluralism a society is at a given time. Initially, an increase in pluralism may well lead to a decline in religious participation. At a later stage, however, a further increase in pluralism may no longer affect plausibility structures, at least not to the same extent. Instead, the positive effects of more choices for the individual may outweigh the possibly negative effects on plausibility structures. And at an even later stage in the development, a further increase in diversity may not add much to the choices already available to "consumers"; in that case, the addition of new "religious firms" may have little effect on participation. Thus, the net effect that an increase in religious pluralism can be expected to have on religious participation will probably depend, i.e., on the level of pluralism in a society. We may add, however, that if an initial effect of emerging religious pluralism should be that participation declines, the explanation need not *necessarily* be that pluralism has undermined plausibility structures. An alternative explanation could be that in the previous monopoly situation, legislation and/or social norms enforcing attendance have kept participation at an artificially high level (see, e.g., Hamberg and Pettersson 1994). In such a case, the emergence of religious pluralism may well lead to a decline in participation to a level where religious "consumption" better corresponds to "real demand."

Changes and Imbalances in the Diversity of Religious Supply and Demand

For reasons developed below, we assume that in a given society, there may exist an imbalance between the diversity of religious demand and the diversity of religious supply. Due to historical developments, a society may have a low level of religious diversity at the supply level and a high level of diversity at the demand level and vice versa.

That such imbalances between supply and demand are conceivable, might, e.g., be inferred from the fact that the organizational structure of the religious market in most countries has a deep and persistent nation-specific historical rooting (Martin 1978), making it more or less resistant to rapid changes, while individual belief systems and religio-moral value structures are far more sensitive to economic and social developments, such as changes in education, communications, and welfare systems, etc. (Inglehart 1997). Undoubtedly, "people's religious choices display a great deal of inertia, due not only to effects of indoctrination and habit formation, but also to the nature of religious commodities" (Iannacconne 1991: 163). However, we find it reasonable to argue that the inertia of the structure of the religious market (the religious supply side) is even more pronounced. People's religious preferences and choices change slowly, but we assume that the structure of the religious market tends to change even more slowly. Hence, we expect that imbalances between supply and demand on religious markets may exist as a result of such timelags.

Processes like secularization, differentiation, individualization, and more recently globalization are often said to make the religious preferences of contemporary mass publics increasingly heterogenous (Halman and Pettersson 2001). As the established social order appears less able to dictate people's religious standards, as growing numbers of suppliers have entered the market for ready-made religious outlooks, and as people have become increasingly free to choose the religious views they prefer, their religious convictions and beliefs are assumed to become increasingly heterogenous and pluralistic. Contemporary society is furthermore said to be increasingly permeated by a wholesale reflexivity to the end that even "the most reliable authorities can be trusted only 'until further notice'" (Giddens 1991: 84) and that fixed guidelines for action become rare. People are seen as continuously entangled in a variety of reflexive acts, and their world views and religious values to be constantly open to debate, reformulation, and change. By such reflexivity, present-day heterogeneity in religious beliefs is assumed to thrive.

In less differentiated societies, the political, economic, legal, and educational systems, etc., were under the presidency of religion. However, due to processes of differentiation, the various social institutions gradually became more specialized. Religion has become more "generalized and abstract, more institutionally separated from and in tension with other spheres." Due to differentiation, the churches relinquished much of their control over other sectors in society, e.g., schools, hospitals, social welfare, registry of births, marriages and deaths, social relations, organization of leisure, etc., with the consequence that the latter institutions developed their own distinct sets of guiding principles. Due to such processes, people in late modernity are said to participate in different systems of meaning, each governed by its own set of values. Like differentiation, individualization is a far-reaching and also a debated process. A common notion is that simultaneously with the individualization processes, religious and moral values have changed fundamentally in the direction of increasing diversity. Thus, the differentiation and individualization processes contribute toward increased diversity in people's religious demands, tastes, and preferences.

Furthermore, religious socialization will be inefficient in societies with low levels of religious participation. In such societies, subjective religiousness will typically be idiosyncratic and heterodox (although far more widespread than organized religious participation [Stark and Finke 2000: 202]). We would expect such societies to be characterized by great diversity of (potential or latent) religious demand, related to the diversity of beliefs. In other words, where religious participation is low, the latent religious demand should tend to be heterogenous. Accordingly, the introduction of a more diversified religious supply may conceivably have more impact on religious participation in a country where a large share of the population only has occasional contacts with the churches, than it would in a country where adherence is high. Hence, an increase in the diversity of religious supply may have more impact in societies where religious participation has reached very low levels than it will in countries where participation is high (and where consequently religious demand is more homogenous).

Imbalances between Religious Supply and Religious Demand: Some Hypotheses

With reference to our definitions and theoretical discussions above, we assume that various imbalances with regard to religious pluralism and diversity of religious demand may occur. Some interesting theoretical consequences of these imbalances can be postulated based on rational choice theory. In order to clarify these, figure 4.1 may be of use. Figure 4.1 combines the results from two different studies. The first study is a cross-national analysis of the consequences of religious market structure (Iannacconne 1991), where the effects of competition on religious activity were studied in 18 countries. The study tested the hypothesis that levels of religious participation are lower in monopolized religious markets than in competitive religious markets. As a measure of the degree of religious monopoly in a country, a Herfindahl market concentration index was used. This was calculated from the data published in Barrett's *World Christian Encyclopedia*. Data on church attendance was taken from the 1981 European Values Study, a survey which asked a number of questions on religious and moral issues among representative national samples from about 30 countries (Harding et al. 1986; Ester et al. 1994; Inglehart 1997).

The results showed the Protestant attendance rates to be "strongly related to market structure but Catholic attendance rates [to be] largely independent of it" (Iannacconne 1991: 169). Thus, religious participation among Protestants was positively related to pluralism in the religious supply (i.e., negatively related to market concentration among the various Protestant churches and denominations). The analysis concluded that Adam Smith's "theory of religious markets constitutes a uniquely economic contribution to research on religion, exposing the weakness of established churches and explaining why nations with similar cultures and economies can have very different levels of religiosity" (Iannaccone 1991: 172–173).

The second study which we relate to investigated the degrees of constraint in extended religious belief systems (Jagodzinski and Dobbelaere 1995). Following Converse's (1964: 207) definition of a belief system as a "configuration of ideas and attitudes in which the elements are bound together by some form of constraint or functional interdependence," the degree of constraint in people's extended religious belief systems was measured by the proportion of variance explained by the first principal component obtained from principal components analyses of eight different belief components. These components were: the number of religious beliefs, the importance of God, the type of God, together with normative moral beliefs about underage sex, homosexuality, prostitution, abortion, and extramarital affairs. The data for ten countries on these components were obtained from the 1981 European Values Study mentioned above. Thus, this second study was based on the same data set as the previous study, and the results from the two studies can therefore be combined. The number of religious beliefs was estimated from answers to seven questions asking the respondents whether they believed in God, the soul, sin, life after death, heaven, the devil, and hell. The type of God was estimated from a question on whether the respondents believed in a personal God, in a more abstract spirit or life force, or if they favored an agnostic or an atheistic image of God. The importance of God was measured by a ten-point scale asking about how important God was in the respondent's life. The moral views on each of the five moral issues were measured by a ten-point scale, ranging from "can never be justified" to "can always be justified." As mentioned, the study reported for each country the degree of constraint in the extended religious belief systems. This measure can easily be transformed into a measure of the degree of diversity in these belief systems. This is simply done by the formula 100 minus (the variance explained by the first component).

The degree of diversity in the extended religious belief systems can then be used as a proxy for the degree of diversity in the religious demand. In this context, it is of interest to note that the national degrees of constraint in the extended religious belief systems were unrelated to the national degrees of secularization. A scatter-plot of the degree of religious pluralism according to the Iannaconne study (100 minus the Herfindahl index for religious concentration) and the degree of diversity in the religious demand estimated from the study by Jagodzinski and Dobbelaere suggests the typology shown in figure 4.1. Diversity of religious demand appears higher in Norway, Denmark, and Great Britain, as compared to Spain, the Netherlands, and (West) Germany. The degree of religious pluralism at the organizational level (diversity of religious supply) appears greater in Great Britain, the Netherlands, and (West) Germany, as compared to Norway, Denmark, and Spain. It should be noted that the latter divisions are based on data on religious pluralism, and not on diversity of religious supply. We assume, however, that religious pluralism at the organizational level is positively correlated with diversity of religious supply. Hence, in the absence of data that directly measure the diversity of supply, we use organizational pluralism as a proxy for diversity of supply.

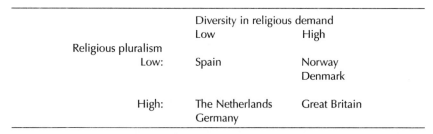

	Diversity in religious demand	
	Low	High
Religious pluralism		
Low:	Spain	Norway Denmark
High:	The Netherlands Germany	Great Britain

Figure 4.1 Religious pluralism and diversity of religious demand in 6 European countries.

Ceteris paribus, one would assume the positive effects on religious participation from an increase in the diversity of supply to be greater in Norway and Denmark as compared to Spain. Since individual religious tastes and preferences are more diversified in Norway and Denmark, an increase in the diversity of religious supply would arguably have greater impact there than it would in Spain, where the degree of religious pluralism is the same (low), but where religious tastes and preferences are less diversified. A similar argument can be made with regard to Great Britain as compared to the Netherlands and Germany. It can also be assumed that, other things being equal, the effects of a more diversified religious supply might be stronger in Spain than in the Netherlands and (West) Germany. The diversity of religious demand is the same (low) in these countries, while the diversity of supply is greater in the Netherlands and Germany. Therefore, it might be assumed that the religious supply in Spain is less "adjusted" to the diversity of religious demand there. Similar arguments can be forwarded with regard to Norway and Denmark in comparison to Great Britain.

Based on our understanding of subjective human rationality, we postulate that the greater the probability that people can find religious activities well adapted to their religious tastes and preferences, the more likely it is that they will choose to participate in such activities. We also postulate that the *greater the heterogeneity* in people's religious tastes and preferences, the greater the probability that they can find religious activities well adapted to their individual tastes, the more pluralistic and diverse the religious supply is. And conversely, *the greater the homogeneity* in people's religious preferences and tastes, the greater the possibility that they can find religious activities well adapted to their individual preferences on a less pluralistic and less diverse religious market. Thus, *ceteris paribus*, the following hypotheses can be deduced: Where there is great diversity of religious demand, religious participation will be higher the more diverse the religious supply. Where there is little diversity of religious demand, however, diversity of religious supply will have less impact on religious participation. (In these hypotheses, it should be noted that the *ceteris paribus* condition includes the degree of competition.) Thus, our hypotheses qualify the assumption that an increase in religious pluralism invariantly leads to higher levels of religious participation. Rather, the positive effects of a diversified religious supply on religious participation can be assumed to be moderated by the degree of heterogeneity in religious beliefs, tastes, and preferences. In this way, we assume interaction effects between religious pluralism and diversity of religious demand.

An Empirical Illustration

In order to find another empirical illustration for our theoretical arguments, we choose again to relate to the cross-national analysis of the consequences of religious market structure mentioned above (Iannaccone 1991). However, in this analysis we will use another version of the measure of diversity in extended religious belief systems described above. As mentioned, the previous measure included moral views on a set of sexual issues. It can be argued that sexual morality is only one of the many components in people's religious-moral outlooks. In order to get a more representative picture from a Judeo-Christian point of view, we therefore prefer another approach. Thus, the questionnaire used in the 1981 European Value Study contained a battery of questions which asked the respondents to say whether each of the commandments applied fully to themselves, applied to a limited extent, or didn't apply at all. From the answers to these questions, we have calculated the number of commandments each respondent found fully relevant to him/herself. Obviously, this component is of the same format as the component covering the number of religious beliefs used in Jagodzinski and Dobbelaere's analysis of the extended religious belief systems. Thus, the extended religious belief systems that we will analyze are based on four components: The number of religious beliefs, the importance of God, the type of God, and the number of commandments said to be fully relevant.

In order to estimate the degree of diversity in these extended religious belief systems, we have performed a set of principal component analyses, one for each country. Based on the results from these analyses, we have then for each country estimated the degree of constraint in the extended religious belief systems. Using the same procedure which we used in connection with figure 4.1, we have then transformed the degree of constraint into a measure of diversity in the extended religious belief system.

With reference to Iannaconne's finding that (only) Protestant attendance rates were related to the religious market structure, while Catholic attendance rates were not, we will only consider countries where the percentage of Catholics is less than 50 percent. Thus, the results presented below concern Britain, Canada, Denmark, Finland, (West) Germany, the Netherlands, Norway, Sweden, and the U.S. In some of the below analyses, Finland is not included because of missing data for the Ten Commandment battery. Australia and New Zealand, which were included in the Iannaconne study, are excluded due to unavailability of the 1981 EVS data. Since the number of countries in our analyses is so small, the empirical findings must only be seen as a tentative illustration of our theoretical suggestions. In order to arrive at safer conclusions, much more thorough analyses are needed.

Figure 4.2 shows a scatter-plot of the nine countries with regard to religious pluralism and weekly church attendance. The results demonstrate an almost perfect relationship between religious pluralism and weekly church attendance. The correlation between religious pluralism and weekly church attendance is .97 ($p < .001$). This result is quite as expected from rational choice theory.

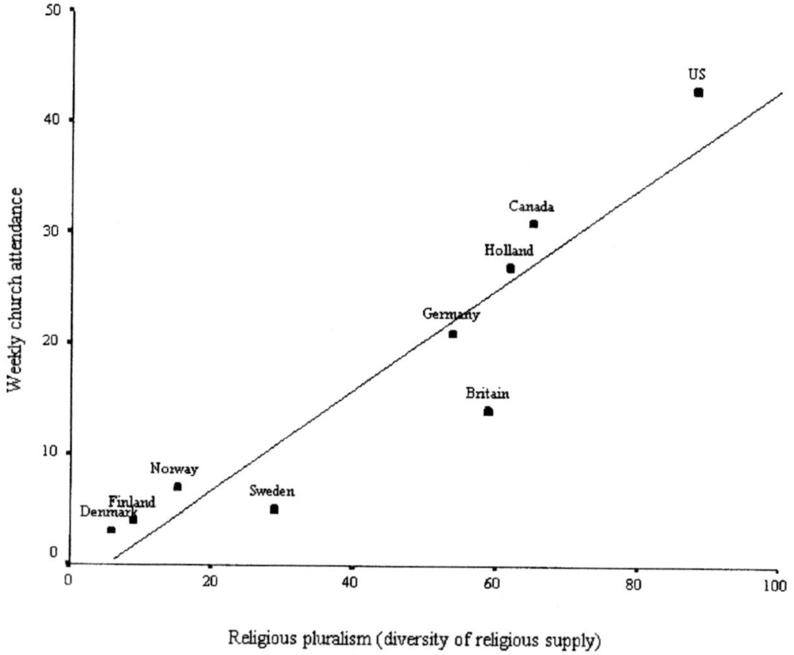

Figure 4.2 Religious pluralism and weekly church attendance in 8 countries.

However, in this article, we are more interested in the impact of diversity in religious demand. As mentioned, our hypothesis is that the positive relationship between religious pluralism and church attendance is moderated by diversity in religious demand. To explore this hypothesis, we have performed a multiple regression analysis, where we introduced the interaction effect between diversity of demand and religious pluralism as a test variable (Jaccard et al. 1990). Thus, we used weekly church attendance as a dependent variable, and diversity of religious demand, religious pluralism, and the interaction effect between diversity of demand and religious pluralism as independent variables. In the first regression analysis with only religious pluralism and diversity of demand as independent variables, the standardized regression coefficients for religious pluralism was .91 ($p < .001$) and for diversity of religious demand .03 (n.s.). R square is .86 ($p < .001$). In these analyses, we used the method of backward exclusion. When however the interaction effect for religious pluralism and diversity of religious demand was introduced, the results changed notably. In this case, only the regression coefficient for the interaction effect was significant (.91, $p < .001$), while the regression coefficients for diversity of demand and religious pluralism turned nonsignificant (.38 and .22, respectively; n.s.). In this case, R square was .84 ($p < .001$). It can therefore be concluded that our tentative analyses were in line with the hypothesis that the relationship between religious pluralism and church attendance is moderated by the diversity of religious demand.

CONCLUSIONS

On the basis of our theoretical arguments and the empirical results presented above, we intend to continue research on the hypothesis that the relationship between religious pluralism and religious participation is moderated by the diversity of religious demand. We see interesting possibilities for further studies of the relationship between religious supply, religious demand, and religious participation. Such studies should focus on areas that are small enough to function as local religious markets (see Stark and Finke 2000: 219). In this way one may also minimize the influence on the results of those factors that are not equal, for instance, differences in religious culture between various countries. While, of course, the *ceteris paribus* condition never can be assumed to be completely fulfilled, it may be more or less approximated, and the impact of those other factors that are not equal should be less, the more homogenous in relevant respects the areas that we study are. The more heterogenous the areas studied, the more those factors that are not equal will influence the empirical results and make it difficult to establish relationships in the statistical analyses. This may be one explanation why the Swedish data, which is available for small, local religious economies, has enabled us in our previous studies (Hamberg and Pettersson 1994, 1997; Pettersson 2001; Pettersson and Hamberg 1997) to find empirical evidence for the existence of the relationships between religious pluralism, religious supply, and religious participation, that we had expected to find on the basis of rational choice theory.

Since the available data seldom permit the estimation of the degree of diversity of religious demand in local religious economies, an alternative might be to use, e.g., the degree of urbanization or the percentage of young well-educated people as possible indicators of the degree of diversity of religious demand (cf. Halman and Pettersson 2001). There might also be other ways to perform such analyses, for instance, to compare the relationship between religious participation and religious pluralism in different subsets of local religious economies which can be reasonably assumed to differ in the degree of diversity of religious demand. In such instances, one would expect stronger relationships between religious participation and religious pluralism in the subsets with the greatest diversity in religious demand (Jaccard et al. 1990: 48). In future studies, we intend to explore this line of research.

We have argued that religious participation is likely to rise as an effect of increased diversity in the religious supply, especially when high diversity in religious demand is coupled with low diversity in religious supply. There is ample empirical evidence that the Scandinavian countries of Denmark, Finland, Norway, and Sweden harbor both high diversity in religious demand and low diversity in religious supply. In these countries, the diversity of religious demand is comparatively high due to the marked developments there towards a postmodern culture (Inglehart 1997; Inglehart and Baker 2000; cf. also our discussion in connection with figure 4.1). "If any societies represent the cutting edge of cultural change, it is the Nordic countries" (Inglehart and Baker 2000: 49). At the same time, the diversity in religious supply is comparatively low in these countries due to the long dominance of the Scandinavian Protestant state churches (Gustafsson and Pettersson 2000). Likewise, church attendance and religious involvement is comparatively low (Pettersson 2001). The Scandinavian countries therefore seem to represent fertile soil where seeds of increased diversity of religious supply are likely to breed increased religious participation.

In this regard, it should be noted that the Scandinavian countries often are described as highly secularized countries. Some of the ingredients of the Scandinavian fertile soil (the high diversity in religious demand, the low rates of church attendance) can be seen as consequences of various secularizing processes (Bruce 1999: 3–29). That we have been able to find substantial empirical support for rational choice theory hypotheses on religious participation in contemporary Sweden may therefore depend on the fact that we have analyzed a comparatively highly secularized context. This is one of the reasons why we do not see rational choice theory as incompatible with evidence of contemporary secularization processes (cf. the introductory discussion on the relationship between rational choice theory and secularization theory).

In future analyses of the relationship between diversity of religious supply and demand, it would also be of interest to relate to research in other fields of relevance. For instance, research on nonprofit organizations and the civil society has suggested that "the greater the degree of diversity of a country's population [ethno-linguistic diversity], the more likely a country's nonprofit sector is to be supported by private giving" (Salomon and Anheier 1998: 232f). Transferred to the religious sector, this conclusion suggests diversity in demand (ethno-linguistic diversity) to be positively related to participation (giving). Other research on the third sector has suggested that the relationship between government and the nonprofit sector may be more cooperative than competitive (cf. the relationship between a large state-regulated church and a small free-church sector), and that there is a positive relationship between the degree of religious diversity in a country and the size of the country's nonprofit sector (Salomon and Anheier 1998: 237, 239). It cannot be excluded that further explorations into such areas of research might shed further light on the relationship between religious pluralism, diversity of religious demand, and religious participation. In this regard, findings from rational choice analyses of political behavior may also be of interest to religious studies. For instance, analyses of political behavior have concluded that "there is plenty that rational choice can be proud of in terms of aiding us in understanding the dynamics of electoral politics, campaigning, and voter choice" (Grofman 1996: 699). It might be argued that at least some forms of political participation are of a similar nature as religious participation, and that the understanding of political participation from a rational choice perspective might improve rational choice understanding of religious participation. Thus, analyses of the relationship between religious participation and diversity of religious supply and demand might also benefit from research in associated fields of human behavior.

In summary, we therefore conclude that we find it more rational and more challenging to pursue the types of research we have described above, and less rational and less challenging to proclaim in advance that rational choice theory is of no use to religious studies.

REFERENCES

Abell, Peter. 1991. "Introduction." *Rational Choice Theory*. Aldershot: Edward Elgar Publishing Limited.

Argyle, Michael and Benjamin Beit-Hallahmi. 1975. *The Social Psychology of Religion*. London: Routledge & Kegan Paul.

Barrett, David. 1982. *World Christian Encyclopedia*. Nairobi: Oxford University Press.

Beckford, James A. 2000. " 'Start Together and Finish Together': Shifts in the Premises and Paradigms Underlying the Scientific Study of Religion," *Journal for the Scientific Study of Religion* 39: 481–495.

Blau, Judith R., Kenneth C. Land, and Kent Redding. 1992. "The Expansion of Religious Affiliation: An Explanation of the Growth of Church Participation in the United States, 1850–1930," *Social Science Research* 21: 329–352.

Bruce, Steve. 1999. *Choice & Religion. A Critique of Rational Choice*. Oxford: Oxford University Press.

Chaves, Mark and David E. Cann. 1992. "Regulation, Pluralism, and Religious Market Structure. Explaining Religion's Vitality," *Rationality and Society* 4: 272–290.

Converse, Philip. 1964. "The Nature of Belief Systems in Mass Publics." In *Ideology and Discontent*. David Apter ed. New York: Free Press.

Ester, Peter, Loek Halman, and Ruud de Moor. 1994. *The Individualizing Society. Value Change in Europe and North America*. Tilburg: Tilburg University Press.

Finke, Roger and Rodney Stark. 1989. "How the Upstart Sects Won America: 1776–1850." *Journal for the Scientific Study of Religion* 28: 27–44.

———. 1992. *The Churching of America 1776–1990: Winners and Losers in Our Religious Economy*. New Brunswick, N.J.: Rutgers University Press.

Finke, Roger, Avery Guest, and Rodney Stark. 1996. "Pluralism and Religious Participation: New York, 1855–1865," *American sociological Review* 61: 203–218.

Friedman, Debra and Michael Hechter. 1988. "The Contribution of Rational Choice Theory to Macrosociological Research," *Sociological Theory* 6: 201–218.

Giddens, Anthony. 1991. *The Consequences of Modernity*. Stanford, Calif.: Stanford University Press.

Grofman, Bernard. 1996. "Political Economy: Downsian Perspectives." *A New Handbook of Political Science*. Robert Goodin and Hans-Dieter Klingeman, eds. Oxford: Oxford University Press.

Gustafsson, Göran and Thorleif Pettersson, eds. 2000. *Folkkyrkor och religiös pluralism—den nordiska religiösa modellen*. Stockholm: Verbum.

Halman, Loek and Thorleif Pettersson. 2001. "Increasing Moral Pluralism." To be published in *Religious and Moral Pluralism*, Karel Dobbelaere and Wolfgang Jagodzinski eds. Forthcoming. Oxford: Oxford University Press.

Hamberg, Eva M. 1976. *Studier i internationell migration*. Stockholm: Almqvist & Wiksell International.

Hamberg, Eva M. and Thorleif Pettersson. 1994. "The Religious Market: Denominational Competition and Religious Participation in Contemporary Sweden," *Journal for the Scientific Study of Religion* 33: 205–216.

———. 1997. "Short-term Changes in Religious Supply and Church Attendance in Contemporary Sweden," *Research in the Social Scientific Study of Religion* 8: 35–51.

Harding, Stephen and David Phillips, with Michael Fogarty. 1986. *Contrasting Values in Western Europe: Unity, Diversity and Change*. Basingstoke and London: Macmillan.

Iannaccone, Laurence R. 1991. "The Consequences of Religious Market Regulation: Adam Smith and the Economics of Religion," *Rationality and Society* 3: 156–177.

———. 1992. "Religious Markets and the Economics of Religion," *Social Compass* 39: 123–131.

Inglehart, Ronald. 1997. *Modernization and Postmodernization*. Princeton, N.J.: Princeton University Press.

Inglehart, Ronald and Wayne Baker, 2000. "Modernization, Cultural Change, and the Persistence of Traditional Values," *American Sociological Review* 65, February: 19–51.

Jaccard, James, Robert Turrisi, and Choi Wan. 1990. *Interaction Effects in Multiple Regression*. Sage University Papers. Quatitative Applications in the Social Sciences. London: Sage Publications.

Jagodzinski, Wolfgang and Karel Dobbelaere. 1995. "Religious and Ethical Pluralism." In *The Impact of Values*. Jan van Deth and Elinor Scarbrough, eds. Oxford: Oxford University Press.

Martin, David. 1978. *A General Theory of Secularization*. Oxford: Basil Blackwell.

Olson, Daniel. 1999. "Religious Pluralism and US Church Membership: A Reassessment," *Sociology of Religion* 60 (2): 149–173.

———. 2000. "Religious Pluralism and Church Involvement: Steps in the Exploration of a Changing Relationship." Paper presented at the May 6th meeting of the Chicago Area Group Studying Religious Congregations, Loyola University, Chicago.

Pettersson, Thorleif. 2001. "Många eller få? Drygt en halv miljon kyrkobesökunder ett veckoslut." *Det religiösa Sverige—Gudstjänst- och andaktsliv under ett veckoslut vid millenieskiftet*. Ingemar Brohed and Margareta Skog, eds. In Press. Orebro: Libris.

Pettersson, Thorleif and Eva M. Hamberg. 1997. "Denominational Pluralism and Church Membership in Contemporary Sweden," *Journal of Empirical Theology* 10: 61–78.

Salomon, Lester and Helmut Anheier. 1998. "Social Origins of Civil Society: Explaining the Nonprofit Sector Cross-Nationally," *Voluntas: International Journal of Voluntary and Nonprofit Organizations* 9 (3): 213–248.

Stark, Rodney and Roger Finke. 2000. *Acts of Faith. Explaining the Human Side of Religion.* Berkeley, Los Angeles, and London: University of California Press.

Stark, Rodney and Laurence R. Iannaccone. 1994. "A Supply-side Reinterpretation of the 'Secularization' of Europe," *Journal for the Scientific Study of Religion* 33: 230–252.

Stark, Rodney and James C. McCann. 1993. "Market Forces and Catholic Commitment: Exploring the New Paradigm," *Journal for the Scientific Study of Religion* 32: 111–124.

5

A Political Economy of Religion

Anthony Gill

Within the economics of religion literature, one of the most interesting findings is that religious competition enhances the overall level of religious practice within a society. The theory explaining this finding rests upon the assumption that religious markets are naturally pluralistic and that one denomination cannot monopolize a country without state assistance (e.g., Stark and Finke 2000: 198–199; Stark 1992; Stark and Bainbridge 1985: 508). This has led several scholars to assert that the level of state regulation over religion negatively affects the degree of pluralism. Empirical research—both qualitative and quantitative—bears out this assertion (Finke 1990; Chaves and Cann 1992; Finke and Iannaccone 1993; Gill 1999a). While we now have a firm understanding that religious freedom enhances denominational competition, thereby promoting pluralism and spiritual vitality, we know little about why governments would liberalize laws governing religion. This puzzle is all the more interesting in that there are varying degrees of religious freedom around the world. Why do some countries maintain relatively high barriers of entry into the religious market for minority faiths, while others pursue more laissez faire policies? What interests do politicians have in regulating churches, particularly those that pose little threat to the common good? And what accounts for changes in laws regulating religions at certain moments in history?

The relatively new "economics of religion" paradigm[1] has yet to provide answers for these questions. Most studies within this theoretical perspective have avoided analysis of political factors. This is not to fault scholars in this field for ignoring politics. The progression of scientific knowledge requires use of the "ceteris paribus" clause; some variables are held constant in order that other potentially relevant variables can be examined in isolation.

Research agendas and knowledge advance by placing these neglected factors under closer scrutiny. To date, religious economy scholars have discovered a great deal about religious pluralism while holding political considerations constant. We are now at a point where it is fruitful to wrestle with the impact of politics on the religious economy in a more rigorous fashion. Fortunately, political factors can be added easily to rational choice studies of religion thereby enhancing their explanatory power.

The goal of this chapter is to introduce political considerations into the mix of variables used in economic analyses of religion, thereby taking the first steps toward constructing a formal *political* economy of religion. I do this by laying out the interests and common incentives faced by politicians and religious lobbying groups. The theory presented below is not intended to be a comprehensive model of all political-religious interactions. Rather, the primary focus is to explain why governments regulate religious markets. For reasons of simplicity, I ignore other potentially interesting topics such as religiously based political mobilization[2] and internal church politics. The model presented below favors interest-based and organizational factors over ideational variables. This is not to say that ideas are unimportant.[3] Granted, if everyone in society believed that religious disestablishment was a grand idea it is unlikely that establishment would persist for long. In reality, however, there typically exists a plethora of ideas regarding the exact nature of church-state relations.[4] Which ideas win out is usually a function of power relations and the institutional environment wherein political battles are fought. My primary concern here is to lay out a deductive framework useful in explaining differences in religious liberty across space and time. I accomplish this by introducing a series of axioms and propositions about the interests and behavior of political actors that builds upon the economic models developed by Stark, Bainbridge, Iannaccone, Finke, and others. Hopefully, this framework will become a part of the wider literature on the economics of religion and prompt further theory building and empirical testing.

RELIGIOUS LIBERTY AS A REGULATORY ISSUE

Despite the fact that much has been written on the topic of religious liberty, scholars have yet to craft a theoretically informed explanation of its origins. Most works on this subject are detailed histories (cf. Estep 1990; Adams and Emmerich 1990) or normative debates about the meaning of various laws or their proper boundaries (cf. Segers and Jelen 1998). Furthermore, religious liberty is rarely seen as a regulatory issue.[5] This may be in part due to the reluctance of most people to view religion as an economic industry, the typical subject of government regulation. But as early as 1776, Adam Smith astutely noted that the rules governing industry were similar in many ways to those placed on religion.

> The laws concerning [agriculture] may every where be compared to the laws concerning religion. The people feel themselves so much interested in what related either to their subsistence in this life, or to their happiness in a life to come, that government must yield to their prejudices, and, in order to preserve the publick [sic] tranquility, establish that system which they approve of. It is upon this account, perhaps, that we so seldom find a reasonable system established with regard to either of those two capital objects (Smith [1776] 1976: 539).

Given that religion fills important needs for many people and has a large public component, it is not surprising to find it come to the attention of legislators and kings. Looking for the origins of religious liberty from a regulatory perspective—i.e., examining the institutional interests of the regulator and regulated—would seem to be a fruitful endeavor.

Any casual conversation with a clergy member involved in the daily operations of his ministry will quickly reveal how many government procedures must be followed, from maintaining tax-exempt status to considering zoning ordinances when expanding a church building (cf. Cleary 2001). While several laws confronting clergy are meant to apply to all citizens, many other rules are directed specifically at religious organizations and their staff. In addition to tax status and zoning laws, a list of regulations applying to religious organizations in any given country might include restrictions on missionaries and their equipment,[6] registration requirements,[7] laws governing property ownership,[8] access to media outlets, and limits on the public display of religion or religious activity.

Preferential subsidies that grant financial favors or public access (e.g., to schools) to one denomination also represent a subtle restriction of religious liberty in that they hinder the recruitment efforts of other denominations (Finke 1990: 615). Consider the example of a government that collects mandatory tithes for one specific denomination (or heavily subsidizes that denomination with general tax revenues). Any person wishing to join an alternative denomination that requires tithing automatically faces a double financial burden. One could expect only the most fervent believers to tolerate such a situation. Potential converts of modest means and mild devotion are likely to be dissuaded.[9]

A regulation will be defined here as any government rule or law that requires specific types of behavior and which therefore alters the relative costs and benefits of at least some individuals and groups in the religious economy. A proscription on foreign missionaries is an obvious example in that it makes it difficult for religions facing a shortage of clergy from spreading their message with help from abroad. Preferential access to pubic schools for one denomination is a less obvious example. Here, the access to young minds and "official endorsement" granted to the favored church makes it more difficult for other faiths to convince people they are a legitimate alternative. Iannaccone's (1990, 1984) theory of religious capital also applies here in that the more exposure youngsters receive to one religion, the less likely they are to convert to other faiths later in life. And, of course, the government's definition of what constitutes a legal religious organization is the perhaps the most important regulation related to religious liberty. If certain liberties are granted to all *legal* churches, but one's own church is not considered legal, members of the illegal faith have less liberty. It should be noted that no nation could be reasonably expected to implement total religious liberty; maintaining a degree of social peace implies outlawing groups that pose a danger to the general populace (e.g., religions practicing human sacrifice). Thus, rather than focusing on absolutes, religious liberty should be conceived of as a continuum wherein total freedom only serves as an anchor point for measurement.

Enforcement of regulations also matters. The reluctance of public officials to monitor and enforce laws applying to churches could indicate a de facto increase or decrease in freedom. Across-the-board nonenforcement of restrictive regulations would imply an increase of religious liberty. For instance, the Mexican Constitution of 1917 imposed restrictions on the wearing of clerical garb in public, which applied to all religions. However, by the mid-1950s this law was largely ignored. On the other hand, selective nonenforcement of laws may result in a reduction in religious liberty for some, if not all, groups. Consider an organization that is legally guaranteed the free and open practice of its faith. If this group suffers continual harassment and physical abuse while state authorities look the other way, there is little doubt that its freedom is reduced. For reasons of analytical simplicity, this chapter will not address the issue of enforcement directly, although the theory presented below could be extended to such issues. With this caveat in mind, we now turn toward a theory of religious liberty.

A POLITICAL ECONOMIC THEORY OF RELIGIOUS LIBERTY

Developing a rational choice theory of church-state relations requires defining the interests and power of actors involved in the religious economy. From this information we can derive a number of theoretical propositions that predict behavior under varying environmental contexts. This last point is important. Rational choice theory is often accused of ignoring "context," generally meaning the rich details of a historical situation. But to the contrary, "context" is central to rational choice analysis in that the various environmental constraints actors face at any given time affect the relative prices of pursuing different strategies (Gill 1998; Geddes 1995: 90–91). The theory developed here is presented in a general form with the intent that it could be applied to a variety of historical situations—from colonial Latin America to contemporary Eastern Europe. The task of the analyst in each empirical situation is to show how the relevant environmental features affect the behavior of the key actors. The most important actors in the development of religious liberty are religious groups (including both dominant and minority churches), secular rulers, and rivals to secular power. Foreign actors may also play a role in the process, but my attention will be mainly on the domestic political situation.

Interests and Incentives in the Religious Economy

Building off the work of Rod Stark, Larry Iannaccone, Roger Finke, and William Sims Bainbridge, and proceeding in a deductive manner, I begin with the following definitions and axioms regarding religious actors.

Def. 1: *Religious goods* are the fundamental answers to the deep philosophic questions surrounding life that have as their basis some appeal to a supernatural force.

Def. 2: A *religious firm* is an organization that produces and distributes religious goods.

Def. 3: A *religious marketplace (economy)* is the social arena wherein religious firms compete for members and resources.

Religious firms obviously offer individuals more than just philosophic answers. Other goods and services provided include fellowship, opportunities for business networking, social welfare, and entertainment activities. All of this may help to bind the group together and thus have important consequences for realizing collective action. However, many of these goods can be produced by other social organizations with varying degrees of efficiency. What differentiates religious organizations is their appeal to supernatural explanations for the mysteries of life (Stark and Finke 2000: 88–96).

Concentrating on the supernatural aspect of religious goods reveals important organizational incentives facing religious firms and, when combined with axiomatic observations about societal preferences and firm behavior, helps to explain firm behavior in the religious marketplace.

Axiom 1: Religious goods are easy to produce and vulnerable to competition.

Since religious goods are essentially ideas, they are relatively easy to produce. They do not require a great deal of up-front capital, though widespread dissemination necessitates some degree of costly organization. The history of religion is replete with examples of upstart religious groups, some of which become phenomenal successes (e.g., Christianity, Islam) and others that do not. Even within successful religions, new variants are constantly being created (e.g., Calvinism, Methodism, and Mormonism within the Christian tradition).

The ideational aspect of religion makes it a special case of what economists call "credence goods"—i.e., goods where the consumer has a difficulty in verifying quality until after the purchase is complete.[10] The difficulty in assessing the quality (and availability—e.g., salvation) of religious goods also makes them easy to produce since "shoddy" goods can be passed off as high-quality brands. Although clergy often take steps to minimize the uncertainty associated with their product—e.g., taking vows of poverty to avoid the appearance of fraud, developing a complex theology—the fact remains that it is difficult for consumers to differentiate between the quality of different religious "brands" (denominations). As a result, religious producers are highly vulnerable to competitive pressures.[11] Consumers unsure of the veracity of any one denomination's claims could potentially be wooed by another denomination.

Competition in the religious economy is enhanced by the diversity of spiritual tastes existing in society, our second axiom.

Axiom 2: Religious preferences in society are pluralistic.

This is a controversial assumption that cuts against the grain of most scholarship on nationalism, which argues that one of the central defining features of a nation is a common religious preference. This line of reasoning, however, may be conflated with the subject of this study—religious regulation. If a religious economy is highly regulated, making it difficult for all but one religion to practice, religious consumers will have little choice but than to join the government-sanctioned denomination. People who would otherwise join some other denomination are forced to declare allegiance to the officially sanctioned faith. The alternative is to be irreligious or significantly reduce participation. Unfortunately, it is methodologically difficult, though not impossible, to discern whether a dominant preference for one religion in society is due to a true preference for that religion or a lack of alternative faiths from which to choose. Survey research in countries with monopoly faiths are not helpful in this endeavor since respondents would not be familiar enough with alternatives to reveal what their true preferences would be under pluralism.

Consider an alternative assumption wherein societal preferences for religion are diverse. It is not unrealistic to assume that within society some people prefer very strict forms of religion that offer highly ritualized practices, while others prefer more liberal styles of worship (see Stark and Finke 2000: 195–198). One could easily imagine other dimensions on which religious preferences could differ (e.g., pantheism vs. monotheism, vengeful gods vs. caring deities, etc.). Evidence for the existence of pluralistic preferences is indirect. Chaves and Cann (1992) and Gill (1999a) demonstrate that religious pluralism is highest where regulation is lowest, implying that once minority religions are allowed to proselytize, they are able to satisfy niches that were not served by a monopoly faith. Finke (1997a, 1997b) and Finke and Iannaccone (1993) also show that when regulations constraining new faiths are liberalized, religious pluralism and participation increase.[12] If religious preferences were homogenous in the countries examined, upstart sects would quickly fail since no one would be interested in joining them.

As one might expect, the inherent competitiveness of the religious market helps to shape the incentive structure of religious firms. This leads us to our next assumption.

Axiom 3: Religious firms are membership (i.e., market share) maximizers or, at a minimum, prefer to minimize membership losses.

If a priest is convinced that his faith's spiritual message is correct, it seems only natural that he would want as many people to believe the same. There are some exceptions to this rule, such as religious groups that view members as a "chosen people" and do not actively seek converts (e.g., Judaism) or "pay-as-you-go" movements (e.g., New Age movements). However, at a minimum, these religious groups still try to avoid losing adherents as such a loss would indicate the clergy are failing to do their job adequately. Declining membership also means a loss of financial contributions and volunteer labor, something most institutions seek to avoid. For purposes of this study, I will limit my attention to proselytizing faiths, which encompasses most of the Western world.

Given the preceding axioms, it is possible to derive a testable hypothesis about the regulatory preferences of religious firms.

Proposition 1: Hegemonic religions will prefer high levels of government regulation (i.e., restrictions on religious liberty), particularly as relates to religious minorities. Religious minorities will prefer laws favoring greater religious liberty.[13]

Religious firms that have achieved a monopoly or dominant market share will defend against membership defections and seek policies that create artificially high barriers to entry in the religious marketplace. Although rhetorically in favor of freedom of conscience, leaders of spiritual monopolies will favor laws requiring minority religions to gain legal permission to proselytize, restrictive visas on missionaries, and zoning regulations that make it difficult for upstart sects to build churches. In contrast, minority religious groups will seek legislation lowering restrictions on religious trade.

The Roman Catholic Church offers an interesting test of this hypothesis. The Catholic Church represents a highly centralized faith that is present in nearly every country of the world. However, it varies in its majority or minority status. An ideational model of religious preferences would predict that policy preferences are determined by Catholic doctrine. Alternatively, Proposition 1 predicts policy differences based on the market context in which the Church finds itself. In Latin America where Catholicism has been dominant for five centuries, bishops have actively sought restrictions on evangelical sects that have been making amazing headway in the region since the 1930s (Gill 1999c). However, in post-Soviet Russia, where Catholics are an expanding denomination, the Vatican has been pressing for greater access against the protests of the historically dominant Orthodox Church (Kutznetsov 1996). This "double standard" reveals an instance where the preferences of religious leaders are determined by their "self-interested" position in the religious marketplace.

Finally, we can further derive from this proposition the preferences of religious groups under pluralistic conditions wherein no single denomination holds a majority market share. Here, all religious firms should prefer a minimum level of religious liberty that allows all *existing* faiths to practice freely. Imposing restrictions on one faith could potentially lead to religious conflict wherein one's own denomination finds itself under repressive legislation. They are, however, likely to oppose complete laissez faire policies that allows new sects to develop unhindered. The case of the United States during the late 1700s is the classic example of this situation. While high degrees of religious regulation existed in the individual colonies favoring different denominations, the impetus to create a larger nation while avoiding a religious war meant all faiths would have to accept the legitimate existence of all others. This significantly weakened government-sanctioned establishments in each state, though religious barriers still remained high for some "foreign" sects, namely Catholicism (Maryland being the exception).

Interests and Incentives in the Political Economy

If religious liberty is a matter of governmental regulation, we should expect the incentive structure of politicians to play a significant role in determining the level (and form) of religious freedom. Why would politicians want to regulate (or deregulate) the religious economy? Answering this question puts the *political* into the political economy of religion. We begin with two basic assumptions about the preferences of policymakers derived from the work of Mayhew (1974), Ames (1987), and Levi (1988).

Axiom 4: Politicians are primarily interested in their personal political survival.

Axiom 5: Politicians want to maximize societal support and neutralize rivals.

Axiom 6: Politicians want to minimize the cost of ruling and maximize revenue intake.

Policymakers may be driven by a plethora of ideological influences, but if they are not in power their goals are largely unachievable. They may also seek power for power's sake (or the fame and fortune it bestows). In whichever case, retaining power is the primary (instrumental) goal to achieving those other ends. Staying in office requires political support from society. This is true for both dictators and democrats. Elected officials (democrats) obviously need votes from supportive constituents. But dictators must also keep society relatively happy lest popular discontent give rise to a palace coup or social revolution. The most preferred form of support is voluntary or quasi-voluntary compliance (Levi 1988, 1997) wherein citizens obey because they believe their leaders are legitimate. Patronage and/or coercion may also be used, though these methods tend to be costly in the long run. Another related way of guaranteeing political survival is to neutralize all possible rivals, either by bringing them into an alliance or severely weakening their ability to challenge the incumbent.

Finally, it must be noted that ruling requires financial resources. Raising taxes or promoting economic growth, which enlarges the tax base of rulers, are the most common means of gathering revenue. The more financial resources a politician controls, the easier it is maintain power, *ceteris paribus:* supporters can be rewarded with treasures, a larger police force and military can be employed to thwart enemies, and/or potential opponents can be bought off. Rulers would prefer to minimize the costs applied directly to securing political survival as this leaves funds available to accomplish other goals (e.g., promote an ideological agenda or stuff one's own bank account). As such, gaining voluntary or quasi-voluntary compliance of the population is the most attractive form of rule as it is the cheapest, as it is much cheaper than patronage (buying supporters) or coercion (maintaining a large army).

To understand the political incentive to regulate the religious economy, we must add one further assumption about the political power of religious firms.

Axiom 7: Successful religions are effective at mobilizing collective action and maintain credible leadership. As such, they are attractive sources of political support or, alternatively, present themselves as potential rivals to authority.

Religious organizations possess several features that are helpful in mobilizing collective action, the basic problem inherent in any mass-based movement supporting or opposing a political regime. Indeed, the successful growth of a religious denomination is a collective action problem itself (cf. Iannaccone 1992, 1994). First, members of a religious community typically hold shared norms, values, and mutual expectations about behavior. This enhances trust among individuals, which in turn lowers the uncertainty associated with mutual cooperation in situations resembling a prisoners' dilemma or assurance games (Chong 1991). Trustworthy leadership is also essential for collective action. Leaders advocating risky action (e.g., protesting a government) will only be successful to the extent that their followers trust their choices. People rarely follow strangers blindly into danger. Numerous other factors also enhance the ability of religious groups to quickly mobilize, including regularized meetings, financial resources, and established networks of communication. For rulers concerned with their political survival, maintaining a tight regulatory control over this potential rival source of authority provides a strong incentive to tamper with laws regulating religious activity. This may entail restricting the freedoms, or reducing the exclusive legal privileges, of particular denominations, especially those that are institutionally aligned with, and unable to back away from a commitment to, a strong rival. Alternatively, religious groups could make for powerful political allies. Coopting a religious group with financial subsidies or preferential legislation that gives it an advantage over rivals represents another political strategy that can shape the degree and nature of religious liberty within a country. For a political leader, decisions related to religious freedom are often affected by the exigencies of maintaining power and obtaining other political goals.

The Politics of Religious Liberty

Predicting whether religious liberty will increase or decrease within a polity, or what form the regulatory regime will take, depends on more specific information about the political and religious environment in question. The bargaining power of political and religious actors will condition the regulatory outcome. Nonetheless, the discussion above points us in the direction of several testable propositions about the relative bargaining power of church and state that can then form the basis for a more historically based narrative. The hypotheses presented below deal specifically with the liberalization of regulatory regimes—i.e., the creation of religious liberty. Nonetheless, the logic of each hypothesis could be modified so as to explain increasing regulation. The most general proposition is as follows.

Proposition 2: To the extent that political survival, revenue collection, and economic growth are hindered by restrictions on religious freedom (or subsidies to a specific church), religious regulation will be liberalized or left unenforced (de facto liberalization).

This hypothesis challenges the notion that religious liberty is the result of a shift in political philosophy or the victory of partisans of a particular philosophy (e.g., Enlightenment liberalism). One of the central failings of ideational explanations is that they typically view the debate over religious liberty in isolation from other concerns in the polity; religious liberty is simply a question of two sides debating "right" versus "wrong," with one side eventually prevailing. In reality, though, legislation rarely is considered in isolation. The reason for specific policy choices in one arena may be connected to seemingly unrelated issues. This proposition directs scholars to look for evidence of potential policy tradeoffs, something ideational perspectives do not do effectively.

Admittedly, proposition 2 is extremely general. The guiding theoretical principle is that some policy tradeoffs affecting a politician's self-interest will be in play during periods of religious deregulation (or increased regulation). This proposition can be made more analytically useful by specifying a set of conditions that may affect political decisionmaking and the ability to bargain. Perhaps the most important condition relates to the presence or absence of viable opponents to power—i.e., the level of political competition. Politicians facing intense rivalries tend to have shorter time horizons and less bargaining power relative to organized social actors than do more secure rulers. Consider first situations where intense political competition exists.

Proposition 3: The presence of viable secular rivals to power increases the bargaining power of religious organizations, *ceteris paribus*.

Proposition 3a: If one religious organization commands hegemonic loyalty within society, and is not institutionally tied to any secular political actor, the bargaining power of that church increases, *ceteris paribus*. Regulatory policy toward religion is likely to favor the dominant church and discriminate against minority denominations.

Proposition 3b: If a church is institutionally linked (or credibly committed) to one political faction, regulatory policy will favor that denomination if the affiliated faction holds power. Conversely, religious deregulation, punishing the dominant church, and rewarding spiritual competitors, is likely when the church's favored party loses.

Proposition 3c: If several competing denominations exist, none with hegemonic dominance, regulatory policy will tend not to discriminate among them (i.e., religious liberty will increase).

Remember, that the ability to organize collective action and deliver political support to politicians or their rivals is the main source of bargaining power for churches.

Where political rivalry is minimal, the goal of political survival becomes less pressing and time horizons lengthen. The political support generated by religious groups becomes less valuable (though by no means valueless) and politicians may be less inclined to give churches what they want.

Proposition 4: As political tenure becomes more secure, the bargaining power of religious groups wanes.

Proposition 4b: Given that restrictions on religious liberty entail monitoring and enforcement costs, politicians will be less likely to enforce them as their political tenure grows secure.

Proposition 4c: As enforcement on restrictions on religious freedom decreases, religious pluralism increases in society (by way of axioms 1 and 2).

In all likelihood, supporting an established church and maintaining legal restrictions on minority religions are relatively inexpensive tasks. For most secure governments, the matter of church regulatory policy will simply be a moot issue. However, if religious pluralism increases and political competition reappears, we are likely to see movement toward religious deregulation. Hence, the best environment for fostering religious freedom is one with religious pluralism and political competition.

Suggestions for Empirical Study

The purpose of the above model was to stimulate an interest in political factors when discussing the religious economy. Space limitations prevent a detailed empirical test of the model. However, a few cases can be noted to demonstrate the prima facie plausibility of the aforementioned propositions.

The creation of the United States (from colonies to sovereign nation in the late 1700s) represents the ideal case for the promotion of religious liberty. Although various denominations had established strongholds in certain areas of the colonies (e.g., Congregationalists in New England), no single faith held majority status over the entire nation. With local states jockeying for power within the new union, political competition was high. Under such circumstances, the least objectionable option for church-state relations was to prohibit a single, established faith and allow for religious liberty at the national level (cf. Finke 1990). The need to promote trade between states and encourage European immigration also played into the hands of increased religious liberty. These economic matters were more important to local leaders than fighting for their state's favored denomination at the national level. Trade and immigration both played an important role in enhancing state revenues at a time when local governments were strapped for cash. As proposition 2 would predict, politicians would be quick to jettison policies favoring one denomination if it interfered seriously with tax revenue and economic growth.

Latin America offers an instructive contrast to the U.S. case. Here, nations were formed during the early nineteenth century amidst violent political competition and religious monopoly. Early in the struggles for independence from Spain, many of the high clergy sided with the monarchy. This would be expected in that the king appointed bishops; thereby the position of Catholic officials was institutionally linked with an unpopular regime. This gave many liberationists an incentive to punish and weaken an "enemy" church (as predicted by proposition 3b). Churches linked to "ancién regimes" during revolutionary times typically do not fare well. Consider the Catholic Church in the late 1700s or the Russian Orthodox Church during the Bolshevik revolution. Nonetheless, the struggle to define national governments was hotly contested with multiple factions trying to secure power. Grassroots clergy, such as Padres Hidalgo and Morales in Mexico, demonstrated an ability to mobilize parishioners in favor of liberation. Although the church was weakened with many bishops fleeing the continent, ideological liberals—who favored separation of church and state along the U.S. or French models—trod lightly when it came to redefining church-state relations until political rivalries were finally settled. An account of Simón Bolívar, an avowed liberal in the French revolutionary tradition, emphasizes this point.

> Notwithstanding his liberal religious views and his unflagging efforts to have [his views on church-state separation] incorporated into the organic laws of Venezuela and New Grenada, Bolívar recognized the political importance of

> clerical support of the Revolution. No one realized better than he the strength of the hold exercised by the Church over the masses of both high and low degree. He therefore was careful not to antagonize the clergy and put aside personal opinion for the general good (Mecham 1966: 45).

Although the "general good" was potentially spared a violent religious war, there were certainly personal political interests at stake here. Bolívar's growing rivalry with General Francisco de Paula Santander over the political shape of "Gran Colombia" led him further to reward the dominant religion with favored legal status.

Changes in the church-state regime did take place in Latin America during the mid-1800s. Throughout this period, new governments sought to continue the *patronato*, an agreement that granted the Spanish crown the ability to appoint bishops, censor papal decrees, and dabble in the financial affairs of the Latin American Church. Not surprisingly, politicians saw this as a powerful tool to control a potential rival to power. However, with most nations in a severe fiscal crisis by midcentury, government leaders went on the "attack" against church privileges and expropriated numerous church landholdings and secularized marriage and funeral services. They also confiscated the church's role maintaining the registry (i.e., the bookkeeping mechanism tracing family lines and property). All of this was to help alleviate government debt. Expropriated landholdings were sold to raise immediate cash and could then be taxed once in secular production. Civil marriages and funerals provided a small revenue stream for the state, and the registry gave the government the bookkeeping infrastructure to levy taxes. In most nations, the church was (inadequately) compensated by an end to the *patronato*, giving the church the institutional autonomy it had demanded since independence.

Restrictions on Protestants were liberalized as Latin American nations sought to boost their economies with trade from Northern Europe and the U.S. Foreign Protestants were allowed to pray freely. However, the church still had enough sway to get prohibitions on non-Catholic proselytizing (including a continued ban on the sale of the Bible to laypersons). Over time, Protestants were able to "sneak" into several countries of Latin America and set up shop. Protestant growth moved slowly at first, but exploded in a number of countries during the mid-1900s. By the end of the century, a return to (reasonably) competitive democracy boded well for increases in religious freedom. Elections became more contested and were often decided by just a few percentage points. Evangelical voting blocs helped to elect presidents in Peru and Colombia, and began to show their weight throughout the region. In many instances, the active Protestant population was equal to that of the active churchgoing Catholic population, diluting the social influence of the church. In response, politicians rewarded Protestant constituents with more guarantees on religious freedom (e.g., less-restrictive zoning regulations, greater access to social institutions such as the military). While Latin America today is by no means a paragon of freedom, religious liberty has increased significantly as predicted by the model above. Gradually increasing religious pluralism and competitive political regimes have enhanced religious freedom.

CONCLUSION

The economic study of religion has provided scholars with a rigorous theoretical framework to study religious behavior at the individual, institutional, and market levels. Because work in this area has proceeded in a deductive manner, explicitly spelling out axioms and propositions, it is possible to add new assumptions, or modify existing axioms, to expand the scope of the theory. This chapter added several assumptions about political behavior that enable us to understand why politicians regulate and deregulate religious markets. The primary assumption is that politicians will make decisions based upon a desire to stay in power and maximize resources available to them. Questions of religious liberty—or more appropriately, religious regulation—need to be seen in light of the various tradeoffs political leaders make in attempting to secure political survival and revenue. Admittedly, this work is still in its infancy. For now, the theory appears best to apply to countries with a Christian tradition. However, with some modifications about the organizational dynamics of non-Christian religions, there is no reason to expect that this model would not apply to the Islamic world or parts of Asia where Eastern religions predominate. As with all scientific theories, the value of a theory is determined by its ability to stand up to repeated empirical scrutiny. I have not answered all of the questions posed in the initial paragraph of this chapter. Nonetheless, I believe that the assumptions and propositions presented above offer a good start to expanding our knowledge of church-state relations and provide a new avenue of research within the economics of religion paradigm. Let the chase begin.

NOTES

1. I am loath to use the word "paradigm" in that it implies rigid theoretical boundaries that cannot be crossed and pigeonholes scholars into preordained categories. In my experience, I have found many of my colleagues reject rational choice theories of religion (and politics) out of hand simply because they use economic theory as a base. While admitting a preference for rational choice modeling (because I think it has a great deal of explanatory power), I am also aware that ideational factors play a significant role in social behavior (see Gill 2000, 1999c). Within the field at large, less

emphasis should be placed on grand paradigmatic battles (which often approach the intensity of religious wars) and more importance given to rigorous empirical (quantitative *and* qualitative) testing. For rhetorical purposes, though, the awkward term "paradigm" will have to suffice.

2. For rational choice studies or the role of religion in political mobilization, see Kalyvas (1996, 2000), Gill (1998), Warner (2000), and Taylor (2001).

3. My interest-based analysis of religious-political interactions does not exclude the possibility that ideas affect social outcomes. However, I am skeptical of assertions (usually found in studies of intellectual history) that ideas are the exclusive or predominant cause of social outcomes. For example, the presence of church-state separation in the United States frequently is attributed to the intellectual arguments made by James Madison and Thomas Jefferson (cf. Noonan 1998: 59–91). But while philosophical arguments for the separation of church and state abounded during the late 1700s, so did intellectual forces favoring religious establishment. In almost all societies, there are a plurality of ideas about how to manage social relations, and which ones eventually win out is not so much a matter of winning intellectual debates as it is garnering the political and economic power to impose one's preferred alternatives on others.

4. A wide range of ideas not only about establishment/disestablishment per se, but also the varying levels and forms of government regulation over religious organizations and belief. Such diversity of opinion still exists in the United States today, despite a general commitment to church-state "separation" among the population. One need only look at the ill-fated Religious Freedom Restoration Act or the controversy surrounding George W. Bush's faith-based funding initiative.

5. See Chaves and Cann (1992), Finke and Iannaccone (1993), Stark and Iannaccone (1994), and Olds (1994) for the rare exceptions.

6. In many parts of Latin America, Protestant missionaries were forbidden from importing copies of the Bible until the middle part of the twentieth century.

7. During the early 1990s, the Hungarian parliament debated which churches should be granted legal status, which in turn brought a host of other privileges, including tax-exempt status. An early law allowed churches with 100 members to legally register. However, the historical churches in the country lobbied for a size limit of 10,000 members and a historical presence in the country of 100 years. See Enyedi (2000).

8. Until 1992, no religious organization could own property in Mexico. This represented a serious disadvantage for any upstart sects since they could only hold services in pre-existing buildings, where space was hard to obtain or too small to build a large congregation (Gill 1999b).

9. This raises an interesting research question. To the extent that subsidies to (or tax collection for) one church are not public knowledge, we should expect little impact on conversion rates. This further suggests that "official" state religions would prefer to keep subsidies hidden. If such subsidies are commonly known, conversion rates should drop. An interesting contemporary test case is Germany, where the government collects tithes for the Catholic and Reformed churches, although the collection is "voluntary." The addition of East Germany, where such taxes were not collected, provides an additional empirical wrinkle to the case.

10. A more formal economic definition of credence goods would include the notion that the producer has greater knowledge of the product's quality than the consumer.

The services provided by an auto mechanic or doctor are typical examples where asymmetric information favors the producer. However, it may be the case that because some of the most basic promises of religion (e.g., salvation) are not verifiable until after death, both consumer *and* producer are unsure of the goods' ultimate quality.

11. Interestingly, while religious production has low barriers to entry, it also benefits from economies of scale, which tends to shield some faiths from competition. The best illustration of this is the old adage that "two hundred fifty million Catholics can't be wrong." In other words, religious consumers use membership figures as a proxy for information about the quality of a good. Large religions thus have an easier time of assuring potential members about the quality of their good as compared to upstart sects (which may explain, in part, why so many upstarts do not succeed). Nonetheless, upstarts can overcome this hurdle and grow large. Size matters, but so do many other factors. Religious economies of scale may only provide a slight advantage for established religions. See Finke and Stark (1992) and Stark (1996) for further discussion on how upstart sects can succeed.

12. Islamic countries would seem to be the exception to this finding as religious participation is seemingly high and alternative faiths are highly circumscribed, implying rather homogenous tastes among society. However, the organizational structure of Islam makes it a highly diverse and competitive religion internally. Individual clerics are responsible for their own salaries ensuring that there is a strong incentive for them to keep their personal followers happy and involved in the faith.

13. Where a traditionally dominant religion exists under an avowed atheistic or anticlerical state (e.g., Soviet Union, Mexico from 1917–1994), the hegemonic faith can be thought of as a minority player in that it does not wield the coercive power to counter the dominant producer of social values and norms.

REFERENCES

Adams, Arlin M. and Charles J. Emmerich. 1990. *A Nation Dedicated to Religious Liberty: The Constitutional Heritage of the Religion Clauses*. Philadelphia: University of Pennsylvania Press.

Ames, Barry. 1987. *Political Survival: Politicians and Public Policy in Latin America*. Berkeley: University of California Press.

Chaves, Mark and David E. Cann. 1992. "Regulation, Pluralism, and Religious Market Structure: Explaining Religion's Vitality," *Rationality and Society* 4 (3): 272–90.

Chong, Dennis. 1991. *Collective Action and the Civil Rights Movement*. Chicago: University of Chicago Press.

Cleary, Caitlin. 2001. "Freeze lifted on churches' size," *Seattle Times* (10 July 2001): B1.

Enyedi, Zsolt. 2000. "Finding a New Pattern: Church-State Relations in Post-Communist Hungary." Unpublished paper presented at the ECPR 28th Joint Sessions of Worshops. Copenhagen, Denmark.

Estep, William R. 1990. *Revolution within the Revolution: The First Amendment in Historical Context, 1612–1789*. Grand Rapids, MI: Eerdmans Publishing.

Finke, Roger, 1990. "Religious Deregulation: Origins and Consequences," *Journal of Church and State* 32: 609–626.

———. 1997a. "The Consequences of Religious Competition: Supply-Side Explanations for Religious Change." In *Assessing Rational Choice Theories of Religion*. Lawrence A. Young, ed. New York: Routledge, 46–65.

———. 1997b. "The Illusion of Shifting Demand: Supply-Side Interpretations of American Religious History." In *Retelling U.S. Religious History*. Thomas Tweed, ed. Berkeley: University of California Press, 108–124.

Finke, Roger and Laurence Iannaccone. 1993. "Supply-Side Explanations for Religious Change in America," *The Annals* 527: 27–39.

Finke, Roger and Rodney Stark. 1992. *The Churching of America: Winners and Losers in Our Religious Economy*. New Brunswick, N.J.: Rutgers University Press.

Geddes, Barbara. 1995. "Uses and Limitations of Rational Choice." In *Latin America in Comparative Perpective: New Approaches to Methods and Analysis*. Peter H. Smith, ed. Boulder, Colo.: Westview Press.

Gill, Anthony. 1998. *Rendering Unto Caesar: The Catholic Church and the State in Latin America*. Chicago: University of Chicago Press.

———. 1999a. "Government Regulation, Social Anomie and Religious Pluralism in Latin America: A Cross-National Analysis," *Rationality and Society* 11 (3): 287–316.

———. 1999b. "The Politics of Regulating Religion in Mexico: The 1992 Constitutional Reforms in Historical Context," *Journal of Church and State* 41 (4): 761–794.

———. 1999c. "The Struggle to Be Soul Provider: Catholic Responses to Protestant Growth in Latin America." In *Latin American Religion in Motion*. Christian Smith and Joshua Prokopy, ed. New York: Routledge, 17–42.

———. 2000. "A Continental Divide: Can Rational Choice Be Reconciled with Cultural Theories in the Study of Comparative Politics?" Paper presented at the Annual Meeting of the American Political Science Association. Washington, D.C.

Iannaccone, Laurence R. 1984. "Consumption Capital and Habit Formation with an Application to Religious Participation." Ph.D. dissertation, University of Chicago.

———. 1990. "Religious Participation: A Human Capital Approach," *Journal for the Scientific Study of Religion* 29 (3): 297–314.

———. 1992. "Sacrifice and Stigma: Reducing Free-Riding in Cults, Communes, and Other Collectives," *Journal of Political Economy* 100 (2): 271–291.

———. 1994. "Why Strict Churches Are Strong," *American Journal of Sociology* 99 (5): 1180–1210.

Kalyvas, Stathis N. 1996. *The Rise of Christian Democracy in Europe*. Ithaca, N.Y.: Cornell University Press.

———. 2000. "Commitment Problems in Emerging Democracies: The Case of Religious Parties," *Comparative Politics* 32 (4): 379–398.

Kuznetsov, Anatoly. 1996. "Ecumenism, Evangelization and Religious Freedom in Russia and the Former Soviet Republics," *Religion in Eastern Europe* 16 (2): 8–14.

Levi, Margaret. 1988. *Of Rule and Revenue*. Berkeley: University of California Press.

———. 1997. *Consent, Dissent and Patriotism*. Cambridge, England: Cambridge University Press.

Mayhew, David. 1974. *Congress: The Electoral Connection*. New Haven, Conn.: Yale University Press.

Mecham, J. Lloyd. 1966. *Church and State in Latin America*. Chapel Hill: University of North Carolina Press.

Noonan, John T. 1998. *The Lustre of Our Country: The American Experience of Religious Freedom.* Berkeley: University of California Press.

Olds, Kelly. 1994. "Privatizing the Church: Disestablishment in Connecticut and Massachusetts," *Journal of Political Economy* 102 (2): 277–297.

Segers, Mary C. and Ted G. Jelen. 1998. *A Wall of Separation? Debating the Public Role of Religion.* Lanham, Md.: Rowman & Littlefield.

Smith, Adam. 1976 [1776]. *An Inquiry into the Nature and Causes of the Wealth of Nations, Vols. I and II.* Indianapolis, Ind.: Liberty Fund.

Stark, Rodney. 1992. "Do Catholic Societies Really Exist?" *Rationality and Society* 4 (3): 261–271.

———. 1996. *The Rise of Christianity: A Sociologist Reconsiders History.* Princeton, N.J.: Princeton University Press.

Stark, Rodney and William Sims Bainbridge. 1985. *A Theory of Religion.* New York: Peter Lange Publishing.

Stark, Rodney and Roger Finke. 2000. *Acts of Faith: Explaining the Human Side of Religion.* Berkeley: University of California Press.

Stark, Rodney and Laurence Iannaccone. 1994. "A Supply-Side Reinterpretation of the 'Secularization' of Europe," *Journal for the Scientific Study of Religion* 33 (3): 230–252.

Taylor, Julie. 2001. "Prophet Sharing: Conflict and Cooperation between Islamic Clerics and the State in the Middle East." Manuscript. UCLA.

Warner, Carolyn M. 2000. *Confessions of an Interest Group: The Catholic Church and Political Parties in Europe.* Princeton, N.J.: Princeton University Press.

6

Competing Notions of Religious Competition and Conflict in Theories of Religious Economies

Daniel V. A. Olson

INTRODUCTION

It is hard to think of many scholars who have contributed as many new ideas to the sociology of religion in the last quarter of the twentieth century as Rodney Stark. This volume, including the contributions of Stark's opponents, is a testament to the influence of his ideas, and the ideas of his close collaborators, primarily William Sims Bainbridge, Roger Finke, and Laurence Iannaccone (hereafter Stark et al.). During the last twenty years in particular, Stark et al. have focussed new attention on old questions dealing with the most basic facts of religion. Why are some people more religious than others? Why are some nations or regions more religious than others? How and why do religious groups differ from one another? Why do some religious groups grow while others decline? Why and how do religious groups change? Is the world becoming more or less religious or both at the same time? Will science, modern life, and education lead to the extinction of religion? These are just a few of the many questions that Stark and his collaborators have taken up.

In order to answer these questions Stark et al., especially Stark himself, have gathered information on religion from a broad range of geographic and historical settings to examine early Christianity (Stark 1996), medieval Europe (Stark 1999), nineteenth-century England and the U.S. (Stark, Finke, and Iannaccone 1995; Finke, Guest, and Stark 1996), Latin America (Stark 1991), twentieth-century Europe (Stark and Iannaccone 1994), international comparisons in the twentieth century (Iannaccone 1991), and the U.S. (Stark and McCann 1993; Stark 1997b). Moreover, Stark et al. have tried, both in articles on specific topics and in several general book-length presentations

(Stark and Bainbridge 1985, 1987; Finke and Stark 2000) to unify these explanations by linking specific results to a common set of core propositions. These core propositions have been variously labeled "rational choice," "supply-side," or "religious economies" models and have been most accessibly summed up in Stark and Finke's recent (2000) book *Acts of Faith*.

While *Acts of Faith* sometimes gives the impression of a research agenda completed and wrapped up, with most major questions resolved, the responses to the Stark et al. agenda are only beginning to kick into high gear. For example, a forthcoming review of their work on pluralism in the *Annual Review of Sociology* (Chaves and Gorski 2001) concludes that most research fails to support Stark et al.'s claims concerning the positive effects of religious pluralism. Increasingly, European scholars (e.g., Bruce 1999) are likely to challenge Stark et al.'s assertions concerning the current and historic religious situation in Europe, especially the relation of the state regulation of religion to religious pluralism and religious involvement. But even in the unlikely event that future scholars were to agree that all the theories of Stark et al. were wrong, the challenge provided by the work of Stark et al. will have served the purpose of reinvigorating interest in a very broad range of research questions, questions whose answers have, for a long time, largely been taken for granted.

The main point of this chapter is not that Stark et al.'s theories about "religious economies" are mostly right or mostly wrong. The main point is that currently it is difficult to reach a clear verdict about many of the model's predictions. The primary obstacle to such a verdict is not the adequacy of the research and statistical methods used (though that is relevant). Nor is it mainly an issue of determining which side has more research results piled up on their side of the balance scale (though that also is relevant). The more basic problem is theoretical. Despite long lists of numbered (and quite interesting) propositions, important theoretical ambiguities and inconsistencies remain in the work of Stark et al. These ambiguities lead directly to many of the current arguments over the interpretation of research results. Researchers can agree on what the results show, but not on what the results mean concerning the theories of Stark et al.

To begin with, the theory's most central concept, religious competition, is nowhere defined and is therefore used very loosely and ambiguously across different explanatory contexts. This makes it difficult for researchers to know whether they have actually measured competition. Thus, for example, Stark and Iannaccone (1994, 1996) can agree with Lechner (1996a, 1996b) that over the past several decades religious pluralism has increased in the Netherlands, but they do not agree with Lechner that religious competition has increased or that competition is related to the declining rates of religious participation over the same time period. In fact, most of Stark et al.'s replies to contrary research results turn on the argument that the research in question does not adequately measure religious *competition* (e.g., Finke and Stark 1989; Stark and Iannaccone 1996; Stark et al. 1995; Finke et al. 1996; Finke and Stark 1998). But without a clear definition of religious competition and agreement on how it should be measured, such arguments are unlikely to be resolved.

The goal of this chapter is partly constructive and partly critical. I first briefly highlight the key assumptions and explanations behind Stark et al.'s work on religious economies and where I stand with regard to these assumptions. I then expand upon these theories somewhat in ways that seem consistent with other things Stark et al. have said. I argue that Stark et al.'s work implies the existence of a more general concept, religious opposition, and that there are two types of religious opposition, religious competition and religious conflict. A careful analysis of these two types of opposition highlights theoretical ambiguities and inconsistencies that lie behind the conflicting interpretations of published research results and identifies areas where future research on religious economies are likely to stumble. I then apply the results of this analysis to the three main areas of research on religious economies: religious market share, the state regulation of religion, and religious pluralism.

I conclude that in two of these three research areas, religious market share and state regulation, most of the current research results are better seen as effects of religious conflict (as broadly defined below) than as examples of religious competition. While Stark et al. imply that religious conflict is simply another form of competition that, in certain circumstances, replaces competition, I argue that conflict and competition are quite different. The mechanisms underlying the response of groups to religious conflict may often (though not necessarily) involve demand-side processes as much or more than the supply-side processes Stark et al. associate with religious competition. I agree with Stark et al. that groups facing religious opposition of both types, but especially conflict, will often experience increased levels of religious, or at least organizational, commitment among their adherents, but I also argue that in many cases this could come at the cost of declining group size. While published research results appear to confirm Stark et al.'s predictions concerning religious conflict, I conclude that the jury is still out concerning religious competition.

KEY ASSUMPTIONS

Three important assumptions underlie the research of Stark et al. over the past twenty years. First, Stark et al. assume that religious behavior is in no way less rational than other types of human behavior. Because of this assumption, Stark et al.'s theories have been called "rational choice" theories.

This label applies most accurately to the work of Iannaccone (e.g., 1990, 1994, 1997). Stark and Finke have recently denied that they are rational choice theorists in the narrow sense of that term (Stark 1997a; Stark and Finke 2000: 41). For example, they explicitly acknowledge the role played by culture and socialization. Nevertheless, their theoretical approach emphasizes that in religious behavior, as much as in other behavior, individuals seek to maximize their benefits and minimize their costs. Thus religious adherents do not make "irrational" sacrifices for their faith simply because their socialization teaches them that they should. They "sacrifice" only when the perceived religious benefits outweigh the perceived costs.

Second, Stark et al. assume that the underlying need for religion is fairly widespread and, on average, fairly constant across populations, across time, and across societies. At the same time they note that different people in society desire different kinds of religion. Thus no single religion or style of religion can satisfy everyone. While stopping short of claiming that religion is a human universal, Stark et al. assume that most people desire certain things that in principle could only be supplied by a supernatural source, for example, life after death (Stark and Finke 2000: 88 ff.). Because religions (by definition) claim to explain how such needs can be met, religious behavior and belief is unlikely to disappear or permanently decline. This second assumption lies behind Stark et al.'s opposition to secularization theories, especially those that posit a long-term decline or near disappearance of individual religious thought and behavior brought on by greater exposure to education, science, technology, and modern life.

The third assumption, the "supply-side assumption," builds on the second assumption. Stark et al. assume that variations in rates and levels of religious involvement are best explained by variations in the supply of religion rather than the demand for religion (Stark and Iannaccone 1994). The number of religious organizations, services, rituals, books, ideas, etc. available to a population (the supply) can change much faster than a population's desire for religion (which, given the second assumption above, is fairly constant). For example, if church attendance rates fall, it may be due to a failure of religious organizations (perhaps caused by state involvement in religious matters), not a declining need for religion (Stark and Iannaccone 1994). If church attendance rates go up, it is because there is a greater number and variety of religious organizations available and they are doing a better job of meeting religious needs (Finke and Stark 1992). To my knowledge, Stark et al. do not rule out the possibility that the demand for religion could slowly rise or fall given long-term increases or decreases in the pervasiveness or effectiveness of religious socialization.[1] But given the second assumption, it is unlikely that religion and the need for religion would permanently decline.

Part of the charge given to authors of these chapters is to state their own positions on these matters. Thus, let me be clear at the start, I am in basic agreement with the first two of these assumptions and my strong inclination is to accept the third, though, as I argue below, I think good demand-side arguments can and should be made.[2] Because of my position on these three assumptions I am also deeply skeptical of secularization theories that posit the eventual permanent decline of individual religious behavior and thought in more "advanced" societies. This is not to say that religion will not decline in some areas during certain times under certain conditions, or even that some countries might have much lower levels of religious involvement than other countries for long periods of time. But I am not convinced that modernity, post-modernity, functional rationality, institutional differentiation, or exposure to science and technical training are the chief causes of these fluctuations or that religious involvement and interest will decline in some permanent or even long-lasting fashion across all or most of the industrialized nations.

Stark et al. argue that these three assumptions function as axioms and thus, by their nature, are impossible to directly disprove (though opponents might disagree). At best, they claim, one can test hypotheses deduced from these assumptions. Stark et al. have developed an extensive list of such hypotheses and have attempted to test them. These hypotheses are sometimes called the religious economies model.

RELIGIOUS ECONOMIES AND COMPETITION

Not all of the work of Stark et al. deals with religious economies. For example, Iannaccone's (1994) arguments about why "strict" churches have greater organizational strength can be called rational choice arguments but they do not directly address religious economies. As used here, theories of religious economies are explanations that use characteristics of the religious environment in a geographic area as independent variables to help explain the religious behavior of individuals and groups in that same area. Individuals and religious groups behave differently in different religious environments. Stark and Finke (2000: 193) define a religious economy as "all of the religious activity going on in any society: a 'market' of current and potential adherents, a set of one or more organizations seeking to attract or maintain adherents, and the religious culture offered by the organization(s)." One could just as easily substitute the term "environment" for "economy" in the phrase "religious economy," but the term "economy" connotes the theoretical directions Stark et al. have taken.

Why do commitment levels and participation rates vary so much over time and space? Drawing on the supply-side assumption described above, the answer must be that there is a greater supply of religion in those areas where commitment levels and participation rates are higher. But why would some areas be better supplied with religious organizations, books, ideas, rituals, etc. than others? Borrowing from economic models of firms and markets, Stark et al.'s explanation turns on the notion of competition. There will be a greater and more diverse supply of religion where greater religious competition is allowed to develop unrestrained by government subsidies or regulation and intervention. The general theory, very briefly, is that where there is more religious competition, religious leaders must work harder to secure adherents (and adherents' time and money) if they are to maintain their religious organizations, including their own jobs/roles as leaders. This motivates religious leaders in more competitive environments to be more creative and more vigorous, which, all else being equal, makes religious groups more efficient and more appealing to adherents and potential adherents. This, in turn, raises average member commitment levels. Since other religious groups in the same area are experiencing the same competition and thus presumably are working harder and more efficiently to attract and secure the commitment of adherents, the average rates of religious participation and commitment should also be higher in areas with greater religious competition. But what exactly is religious competition?

While discussing the central importance of "ritual" in the work of many early anthropological studies of religion, Stark and Finke (2000: 107–108) complain that these works almost never actually define what ritual is. This makes it possible to mold the term to mean any number of things that might be needed to support a particular claim about the importance of ritual. It is ironic therefore that despite repeated assertions that religious competition is the most central variable in their theoretical approach, Stark et al. seem to skip over the task of defining what religious competition means. I ask their forgiveness in advance if I have overlooked or forgotten some key passage, but religious competition is not one of the 36 terms given formal definition and listed in the appendix of Stark and Finke's very helpful summary (2000) of their theorizing on religion. They do note (218) that "unfortunately, competition is one of those concepts that is very difficult to measure, except indirectly" (using measures such as pluralism and market share).

Even if the term is somewhere given formal definition, it is clear that part of the difficulty in measuring the concept, even indirectly, is that competition means different things in different explanatory contexts. Without a clear idea of what religious competition is, it is hard to know if one has actually measured it and whether particular research results (e.g., research on the effects of religious pluralism or religious market share) support, contradict, or have no bearing on the idea that religious competition increases religious commitment. For this reason a large part of this chapter explores the different meanings Stark et al. associate with religious competition. But first I argue that their work implies a more encompassing concept, religious opposition, within which religious competition can be seen as but one subtype.

RELIGIOUS OPPOSITION

In order to explain why some countries and regions such as Ireland, Poland, Quebec, and Iran have very little religious competition (as measured by religious pluralism) and yet have, or have had, very high levels of religious involvement, Stark et al. (e.g., Stark and Iannaccone 1996; Finke and Stark 1998; Stark and Finke 2000: 219, 239 ff.) argue that "under special circumstances, conflict can substitute for competition in generating high levels of religiousness. For example, when a church serves as the organizational basis for ethnic conflict . . . or provides the rallying point for resistance to external repression (as was the case in Poland), a 'monopoly church' can generate immense support" (Stark and Finke 2000: 219). Such statements suggest that there is a more general concept that includes both "conflict" and "competition."

I call this more general concept *religious opposition* and define it as behavior (or threatened behavior) that obstructs (or is believed to obstruct) a religious group's attainment of its goals. Additionally, when a religion becomes a core element in the shared identity of some social category (e.g., an ethnic group, a nationality, or a social class) religious opposition can occur when that identity group's goals are obstructed or thought to be obstructed. Drawing from Stark et al.'s various assertions, the general argument is that where there is opposition to a religious group's goals (even if this opposition is more imaginary than real) this opposition will elicit greater effort and commitment either from the group's leaders, its adherents, or both. In contrast, groups facing no opposition, and especially those that receive state subsidies, will have lower levels of religious commitment and involvement. Religious leaders of such groups tend to become lazy and secure in their positions (Finke and Stark 1988; Iannaccone 1991) and thus fail to inspire much zeal in their adherents.

My definition of religious opposition includes the phrases "or threatened behavior" and "or is believed to obstruct" in order to emphasize that the hypothesized energetic response can occur even if a group only believes its goals or its identity are being threatened. For example, Smith (1998) argues that American Evangelicals are thriving because they believe themselves to be "embattled" by the "the world," "the media," and "secular humanism." Likewise, Stark and Finke (2000: 248–249) argue that the current religious vitality of many Islamic states derives from a perception among Islamic intellectuals that these states lost much of their former strength and independence due to the secular influences of cooperation with "the West." The way to restore this former greatness is to combat these secular influences by returning to a more vigorous form of Islam. Whether or not secular humanists are actually seeking to undermine Evangelical values and whether or not organizations in the West have set out to weaken Islamic states is less important than the fact that both Evangelicals and Islamic intellectuals believe that they are under attack.

In the work of Stark et al. there are at least two kinds of religious opposition, religious conflict and religious competition. In religious conflict the intent of the obstructing behavior (or imagined behavior) is to obstruct the attainment of a religious group's goals (or its associated identity group's goals). In the most severe cases, a religiously based war or inquisition, one side seeks to destroy another religion's influence and adherents. Somewhat less severely, a political body may outlaw or limit the practice of some particular religion. Or, as in the example above, American Evangelicals may believe that opposing groups, e.g., the "homosexual lobby," are intent on eliminating "Christian values" from the public schools. In all cases, the behavior, or imagined behavior, is aimed at undermining the goals of a religious group or the associated identity group. As should be clear from the examples above, religious conflict, real or imagined, can originate from any number of sources, (e.g., government bodies, interest groups, social movements, even other nations), not just opposing religious groups. Using this definition of religious conflict, many of the processes that Stark et al. associate with competition, e.g., government regulation,[3] are arguably better seen as examples of religious conflict than as competition.

In contrast, religious competition (the concept to which Stark et al. have given the most attention) comes only from other religious groups. Moreover, in religious competition, the main intent of the obstructing behavior is not to harm the interests of some religion; rather the obstruction occurs as a byproduct of other religious groups pursuing their own goals. For example, Stark et al. state that religious competition exists when there are many religious groups in the same area and many groups are striving to increase the number of their adherents and their share of adherents' time and money resources. Since the total potential adherents in an area is limited, one group's organizational success is automatically an obstacle to the success of other groups.

One could make a plausible argument that religious groups are competing not only with other religious groups, but also with every other organization that seeks adherents' finite time and money resources, e.g., employers, governments, retailers, families, professional sports teams, etc. Aside from the difficulties in measuring competition defined in this way, Stark et al. have tended not to focus on this type of competition (from outside the religious market) since (under the second assumption above) religious needs are qualitatively different from other needs and can only be addressed by groups and idea systems that explain how supernatural means are available to satisfy these otherwise unsatisfiable needs. Ultimately, professional sports teams and video rental outlets cannot fully compete in the same market with religious groups since they can satisfy only some of the needs that religions satisfy. However, one could apply economic models, as Iannaccone has done (e.g., 1997), to analyze how individuals' resources and situations affect the proportion of the time and money individuals devote to religion versus other activities. Similar economic models explain why some persons will spend more of their budget on entertainment and less on housing even though new home contractors and apartment complexes do not "compete" with video rental outlets and professional sports teams.

Stark et al. suggest that religious conflict and competition are fairly similar. As noted above, they argue that in some situations conflict can "substitute" for competition. A major section of the chapter on "Competition and Commitment" in *Acts of Faith* is titled "Conflict *as* Competition" (emphasis added, Stark and Finke 2000: 239). I agree with Stark et al. that both competition and conflict have the potential to increase religious commitment. However, as will become clear below, I argue that competition and conflict operate through quite different causal mechanisms. But first there is the problem of how to measure religious competition.

COMPETITION: SUBSTITUTABILITY OR DIVERSITY

Even if one chooses, as I do, to consider only other religious groups as a source of religious competition, the issue of which religious groups to count as competitors is far from clear. The problem arises because of ambiguities built into the way Stark et al. have described competition. One can identify at least two, somewhat contradictory, factors that enter into determining which religious groups are in competition and how much competition there is: substitutability and diversity.

I give credit to the anonymous author of a manuscript I recently reviewed who suggested that the competition facing any religious group should be defined as the number of nearby *substitutes* for that religious group. Thus, if congregation B is the only other nearby congregation that people attending congregation A would want to or be able to attend, then congregation A faces less competition than another congregation, call it C, for which there are four nearby congregations that its attenders might also attend. Although, to my knowledge, Stark et al. nowhere propose such a definition, it seems quite consistent with many of their assertions. Thus, the greater competition created by the larger number of substitutes facing congregation C would force congregation C, especially its leaders, to work harder if they hoped to attract new adherents and maintain the support of their current adherents. The idea of substitutability implies that two religious groups are in competition to the extent that there is some group of potential adherents (a market) who could conceivably chose to join either one group or the other.

But is there only one religious market in which all religious groups compete as potential substitutes? In their early work Stark et al. (e.g., Finke and Stark 1988; Stark et al. 1995; Finke et al. 1996) use the pluralism index to measure competition and apply it to all the countable religious groups in a geographic area.[4] This use of the pluralism index (described below) implicitly assumes that all the countable religions in an area are potential substitutes and competitors for one another. But one might reasonably ask whether a local mosque[5] should be considered a substitute for a nearby Lutheran church. Is there a market of potential adherents who would be likely to attend either the mosque or the Lutheran church?

The notion of substitutability suggests that there may be submarkets or market niches in religion just as there are submarkets within many commercial industries. Just as Ford mini-vans don't compete with Kenilworth trucks though both provide transportation, the Lutheran congregation mentioned above may not be in competition with the nearby mosque though both try to meet religious needs. In fact, Stark et al. explicitly raise the issue of submarkets[6] in religion when they note that sometimes the pluralism index applied to a whole society may be inappropriate. They (e.g., Stark and Finke 2000: 201) give the example of a caste-based society in which there is one religion for each caste, and people can only be adherents of the religion serving their caste. In such a situation, the different caste-based religions would not be in competition for the same set of adherents and thus would not be substitutes. Despite the pluralism of religion in the society as a whole, there would be no competition in any of the submarkets, and thus no religious competition in the society.

The difficulty of relying only on the notion of substitutability to measure competition becomes apparent if one extends it to its most extreme, but logical, conclusion. In that case, the best substitute for a Presbyterian congregation might be another nearby Presbyterian congregation, and the best measures of the competition facing Presbyterian congregations would be the number of nearby Presbyterian congregations. If competition increases religious commitment, then those Presbyterian congregations with the most nearby Presbyterian congregations should also exhibit the highest levels of member commitment.

However, competition defined in this way leads to contradictions both with previous research results and with other claims made by Stark et al. As Stark and Finke (2000: 244 ff.) point out, most of the research examining religious market share (the proportion of religious adherents in an area belonging to a particular denomination) shows that adherents are most committed in areas where their denomination has a smaller market share and where, presumably, there would be fewer nearby congregations from the same denomination. For example, Catholics have higher commitment levels in non-Catholic regions of the U.S. (Stark and McCann 1993; Perl and Olson 2000). But if competition is defined as the number of available substitutes and the best substitutes are other nearby congregations in the same denomination, then one would expect to find (contrary to empirical results so far) that the highest levels of Catholic commitment would be in regions where Catholics are most common and Catholic parishes are most densely concentrated and offering one another the most competition.[7] Not only do these research results run contrary to the implications of competition defined only as substitutability, but this definition of competition (in its most extreme form) runs directly contrary to Stark et al.'s claim (discussed below) that small market share reflects *higher*, not lower, competition. Stark et al.'s claim that small market share reflects higher competition rests on the assumption that the competing religious groups are denominations rather than congregations (another issue that is quite ambiguous in the various claims of Stark et al.[8] and an issue I address below).

Moreover, defining competition purely as substitutability also leads to contradictions with other assertions made by Stark et al. in which competition and its effects are seen to be dependent not upon substitutability but rather upon the *diversity* of religious groups and the choices that such diversity gives to potential adherents. For example, Stark and Finke implore their readers to "Notice our theoretical emphasis on competition. Religious pluralism (the presence of multiple suppliers) is important only insofar as it increases choices and competition, offering consumers a wider range of religious rewards and forcing suppliers to be more responsive and efficient" (Stark and Finke 2000: 201). If all the religious suppliers in an area were identical, totally substitutable for one another, they would then offer consumers no real choices (other than their location) and, according to this statement, there would be no competition.

It is not entirely clear whether Stark et al. see religious diversity and the choices it implies as an *element* of competition (as the passage above seems to imply) or if they view religious diversity as a separate variable that is the *result* of competition. (For example, fierce competition among close substitutes could encourage a religious entrepreneur to found a new religion in a different, less competitive, religious niche, thus increasing religious diversity.) But either way, it is clear that Stark et al. see religious diversity as being closely associated with competition and important for explaining rates of religious involvement.

It is worth noting that Stark et al. emphasize somewhat different causal mechanisms when describing the effects of substitutability and the effects of religious diversity. As noted above, the presence of close substitute groups forces religious leaders to work harder and more creatively to attract and maintain committed adherents. When describing the effects of diversity, they argue (e.g., Finke and Stark 1988; Stark and Finke 2000: 196 ff.) that people have differing underlying religious needs, tastes, and religious desires. No single religion can provide the variety necessary to satisfy the breadth of demand for religion in human populations. Thus the religious needs of a population can be fully met only by a diversity of religious groups. A diversity of religious groups increases the chance that any single potential adherent will find some particular religious group with which they can affiliate. This, in turn, should raise overall affiliation rates. Note that in contrast to their explanation of how close substitute groups affect each other, their explanation of diversity's effect depends less on the energetic response of religious leaders.[9] Instead greater diversity simply allows for a better fit between the diverse religious desires of potential adherents and the religious groups available to them. It is a matter of religious supply conforming to religious demand.

These two implicit meanings of religious competition (substitutability and diversity) may actually be contradictory. In order to be substitutes, two religious organizations would need to be fairly similar. If competition is measured by the number of available substitutes for a religious group in an area, groups that are quite different from one another (say a Southern Baptist congregation and a Catholic church) should not be seen as competitors since they appeal to different submarkets of the religious economy. However, the greater the differences among the groups in an area, the more real choices they offer to potential adherents. Substitutability implies similarity, diversity implies difference. Presumably the most competitive situation would be one in which there were many close substitutes across a broad range of religious submarkets.

CONSCIOUS CONFLICT AND UNCONSCIOUS COMPETITION

In the discussion above, I distinguish between religious conflict and religious competition not only because Stark et al. distinguish them, but also because the causal mechanisms behind their hypothesized effects are quite different. Most of these differences are due to the fact that religious conflict usually involves *conscious* opposition whereas religious competition can operate without religious groups being aware of their competitors. One could make a good argument that religious conflict will not stimulate greater religious commitment unless a group's leaders and adherents are conscious that their religious group, its ideas, or the associated identity group's interests are being threatened. This is why, in religious conflict, the perception of threat is as important as the existence of any actual threat.

In contrast, competition can be unconscious. It can occur when religious groups are unaware of whom their competitors are, even when a group is not trying to "compete" for members, when membership growth is not one of a group's intended goals. For example, in a large metropolis, many congregations may draw from the same large pool of potential attenders. At a particular congregation, some attenders may come and go from week to week without anyone being very sure what other congregations these people might be attending. However, if attendance were to steadily decline, it wouldn't matter whether church leaders could correctly identify the competing congregations, the results would be the same. Religious leaders would have to work harder and more creatively to win back adherents or face the demise of the religious organization, and with it their jobs and roles as leaders. Of course, they could choose to do nothing and allow the organization to dissolve. But even in a scenario where the groups were not seeking to increase their membership there could be a positive association between competition and general commitment levels since the groups that survived and dominated in more competitive environments would tend to be the ones that did a better job of attracting and securing adherents' commitments.

This difference between conscious and unconscious opposition has several important implications for research and theory concerning religious economies. In particular these two types of opposition 1) operate via different causal mechanisms, 2) have effects that differ in their potential geographic scale, 3) are best measured using different variables, and 4) draw on different types of explanations taken from quite different theoretical traditions.

First, when religious opposition is conscious (as in religious conflict) the *causal mechanism* that increases religious commitment may often (though not always) lie as much or more in the agency of the religious adherents as in the actions of religious leaders. If so, the higher commitment levels associated with religious conflict may be more a demand-side than a supply-side phenomenon. Perceiving themselves to be the target of religious conflict, adherents may, without appeals from religious leaders, turn to the religious group as a source of organizational strength and as a means to protect and further their interests, many of which may be linked to the religious or associated identity group. Though I do not know the details of Polish religious history, I would guess that the high rates of mass attendance that occurred under communist rule were not primarily the result of the hard work and creativity of Polish priests. Rather, the threat to Polish and Catholic identity posed by communism probably increased the demand for involvement in the Catholic Church among laypersons. Undoubtedly Catholic leaders experiencing the same threats from communism acted to channel the increased demand for involvement in the Catholic Church. But the overall increase in mass attendance was probably more a *demand-side* phenomenon than the result of a successful marketing campaign and an increased supply of masses scheduled by innovative and vigorous Catholic priests. Even when religious leaders consciously manipulate the perception of threat in order to motivate higher levels of commitment from their adherents, they increase religious involvement by increasing the demand for religion, not by first making religion more available.[10]

In contrast, when religious opposition is *unconscious* (as it may largely be in many cases of religious competition) Stark et al. suggest that agency is primarily located in the responsive or unresponsive actions of religious leaders. In order to test whether this is correct, researchers need to be sensitive to these different causal mechanisms. Ideally, tests of competition's effects should measure the behavior of religious leaders separately from the behavior of adherents. For example, one could examine whether congregations facing greater competition from nearby congregations institute more programs of outreach (per existing member) than do congregations in the same denomination located in areas with fewer nearby substitute congregations. While the initiative for outreach programs could originate with members, such programs would seem more likely to reflect the directions set by church leaders.

Second, conscious and unconscious religious opposition differ in terms of the *geographic scale* at which their effects can operate. This too has been a contentious issue in research on religious economies (e.g., Finke et al. 1996; Olson and Hadaway 1999). When religious opposition is unconscious, as in many instances of religious competition, its effects must largely be local, limited in scope to the distance that potential adherents could reasonably travel to participate in the activities of a religious group. A congregation in San Francisco could achieve an average attendance of thousands without threatening the attendance or resources available to a church in Los Angeles. The two congregations could not be considered substitutes from the point of view of a potential attender. However, when religious opposition is conscious the effects could be much broader geographically, perhaps regional or national. Thus Wiccans throughout the U.S. may have experienced a heightened awareness and commitment to their religious identity when U.S. representative Bob Barr of Georgia attempted to attach an amendment to a defense spending bill that would have banned Wiccan ceremonies from taking place on U.S. military bases (Holley 1999).

Third, *different kinds of measures* are needed for conscious versus unconscious religious opposition. When religious opposition is conscious, the best measures may be those that assess the degree of *perceived* threat experienced by the leaders and adherents of a religious group. Without a perceived threat, the hypothesized increase in religious commitment is unlikely to occur. Such measures might be included on questionnaires given to adherents or leaders, or they might be gleaned from content analysis of a group's publications, interviews, participant observation, etc. But when religious opposition is unconscious, as it often is in religious competition, the best measures are ones that are based on accurate counts of the number, types, and sizes of competing religious groups in a local area limited to the distances people could travel to participate in religious services.

Fourth, explanations of how conscious and unconscious opposition affect religious behavior draw on *different theoretical traditions.* Explanations of how unconscious opposition (as in religious competition) affect behavior have drawn heavily and fruitfully from analogous theories of competition in economic markets. In contrast, explanations of the mechanisms behind the hypothesized effects of conscious opposition draw more on social-psychological theories of how social identities are constructed and maintained and why people rally to defend these identities. Such theories might still be considered rational choice theories, loosely defined. That is, people construct identities and rally to their defense as a way of promoting their self-interests. Nevertheless, economic analogies may not prove as useful for understanding religious conflict as for understanding religious competition. Thus, for example, Smith (1998) explains the high commitment levels of American Evangelicals (even in areas dominated by Evangelicals) primarily by drawing on theories of how subcultural identities are constructed and changed over time.

As I argue below, many of the results that Stark et al. attribute to the largely unconscious effects of religious competition, e.g., the effects of Catholic market share, may actually have more to do with conscious religious opposition in which adherents (as much or more than leaders) rally to the cause of their Catholic religious identity when they find themselves a minority surrounded by a non-Catholic majority.

EFFECTS OF OPPOSITION ON GROUP SIZE AND COMMITMENT

Stark et al. argue that opposition will generally increase the rates and levels of religious involvement and commitment in a geographic area and that within each religious group, greater opposition will lead to higher average commitment levels. But what about the effects of religious opposition on the size of particular groups? Here the implications of Stark et al.'s theories are more ambiguous and have yet to be fully worked out. These ambiguities have important implications for how one interprets research results, especially those dealing with market share.

Two outcomes of religious opposition on group size seem plausible. One could imagine that the *indirect effects* of religious opposition (via commitment levels) would be to increase the size of a group. That is, if religious opposition leads to heightened commitment levels among leaders and adherents, all else being equal, these higher commitment levels should, in turn, attract more adherents and increase the size of a group (Iannaccone, Olson, and Stark 1995).

But what about the *direct effects* of conflict and competition on group size? One could imagine that religious conflict, if it is serious, would cause some people to leave a religious group. For example, some European Jews facing various forms of discrimination (religious conflict) chose to convert to Christianity or at least minimize their Jewish involvements and identity. Competition could have a similar effect. If many religious groups are competing for the same potential religious adherents in a local religious market, not all of these religious groups can grow large. Even if the overall percentage of the population involved in religion increases as Stark et al. predict, some of the competing religious groups are likely to be smaller than they would be if there was little religious competition. Depending on the relative importance of the direct and indirect effects of religious opposition (described above), the overall effect of religious opposition could be to diminish the size of particular religious groups.

If the *direct negative effects* of opposition on the growth of religious groups more frequently outweigh the possibly *indirect positive effects*, one might posit, that all else being equal, the ability of any one particular religious group to grow (increase its number of adherents) is inversely related to the degree of religious opposition (either competition or conflict) it faces. Where religious opposition (either conflict or competition) is weak, particular religious groups can grow more easily and rapidly. Where religious opposition is greater, the growth of any particular group is more difficult and slow and the loss of adherents is more likely.

MARKET SHARE

Up to this point I have considered the effects of religious competition and conflict in a very general way. However, in actual research Stark et al. (and their opponents) have used three other variables both as predictors of religious competition and as measures of religious competition: market share, state regulation, and religious pluralism. In the remainder of this chapter I consider what the above analyses suggest concerning research on each of the three variables.

Market share is the percentage of all religious adherents (or, alternatively, percentage of the total population)[11] in an area that belongs to a particular religious group (usually a denomination). Stark et al. argue that "Individual groups will be more energetic and generate higher levels of commitment to the degree that they have a marginal market position—lack market share" (Stark and Finke 2000: 219). Although this particular statement does not identify a mechanism behind this predicted regularity, as noted above, Stark et al. generally see market share as an inverse measure of religious competition. In response to the greater competition they face, small groups will tend to be more energetic. In contrast, large groups will tend to become complacent.

Nearly all of the research so far, with the exception of Phillips (1998), finds that small market share is associated with higher levels of religious commitment among current members of a particular religious group (e.g., Rabinowitz, Kim, and Lazerwitz 1992; Stark and McCann 1993; Zaleski and Zech 1995; Perl and Olson 2000). What remains to be examined are the possible mechanism(s) behind this empirical regularity (and its exceptions). In light of the analyses above, there are at least three possible explanations that need to be considered, 1) unconscious religious opposition (as in religious competition), 2) conscious religious opposition (as in religious conflict), and 3) the tendency of the least-committed members to be the first to leave a group experiencing opposition and membership losses.

Two characteristics of published research results favor the theory that market share involves conscious religious conflict rather than unconscious competition for adherents. First, levels of member commitment are usually *inversely* associated with denominational market share. This pretty much rules out the notion that competition with close substitute congregations is involved.

As noted above, market share is likely to have a close positive association with the number of nearby congregations in the same denomination, congregations that would be close substitutes competing for the same potential adherents. If competition from close substitute congregations were involved, one would expect denominational market share to reflect greater competition and be *positively*, not inversely, related to member commitment levels.

What about competition for adherents with other *denominations*? Could the inverse relationship reflect competition with other denominations, as Stark et al. seem to imply? It is true that, in general, as market share increases, the number and size of other denominations will tend to decrease, thus lowering potential opposition from other denominations. But is opposition from other *denominations* likely to take the form of competition or is it more likely to involve the conscious processes found in religious conflict? At the very least, opposition from other denominations, especially very different denominations, is unlikely to involve much competition for adherents. This is because, as Stark and Finke note, "Research shows that most people . . . remain within the religious organization in which they were raised" (2000: 119). A substantial research literature cited by Stark and Finke shows that most people seldom switch denominations and that when they do switch, they usually switch to a very similar denomination (2000: 119 ff.). The relative lack of switching between denominations necessarily limits the level of actual *competition* between denominations for adherents. Most of the competition among different denominations would be limited to competition to win the allegiance of the religiously unaffiliated who have no predisposition or attachment to any religious tradition. In the U.S., such persons are a small minority of the population. It also seems likely (though further research is needed) that even in countries with only a few large denominations/groups and many persons whose level of religious activity is low, e.g., Germany, there are relatively few people without some social and psychological ties that would make them unlikely to switch to another denomination (e.g., switching from German Lutheran to German Catholic).

The relative lack of switching among denominations makes it unlikely that the opposition faced by denominations with small market share involves competition for adherents with other *denominations*. What competition there is for adherents is more likely to come from close substitute *congregations*, but, as noted above, the inverse empirical relationship found between market share and levels of religious commitment runs contrary to the positive relationship one would expect if competition from close substitute congregations is involved. It seems unlikely that competition for adherents explains the research results on market share.

In contrast, religious conflict, or related conscious processes, could well lie behind market share results. Religious conflict could be aimed at whole denominations. Smaller denominations might more often be the target of religious conflict and/or adherents of smaller denominations might be more likely to believe that the interests of their religious identity are being threatened. If so, processes related to conscious religious conflict might explain the inverse relationship of denominational market share and commitment levels.

For example, even though Catholics living in South Carolina and Georgia may no longer be targets of overt religious discrimination, there are so few Catholics in these states that Catholics might believe that others see them as different or strange. Catholics who felt either stigmatized or special because of their peculiar religious identity might then attend mass more regularly as a way of seeking support from similar others. They might also give greater support to Catholic organizations as a way to defend their Catholic identity group interests (Perl and Olson 2000). Though the levels of threat and heightened religious identity might be significantly lower than among Polish Catholics under communism, the processes might be qualitatively similar.

A second, but less compelling, reason for believing that market share effects involve conscious opposition is the geographic scale at which market share effects appear to operate. If market share works primarily via unconscious competition, the effects of market share would mostly be local, limited to the distance that adherents can travel to participate in religious activities. In that case, the best measures, and the strongest results, would be found in research that measures market share using small geographic areas like towns and counties. States and whole nations would be too large to accurately measure the competition reflected by market share since religious groups at opposite ends of a state or country could not be competing for the same market of potential adherents. But when market share operates through conscious opposition, the scale at which it operates, and the scale at which it should best be measured, will probably depend on the nature of the opposition but may be as large as regions of countries or whole nations.

While some studies (e.g., parts of Stark and McCann 1993; Zaleski and Zech 1995; Perl and Olson 2000) measure market share at a relatively small scale, counties and Catholic dioceses, other studies (e.g., Stark 1992; parts of Stark and McCann 1993) have measured market share at a national or state level and found quite strong market share effects. The fact that national level and state level tests of the market share hypothesis appear to match the predictions of Stark et al. suggests that many if not most of the mechanisms underlying this regularity have to do with conscious conflict rather than unconscious market competition among religious groups.[12]

As noted above, to the extent that market share effects result from conscious opposition, they may be due to demand-side factors originating in the motivations of lay adherents as much as supply-side factors originating in the needs and desires of the religious leaders to secure the survival and expansion of their religious organizations. Further research is needed to resolve these issues.

There is yet another mechanism (implied by Stark et al.'s models) that could generate the inverse relationships between group size and religious commitment reported in most published research on the topic. In the previous section I argued that religious opposition (either conflict or competition) could lower the sizes of particular religious groups when the direct negative effects of opposition outweigh the indirect positive effects (via higher commitment levels). If true, it would greatly complicate the interpretation of results showing that groups with small market share have higher commitment levels.

The average commitment levels of a group's adherents might rise simply because the least-committed members are the first to leave and the least likely to join a group facing opposition. If the least committed leave first, the average commitment levels of the remaining members automatically goes up without changing the actual commitment levels of any members. In a similar way, a basketball team could raise the average height of its players simply by kicking the shortest players off the team. But such an action won't increase the height of any individual player or help the team win the next game. Thus, for example, Olson and Caddell (1994) found that among United Church of Christ congregations the congregations with the highest per capita financial giving were the congregations that were losing members most rapidly. My own, unpublished analysis of data from the *Yearbook of American and Canadian Churches* suggests that the denominations showing the greatest increases in per-member giving (adjusted for inflation) in the latter half of twentieth century were the same denominations that lost members most rapidly over this same time period.

Even though this causal mechanism is quite different from what Stark et al. hypothesize, a loss of less-committed members among groups facing greater opposition would lead to the same inverse empirical relationship between group size and group commitment predicted by Stark et al. For example, Stark and McCann (1993) find that young Catholic men are more likely to seek the priesthood if they live in areas of the U.S. where Catholics are a smaller proportion of the population. Is this because being a minority faith is a source of perceived religious conflict that causes leaders and adherents to increase their religious commitment, thus producing more candidates for the priesthood? Or does it result because, in areas with few Catholics, the less-committed Catholics (including the young men) are more likely to leave, possibly through intermarriage with non-Catholics? This would leave only the more committed young men who would be more likely to seek the priesthood. Cross-sectional research, research based on data collected at one point in time, would have difficulty discerning which of these processes has the most effect on average commitment levels. In order to avoid this problem, future research will need to measure religious commitment in ways that can distinguish increases in existing adherents' commitment levels from processes that simply weed out the less committed. So far, this issue has not been addressed in any significant way in existing research.

To sum up, research on religious market share is mostly consistent with Stark et al.'s claim that commitment levels should be highest where market share is lower. However, it is not yet clear whether the higher commitment levels of small denominations reflect greater competition (and supply-side processes), greater conflict (and demand-side processes), or simply a process whereby only the most committed persons join and/or remain adherents of small groups. I argue that research results currently seem more consistent with the last two explanations.

REGULATION

The regulation of religion as described by Stark et al. (e.g., Iannaccone 1991; Finke and Iannaccone 1993; Stark and Iannaccone 1994; Iannaccone and Finke 1997; Finke and Stark 1998; Stark and Finke 2000) refers to actions by government bodies that either restrict or aid (e.g., through tax support or subsidies) religious groups. In general, Stark et al. argue that state regulation of both types lowers the number and variety of religious groups in a society and thereby lessens competition (especially competition defined as diversity) among religious groups. With less competition there will be lower rates of religious involvement and commitment (for reasons discussed above). For example, Finke and Iannaccone (1993) and Iannaccone and Finke (1997) interpret the first and second "great awakenings" of U.S. religious history (in the early to mid-1700s and the early 1800s) as the result of progressive government deregulation of the U.S. religious economy.

Although, in general, Stark et al. argue that the less government regulation the better, it is worth noting that they implicitly assume at least a small amount of even-handed state regulation of religious matters. They assume that governments will regulate and punish the most serious forms of religious conflict among religious groups. For example, the state should prosecute religious groups that burn down the places of worship belonging to other religious groups. While this might seem a trivial point, one can imagine that in countries where there is no such regulation, or more likely, where such regulation is not applied even-handedly to all religions, a dominant religious group could stifle the growth of potential competitors by threats and intimidation. In such a setting pluralism and competition are unlikely to thrive. Conflict in the form of state regulation is merely replaced by conflict originating in other religious groups. Thus, following the logic of Stark et al. the optimum religious diversity and competition will be reached when the regulation of religion is low, applies to all groups equally, and prevents religious groups from undertaking actions against one another that would be criminal if done by nonreligious groups (e.g., burning down buildings).

By this standard, there would be very few nations that Stark et al. describe as approaching the optimum (low) levels of religious regulation. The U.S. appears to come close (Finke and Stark 1992) but even most western European societies are described by Stark et al. as having substantial levels of religious regulation (e.g., Stark and Iannaccone 1994; Stark and Finke 2000: 228–236) despite the fact that European scholars of religion might disagree (e.g., Bruce 1999).

Most of the things Stark et al. identify as regulation of religion fall under the heading of religious conflict (as opposed to competition) as defined above, behavior where the intent (or unintended effect) is to obstruct the attainment of a religious group's goals (or its associated identity group's goals). In this case the opposition comes from the state. Although state subsidies do not neatly fit this definition of conflict, subsidies might well be perceived as conflict by religious groups that do not receive them.

If government regulation is a form of religious conflict, one would expect to see the same conscious demand-side processes at work in groups that are the target of government discrimination as one would see among other groups facing conscious religious conflict, e.g., groups involved in a religiously based ethnic conflict. Adherents, those that are not driven away, are likely to rally, via demand-side processes, to the cause of their faith and religious identity. In keeping with the general assertions made above concerning the effects of religious conflict on group size, such groups would often (but not always)[13] be smaller in size, but exhibit higher levels of religious commitment.[14] In contrast, the groups receiving subsidies and experiencing no religious opposition are likely to be larger in size but have adherents with lower commitment. The very low average commitment levels among members of the huge state Lutheran church of Sweden and the high commitment levels exhibited by members of the tiny Swedish free churches provide an excellent case in point (Iannaccone 1991).

Viewing regulation as a form of religious conflict highlights an otherwise implicit relationship built into the structure of Stark et al.'s theoretical structure. Religious conflict and religious competition may often be inversely related. A reduction in religious conflict (in this case from state regulation) can lead over time to an increase in religious competition. If conflict in the form of regulation is lowered for all types of religious groups, then all groups should have a better chance of increasing their numbers. All else being equal, this growth may at first be accompanied by a drop in average commitment levels among existing religious adherents (because of the reduced opposition). However, if existing groups continue to grow and new groups form (because there is little opposition), the religious groups will eventually begin to compete for the same unaffiliated or weakly affiliated adherents, and religious competition (measured as diversity) will increase. Stark et al. highlight how this works for regulation, but it may apply more generally to all types of religious conflict including ethnically based conflict. It is difficult for competition (measured by the number and diversity of religious groups) to develop where religious conflict is strong and suppresses the growth of potential competitor religions.

One implication of an inverse relationship between religious conflict and competition is that by Stark et al.'s own assessments, competition may not play much of a role in the religious economies of most countries in the world. If, as Stark et al. suggest, there are few countries without substantial degrees of religious regulation, it may be that the full processes of religious competition operate in only a very few countries like the U.S. In most countries of the world, religious economies are affected more by religious conflict than by competition. To extend this logic even more speculatively, if government regulation is a form of religious conflict and the invigorating effects of conflict operate primarily through conscious demand-side, rather than supply-side, processes, then it may be that demand-side, rather than supply-side, processes dominate most of the world's religious economies. This is an area that future research should consider.

The interesting and theoretically important inverse relationship between religious conflict and religious competition has sometimes been obscured in the work of Stark et al. by the tendency to view regulation as an inverse *measure* of competition rather than as a potential inverse *cause* of competition. For example, Stark and Finke (2000: 219) assert that "To the extent that pluralism or regulation are adequate inferential measures of competition, the overall level of religiousness will be higher where pluralism is greater or where regulation is lower." Setting aside for the moment the issue of pluralism, such a statement assumes either that the (low) level of regulation is but one manifestation of competition (the same thing as competition) or it assumes the truth of a negative relationship between regulation and competition as a given, not requiring empirical examination. Either assumption does away with the need to examine whether, in fact, lowered state regulation generally increases the number and variety of religious groups. My point here is that it may be more consistent with the rest of Stark et al.'s theoretical scheme to view regulation not as a measure of competition, but as but one form of religious conflict and as a key exemplar of the negative effects of religious conflict upon religious competition.

What do research results suggest concerning the effects of state regulation on religion? Studies of state regulation have been of two types, international comparisons of many nations at one point in time (cross-sectional studies), and historical studies of changes in a single nation over time. International comparisons (e.g., Chaves and Cann 1992; Chaves, Schraeder, and Sprindys 1994) generally find that higher rates of religious participation are found in countries with lower levels of religious regulation. Other research (e.g., Iannaccone 1991) attempts to explain international cross-sectional differences in religious participation rates, but the independent variable in these analyses is pluralism, not government regulation.

While international comparisons of religious regulation and rates of religious participation generally seem consistent with Stark et al.'s predictions, future research is more likely to challenge the regulation hypothesis using historical, longitudinal studies of single countries (e.g., Bruce 1999). These historical studies need to focus on the question of causal order. Even if cross-sectional international comparisons find an inverse relationship between regulation and competition measured as pluralism, one may well ask whether the changes in regulation precede or follow the changes in religious pluralism.

Put another way, does pluralism emerge only when regulation declines (as Stark et al. argue), or are governments forced into deregulating religion only when faced with a diversity of strong religious groups? It may be that when there is a single majority religion, governments find it expedient to favor this religion and regulate all others. Where there is an oligopoly of a few equally strong religions, it might be in the government's interest to protect these few religions and regulate against all others, as was true in the Netherlands. It may be that where pluralism is already lush, deregulation breaks out. Finke and Iannaccone (1993) argue that progressive deregulation preceded the first and second Great Awakenings of U.S. religious history, but the reverse point could also be made. For example, one could make a good case that the first amendment to the U.S. constitution which deregulated religion at the federal (but not the state) level was added mainly to gain support for the constitution from an already religiously diverse group of colonies. It may also be that regulation and pluralism are entwined in a causal loop, with each variable negatively reinforcing the another. Historical research is needed to disentangle this relationship.

To sum up, I argue that state regulation is best seen as a form of religious conflict (rather than competition) and that as a form of religious conflict, the effects of regulation itself may operate primarily through demand-side processes. However, I agree with Stark et al. that lowered state regulation can lead to greater religious competition (at least greater diversity) and thus could enhance the functioning of the supply-side processes that Stark et al. emphasize. I extend this point to argue that this is but one example of a more general inverse relationship between religious conflict and religious competition. If, as Stark et al. claim, most religious economies have substantial degrees of state regulation, then most religious economies may be dominated by the conscious supply-side processes associated with religious conflict more than the demand-side processes that Stark et al. associate with competition.

PLURALISM

Religious pluralism has played a key role in the religious economies model from the very beginning (e.g., Finke and Stark 1989; Stark et al. 1995; Finke et al. 1996). It is the measure that most closely approximates the definition of religious competition as *diversity*. Finke and Stark's (1988) first influential presentation of the religious economies model in the American Sociological Review emphasized the key test provided by pluralism. Stark, Finke, and Iannaccone argued that "the crucial hypothesis" that follows from a series of propositions concerning religious economies is that "within any appropriate set of aggregate (or ecological) units, other things being equal, there will be a positive correlation between religious pluralism (or diversity) and overall levels of religious participation" (Stark et al. 1995: 433).

It is not surprising that Stark et al. chose to highlight pluralism. It is the point at which the religious economies model most directly confronts secularization theories. Many secularization theories implicitly or explicitly argue that religious pluralism will undermine religious belief. As modernization brings diverse peoples and religions into closer contact, people realize that different religions have different, and sometimes contradictory, versions of religious truth. Increasingly they ask, "How can they all be right?" Doubt increases, conviction wanes, and religious participation declines. But the religious economies model makes exactly the opposite prediction. As religious pluralism increases so does religious competition. Competition forces religious groups to work harder, potential adherents have more choices, and religious participation rates increase.

Nearly all of the research examining pluralism measures pluralism using the pluralism index, an index based on the Herfindahl index long used in economics to measure market concentration. The pluralism index equals one minus the Herfindahl index or $1–Ep_i^2$ where p_i is the proportion of all religious adherents in an area belonging to the *i*th religious group. This index ranges from 0 (zero) when there is a just one religious group in an area (a religious monopoly) to just less than 1 (one) when there are many religious groups of equal size. The pluralism index increases both with the *number* of groups and with the *evenness* of the sizes of the religious groups in an area. It reaches its highest value at just slightly less than one in the theoretical situation where each person in an area constitutes his or her own religious "group."[15]

The pluralism index is actually a good measure of several theoretically important phenomena. For example, it is a good measure of competition when competition is defined as *denominational diversity*. Because the pluralism index takes into account the evenness of the group sizes, the pluralism index is probably a better measure of the real choices available to most potential adherents than simply counting the number of groups. Thus the pluralism index remains low, as it should, when one or two religious groups dominate a religious market even though there might be hundreds of tiny religious groups in an area that most potential adherents have never heard of and would be unlikely to join. This is consistent with Stark and Finke's recent (2000: 199) definition of "pluralistic" as "the number of firms active in the economy; the more firms there are with *significant* market shares, the greater the degree of pluralism" (emphasis added).

The pluralism index is also a good measure of phenomena highlighted by some secularization theories. As Finke et al. (1996) pointed out, the pluralism index can also be thought of as the probability that any two religious adherents chosen at random will belong to *different* religious groups. In the case of a religious monopoly, this probability would equal zero as would the pluralism index. In the case of two groups of equal size, this probability would equal .5 as would the pluralism index. If, as some secularization theories suppose, contact with persons from other religious groups tends to lessen religious convictions and commitment, then, all else being equal, such contact is likely to increase as the pluralism index increases and the probability of encountering such persons increases.

What do research results show concerning the relationship of pluralism and religious involvement? In a review article Chaves and Gorski (2001) examine 82 valid[16] published tests of the relationship between pluralism and rates of religious involvement. All of these studies are based on large-scale studies of the religious pluralism and the rates of religious involvement across many geographic areas collected at one point in time. Of these 82 tests of the pluralism hypothesis, Chaves and Gorski conclude that only 11 tests originating from four separate settings give support to Stark et al. The rest either contradict Stark et al.'s predictions or show no relationship between pluralism and rates of religious involvement.

Stark et al. have raised three objections to studies of pluralism finding results contrary to their predictions. First, they object (e.g. Finke and Stark 1988, 1989) that in order to detect the true effects of pluralism, statistical controls are needed to account for the influence of the percent Catholic on rates of religious participation. Second, they object (e.g., Finke and Stark 1989; Finke et al. 1996) that the geographic areas used in many (but not all) studies of pluralism (e.g., counties) are too large to accurately measure the pluralism of real religious markets and thus such studies should be discounted. Third, they argue that "above a certain level, pluralism becomes redundant. . . . We have discovered that there is a 'ceiling effect'—that beyond a certain point, the market is saturated and additional competition and diversity do not increase the overall level of religious participation" (Stark and Finke 2000: 219). Because I deal with the first two of these issues in detail in separate publications (Olson and Hadaway 1999; Olson 1999), and because much of the evidence and counterevidence used to debate all three of these issues has been rendered moot by Voas, Olson, and Crockett (2001), I do not discuss these objections here.

Recently Voas, Olson, and Crockett (2001) suggest that other, quite serious, difficulties beset past research on pluralism. Nearly all of this research uses cross-sectional data (data collected for many areas at a single point in time) to examine whether rates of religious involvement (e.g., church membership or church attendance rates) are higher or lower in areas of greater religious pluralism. Voas et al. argue that because of previously overlooked mathematical relationships between the independent variable (the pluralism index) and the dependent variable (participation rates), the correlation between these two variables will usually not be zero even when there is no causal influence of pluralism on religious participation. They point out that when pluralism has no causal influence on participation rates, the value of the correlation between these variables could still be strongly positive or negative depending on the nature of the size distributions of the denominations across geographic areas in a particular data set. If the variation in the size of the larger denominations is greater than the variation in the size of the smaller denominations (as it often is in real data), the correlation between pluralism and participation rates will tend to be negative, making it appear that greater pluralism leads to less religious involvement. This is because increases in the size of the larger denominations simultaneously reflect both higher participation rates and *lower* pluralism. If the variation in the size of the smaller denominations is greater than the variation in the sizes of the larger or largest denomination (as it sometimes is in real data sets), the correlation will tend to be positive, making it appear, as Stark et al. argue, that pluralism boosts religious involvement. This is because increases in the smaller denominations simultaneously reflect higher participation rates and *greater* pluralism. Voas et al. argue that the strong positive and negative correlations reported in previous studies mostly reflect the size distributions of the denominations that happen to be found in these data sets and do not reflect real causal influences of pluralism on participation rates. If Voas et al. are correct, most of the quite substantial body of previous research on pluralism will have to be abandoned.

Because of the theoretical importance of pluralism, Voas et al. argue that research on pluralism should go forward using methods that avoid the pitfalls described in their paper. For example, they suggest that it may be possible to use data collected at multiple points in time to examine whether and how pluralism at one time affects *later changes* in participation rates. Until such studies are undertaken, it would appear that the jury is out concerning the effects of religious pluralism.

CONCLUSIONS

Theoretical ambiguities remain the key obstacle to reaching a clear verdict concerning Stark et al.'s theories of religious economies. The most crucial of these ambiguities is the failure to define religious competition, the theory's key independent variable. Secondarily, Stark et al.'s opponents (e.g., Lechner 1996a) argue that the notion of religious conflict is brought in on an ad hoc and unsystematic basis (e.g., Ireland, Quebec, Poland, Iran) to bail out the theory when predictions based on religious competition appear unsupportable.

I argue instead that both religious conflict and religious competition can be seen as different types of a larger category, religious opposition. I agree with Stark et al. that both types of religious opposition (conflict and competition) have the potential to raise levels of religious commitment, in particular religious groups (though perhaps at the price of declining group size). However, critics of Stark et al. are right to point out that the causal mechanisms operating in religious conflict are quite different from the mechanisms Stark et al. describe for religious competition. The mechanisms behind the effects of religious conflict may lie more in the demand-side needs of religious adherents to protect and advance the interests of their religious and/or social identity whereas Stark et al. claim that the mechanisms behind the effects of competition lie more on the supply-side, with the need of religious leaders to better supply followers with ways to satisfy their religious needs and thus secure the future of the religious group and the leader's positions.

I further suggest that religious conflict and religious competition may be inversely related. Religious competition can flourish only where religious conflict is low. I argue that Stark et al.'s assertions concerning the deleterious effects of state regulation on religious competition is but one example of this more general principle. Moreover, if state regulation is, in fact, a form of religious conflict, and there are, according to Stark et al., few areas of the world without significant state regulation of religion (a point some European sociologists would dispute), it may be that there are few religious economies in which religious competition plays a very significant role. Religious conflict, not competition, may be the most dominant factor in most of the world's religious economies.

Of course, the major potential flaw in this argument is that while conflict might suppress religious competition, lack of religious conflict might not always lead to outbreaks of new religious competition. Secularization theorists might argue, for example, that Western Europe has neither high levels of religious conflict nor much religious competition simply because there is no religious demand to support a growth of new religious competition. More study of the Western European situation and comparison with the Eastern European situation (where levels of state regulation are rapidly changing) will further advance understanding of these issues.

Do religious conflict and competition actually increase religious involvement and commitment? Turning first to conflict, the answer clearly seems to be yes, especially in the case of religio-ethnic-national conflicts such as Quebec, Ireland, and Poland. This point was made earlier by Martin (1978) and even by some (e.g., Bruce 1999) who see religious conflict within a larger framework of secularization theory. Research by Smith (1998) on American Evangelicals suggests that processes involving consciously perceived conflict may act to invigorate religious commitment even in more mundane social settings where religious conflict only reaches the level of cultural tension and there are no actual martyrs or terrorist attacks. Somewhat more speculatively, I suggest that conscious, demand-side processes like those involved in religious conflict may also explain results showing higher levels of time and money commitments among adherents of denominations with small market share. That is, religious adherents of minority religious groups (those who do not leave the group) rally to the defense of their minority religious identity and thus give more time and money to their churches. However, further research is needed to determine the mechanisms that best explain the results of research on religious market share.

Turning from religious conflict, one may ask whether religious competition increases religious involvement and commitment. Here the jury is still out. The question cannot be decided without a clear understanding of what religious competition is and how it should be measured. I have suggested two, somewhat contradictory, meanings of competition that seem consistent with various of Stark et al.'s claims concerning competition: substitutability and diversity. Of these, competition defined as diversity has received the most attention in published research. The pluralism index used in this research is a good measure of denominational diversity. However, recent work by Voas et al. (2001) suggests that most of the past work on religious pluralism is flawed and should be abandoned. Research on pluralism is therefore back at square one, needing to begin again with new methods not subject to the problems identified by Voas et al. To my knowledge, there is no published research using measures of competition defined as the number of nearby substitutable religious groups (unless one were to count market share research as evidence against competition defined as substitutability). Here again, the jury is still out concerning the effects of religious competition.

In much the same way that Stark et al. claim that competition increases religious commitment, the intellectual competition posed by Stark et al.'s assertions concerning religious economies has greatly invigorated the sociological study of religion. Nevertheless, the issues raised by their work are far from settled. Future theoretical and empirical analysis are needed to work through these many questions. If the history of social science research is any guide, the results will turn out to be both more interesting and more surprising than either Stark et al. or their most strident opponents would have guessed.

NOTES

Direct all correspondence to Dan Olson, Department of Sociology, Indiana University, South Bend, IN 46634, dolson@iusb.edu. Thanks to Mark Chaves, Fred Kniss, Chris Smith, and David Voas for comments on earlier drafts.

1. Usually, however, Stark et al. view these changes as the result of changes in religious capital (Iannaccone 1990) rather than a change in the underlying desire for religion.

2. In particular, good arguments can be made that people may seek greater or lesser religious participation based on differences in the nonreligious rewards and sanctions that are associated with participation (e.g., acceptance, status, participation in social community, etc.).

3. It is not clear if Stark et al. view government regulation as a form of competition (though at times they refer to it as an inferential measure of competition) or whether they see its absence as a cause of religious competition.

4. My own recent work has employed the pluralism index in this same fashion.

5. In fairness to Stark et al. most of their applications of the pluralism index has been only to Christian religious groups, which in principle, seem more substitutable. But even then, the question is the same. How much of a common market of potential adherents is there for an Assemblies of God congregation and an Episcopalian congregation with very high church, liturgical, worship services?

6. Recently Stark and Finke (2000) have argued that there are "niches" in all religious markets that vary in terms of their tension with society. Though Stark et al. use

the concept of niches for a somewhat different theoretical purpose, niches might also function as submarkets for religious competition.

7. Perl and Olson (2000) show that some of the effects of market share are due to congregation size. In areas with small market share, congregations tend to have fewer members. Small congregation size is known to be associated with higher commitment levels. In very Catholic areas, parishes are very large and commitment levels are lower. In less Catholic areas, parishes have fewer members and commitment is higher. Perl and Olson (2000) found that congregation size accounted for the relationship between market share and attendance rates (among five denominations) but that congregational size did not account for the apparent effects of market share on per capita giving (controlling for income).

8. It is worth noting in passing that ambiguities concerning whether competition is primarily between denominations or between congregations (and other suborganizations of denominations) also partly underlie Stark et al.'s conflicting observations concerning large Catholic market share. On the one hand, Stark and McCann (1993) and Stark (1992, 1998) argue that large Catholic market share reduces competition and commitment among Catholics. But elsewhere, Stark et al. argue (e.g., Finke and Stark 1989; Iannaccone 1992) that Catholics have an especially high degree of internal diversity and that this leads to competition "from within" (e.g., different religious orders, parishes with quite different ethnic identities, etc.) which can invigorate Catholic commitment levels even in countries or large 1906 U.S. cities where Catholics had a very high market share. Thus, while Stark et al. use large Catholic market share as an indicator of lower competition when studying market share, they elsewhere use large Catholic market share as a proxy for *greater* competitiveness in an overall religious market.

9. Of course, if a religious group is very different from other religions that are accepted by a given society, the leaders of such groups would have to struggle very hard to overcome the prejudice and negative preconceptions that potential adherents might have.

10. Admittedly, the distinction between supply and demand becomes a bit fuzzy in this situation. If leaders were concerned by flagging membership and commitment levels (and the effect that such changes might have on their jobs) they might "whip up" a "conflict" with some potential enemy group, convince adherents that their interests are being threatened, and argue that adherents needed to "rally round the flag" to support the religious group and its interests. One could argue that this is a demand-side process (since it is demand that first increases), but the originating causal mechanism lies more with the motivations of the leaders than with adherents.

11. When used to measure competition, religious market share is probably better measured as the percent of adherents who belong to a denomination. This is because competition (for adherents) comes only from other religious groups (unless nonreligion is viewed as a "religious group"). When used to measure potential religious conflict, religious market share is probably best measured as the percent of the population belonging to a group since the conflict a group faces (e.g., discrimination) could come from nonreligious as well as religious segments of the population.

12. Of course, one could argue that national-level market share measures might still reflect local-level unconscious competition simply aggregated to the national

level. This is plausible, especially if the nations in question were relatively homogeneous in terms of the geographic distributions of religious groups. Then the results for the whole nation might simply reflect the average or typical situation in local religious markets. But religious groups are seldom so homogeneously distributed. More often religious groups are concentrated, for historical and cultural reasons, in particular regions of a nation (e.g., Kosmin and Lachman 1993). In that case, the percent of the national population belonging to a particular religious group would tend to be much smaller than the typical percentage belonging to that group in the local areas where most of the group's adherents live.

13. In the case of ethnic conflict where one cannot voluntarily give up one's ethnic identity, conflict will not reduce the size of the ethnic-religious groups.

14. This assumes that the direct, negative effects of opposition on group size outweigh the indirect, potentially positive effects in which oppositions heightens commitment levels which, in turn, attracts new members.

15. For a fuller discussion of how to calculate the pluralism, index, see my paper delivered at the Chicago Area Group for the Study of Religious Communities (CAGSRC), May 6, 2001, available at http:/www.iusb.edu/~dolson/Papers/OlsonCAGSRC.htm.

16. Chaves and Gorski only count as valid tests those tests that are not compromised by including inappropriate statistical controls for the percent of the population that is Catholic, a problem discussed both in Chaves and Gorski (2001) and Olson (1999).

REFERENCES

Bruce, Steve. 1999. *Choice & Religion: A Critique of Rational Choice Theory*. New York: Oxford University Press.

Chaves, Mark and David E. Cann. 1992. "Regulation, Pluralism, and Religious Market Structure: Explaining Religion's Vitality," *Rationality and Society* 4: 272–290.

Chaves, M., P. J. Schraeder, and M. Sprindys. 1994. "State Regulation of Religion and Muslim Religious Vitality in the Industrialized West," *The Journal of Politics* 56: 1087–1098.

Chaves, Mark and Philip S. Gorski. Forthcoming 2001. "Religious Pluralism and Religious Participation," *Annual Review of Sociology* 27.

Finke, Roger, Avery M. Guest, and Rodney Stark. 1996. "Mobilizing Local Religious Markets: Religious Pluralism in the Empire State, 1855 to 1865," *American Sociological Review* 61: 203–218.

Finke, Roger and Laurence R. Iannaccone. 1993. "Supply-Side Explanations for Religious Change," *Annals of the American Academy of Political and Social Science* 527: 27–40.

Finke, Roger and Rodney Stark. 1988. "Religious Economies and Sacred Canopies: Religious Mobilization in American Cities, 1906," *American Sociological Review* 53: 41–49.

———. 1989. "Evaluating the Evidence: Religious Economies and Sacred Canopies," *American Sociological Review* 54: 1054–1056.

———. 1992. *The Churching of America, 1776–1990: Winners and Losers in Our Religious Economy*. New Brunswick, N.J.: Rutgers University Press.

———. 1998. "Religious Choice and Competition (Reply to Olson)," *American Sociological Review* 63: 761–766.

Holley, Joe. 1999. *U.S. News & World Report* 126 (23 June 14): 27.

Iannaccone, Laurence R. 1990. "Religious Participation: A Human Capital Approach," *Journal for the Scientific Study of Religion* 29: 297–314.

———. 1991. "The Consequences of Religious Market Structure: Adam Smith and the Economics of Religion," *Rationality and Society* 3 (2): 156–177.

———. 1992. "Response to Box-Steffensmeier," *Rationality and Society* 4: 247–251.

———. 1994. "Why Strict Churches Are Strong," *American Journal of Sociology* 99: 1180–1211.

———. 1997. "Skewness Explained: A Rational Choice Model of Religious Giving," *Journal for the Scientific Study of Religion* 36: 141–157.

Iannaccone, Laurence R. and Roger Finke. 1997. "Deregulating Religion: The Economics of Church and State," *Economic Inquiry* 35: 350–364

Iannaccone, Laurence R., Daniel V. A. Olson, and Rodney Stark. 1995. "Religious Resources and Church Growth," *Social Forces* 74 (2): 705–731.

Kosmin, Barry Alexander and Seymour P. Lachman. 1993. *One Nation under God: Religion in Contemporary American Society*. New York: Harmony Books.

Lechner, Frank. 1996a. "Rejoinder to Stark and Iannaccone: 'Heads, I Win...': On Immunizing a Theory," *Journal for the Scientific Study of Religion* 35: 272–274.

———. 1996b. "Secularization in the Netherlands?" *Journal for the Scientific Study of Religion* 35: 252–264.

Martin, David. 1978. *A General Theory of Secularization*. New York: Harper & Row.

Olson, Daniel V. A. 1999. "Religious Pluralism and U.S. Church Membership: A Reassessment," *Sociology of Religion* 60 (2): 149–173.

Olson, Daniel V. A. and David Caddell. 1994. "Generous Congregations, Generous Givers: Congregational Contexts that Stimulate Individual Giving," *Review of Religious Research* 36: 168–180.

Olson, Daniel V. A. and C. Kirk Hadaway. 1999. "Religious Pluralism and Affiliation Among Canadian Counties and Cities," *Journal for the Scientific Study of Religion* 38 (4): 490–508.

Perl, Paul and Daniel V. A. Olson. 2000. "Religious Market Share and Intensity of Church Involvement in Five Denominations," *Journal for the Scientific Study of Religion* 39 (1): 12–31.

Phillips, Rick. 1998. "Religious Market Share and Mormon Church Activity," *Sociology of Religion* 59: 304–316.

Rabinowitz, Jonathan, Israel Kim, and Bernard Lazerwitz. 1992. "Metropolitan Size and Participation in Religio-Ethnic Communities," *Journal for the Scientific Study of Religion* 31: 339–345.

Smith, Christian, with Michael Emerson, Sally Gallagher, Paul Kennedy, and David Sikkink. 1998. *American Evangelicalism: Embattled and Thriving*. Chicago: University of Chicago Press.

Stark, Rodney. 1991. "Modernization, Secularization, and Mormon Success." In *In Gods We Trust: New Patterns of Religious Pluralism in America* Second Ed. Thomas Robbins and Dick Anthony, eds. New Brunswick, N.J.: Transaction Publishers.

———. 1992. "Do Catholic Societies Really Exist?" *Rationality and Society* 4: 261–271.

———. 1996. *The Rise of Christianity: A Sociologist Reconsiders History*. Princeton, N.J.: Princeton University Press.

———. 1997a. "Bringing Theory Back in." In *Rational Choice Theory and Religion*. Lawrence A. Young, ed. New York: Routledge, 3–23.

———. 1997b. "German and German-American Religion: Approximating a Crucial Experiment," *Journal for the Scientific Study of Religion* 36: 182–193.

———. 1998. "Catholic Contexts: Competition, Commitment, and Innovation," *Review of Religious Research* 39: 197–208.

———. 1999. "Secularization. R.I.P.," *Sociology of Religion* 60: 249–273.

Stark, Rodney and William Simms Bainbridge. 1985. *The Future of Religion: Secularization, Revival, and Cult Formation*. Berkeley and Los Angeles: University of California Press.

———. 1987. *A Theory of Religion*. New York: Peter Lang.

Stark, Rodney and Roger Finke. 2000. *Acts of Faith: Explaining the Human Side of Religion*. Berkeley and Los Angeles: University of California Press.

Stark, Rodney, Roger Finke, and Laurence R. Iannaccone. 1995. "Pluralism and Piety: England and Wales, 1851," *Journal for the Scientific Study of Religion* 34 (4): 431–444.

Stark, Rodney and Laurence R. Iannaccone. 1994. "A Supply-Side Reinterpretation of the 'Secularization' of Europe," *Journal for the Scientific Study of Religion* 33 (3): 230–252.

———. 1996. "Recent Religious Declines in Quebec, Poland, and the Netherlands: A Theory Vindicated," *Journal for the Scientific Study of Religion* 35: 265–271.

Stark, Rodney and J. C. McCann. 1993. "Market Forces and Catholic Commitment: Exploring the New Paradigm," *Journal for the Scientific Study of Religion* 32: 111–124.

Voas, David, Daniel V. A. Olson, and Alasdair Crockett. 2001. "Studies of Religious Pluralism and Participation: Was Everybody Wrong?" Paper presented at the annual meetings of the Society for the Scientific Study of Religion, Columbus, Ohio, October 18–21.

Zaleski, Peter A. and Charles E. Zech. 1995. "The Effect of Religious Market Competition on Church Giving," *Review of Social Economy* 53: 350–367.

7

The Poverty of Economism or the Social Limits on Maximizing

Steve Bruce

INTRODUCTION

There is no need to summarize the rational choice approach to religion; other essays in this volume have done that.[1] My purposes are to draw attention to the new paradigm's lack of explanatory success and to identify the primary cause of that failure. There are two elements to the rational choice model: a macro-economic story about the virtues of competition and a micro-economic story about human capital. Each will be considered before I turn to the general inadequacies of the whole approach.

RELIGIOUS ECONOMIES

Stark and his associates believe that there is strong evidence for a general connection between the freedom of a religious economy and religious vitality. They say: "Of 13 published empirical tests of the proposition that that religious pluralism results in higher rates of religious participation, only a study based in the 1851 religious census of England and Wales reported contrary results" (Stark et al. 1995: 431) and "evidence for the hypothesis that religious competition increases religious mobilization is now quite substantial" (Stark et al. 1995: 442). I will now question that confidence.

The United States

Finke and Stark (1988) used the 1906 U.S. Census of Religious Bodies to examine the relationship between church membership and religious diversity[2] in the 150 largest towns and cities of the United States. The results were presented as strong evidence that competition in religion, as in car production, increased rather than undermined consumption. However, as commentators were quick to point out, their own statistics cast doubts on their claims. Taken on its own, the link between diversity and vitality was very strongly negative. The more diverse places had the lower rates of church membership.[3] Finke and Stark only managed to produce statistics that suited their argument by controlling for the percentage Catholic in their regression equations. When others tried to replicate Finke and Stark's work they failed. Land and colleagues analyzed county-level data for over 700 counties and for a subset of counties that contained the 150 cities studied by Finke and Stark (Land et al. 1991). In both cases they came to quite the opposite conclusion. For the large sample they found that diversity was associated with low rates of church adherence, even when the percentage Catholic was figured into the regression equation. On the smaller sample of just the counties containing the big cities, they found that the direct effect of diversity was negative, until they entered the percentage Catholic into the equation, when it became positive but only very weakly so. When they added data from the 1920s and 1930s so that they could see the effects of diversity on church membership over time, they found that the negative effect of diversity was even greater. Only for a small sample containing the big cities could anything like the relationship posited by Finke and Stark be found and that was so weak as to be statistically insignificant. As the team put it: "Our conclusion is that religious monopoly—not diversity—fuels religious expansion . . . [and] ethnic homogeneity is also conducive to religious expansion" (Blau et al. 1991: 329).

Breault applied the Finke and Stark model to 1980 data and found that religious diversity had a persistent, negative, and statistically significant effect on the rate of adherence (1989a, 1989b). In subsequent exchanges, the supply-siders tried to answer these criticisms but they failed to satisfy other scholars that the statistical manipulation of the data which produced their confirming results was justified. Olson, who has considerable sympathy for elements of the rational choice approach, took seriously the problem of multi-collinearity and demonstrated convincingly that the positive effects produced by Stark and colleagues were a statistical artefact of controlling for the proportion of Catholics and that the same positive effects could be produced by controlling for the largest group (whatever it was) and by inventing an entirely spurious large obviously irrelevant "denomination" by grouping together very different organizations (Olson 1999).

Rather than going through all the contested studies, I will defer to my colleagues Chaves and Gorski, who have recently evaluated twenty-six published articles or chapters which analyze the links between religious pluralism and religious participation. Ten of those (seven of them authored by some combination of Stark, Finke, and Iannaccone) found a positive relationship. Eleven found a negative relationship. Five found null effects. Within these outputs, they found a total of 193 separate analyses and of these only twenty-four (12 percent) yield results which appear to support the new paradigm. After painstaking secondary analysis, Chaves and Gorski conclude: "The empirical evidence contradicts the claim that religious pluralism is positively associated with religious participation in any general sense" (Chaves and Gorski 2001: 279).

Pluralism in Europe

There are obvious advantages in trying to compare countries that have much in common and differ primarily in degree of religious pluralism. I have tried this with two clusters: the three Baltic states and the four Nordic countries (Bruce 1999: 92–104). The results offer no support at all for the supply-side argument. In the case of the Baltic states, religiously homogeneous Lithuania has a much higher church adherence rate than the more mixed Estonia and Latvia. In the case of the Nordic countries, Finland stands out as the most religious. In both clusters, the most religious country is the one in which the greatest threat to national integrity (from the Soviet Union in both cases) coincides with the greatest degree of internal homogeneity. The strength of religion seems related to its place at the heart of national identity, a place it can only sustain when there is little or no pluralism.

The Lithuanian example leads us on to the Catholic problem. If competition is so beneficial then the success of Catholicism in Europe is a mystery. The most churched country in western Europe is the Republic of Ireland, which is so thoroughly Catholic that until very recently (church attendance began to decline rapidly in the late 1970s) the church enjoyed the status of *de facto*, if not *de jure*, establishment. In eastern Europe, the most religious country (and the one that provided the most powerful resistance to Soviet imperialism) was Poland, again overwhelmingly Catholic. Iannaccone admits that "Protestant attendance rates are strongly related to market structure but Catholic attendance rates are largely independent of it" (1991: 169) but does not see this failure to explain the behavior of the largest bloc of Christians as a problem for what claims to be a general theory.

A Statistical Aside

It may well be that all the above studies that involve correlations between pluralism and participation in cross-sectional data are meaningless. Voas et al. have argued (convincingly to someone who is not an expert statistician) that "the associations reported reflect not the effects of pluralism, but a previously overlooked mathematical relationship. . . . Using simulations we show that even when pluralism has no effect on participation, a mathematically necessary non-zero correlation between the variables will emerge. . . . The sign and magnitude of this correlation depend on the nature of the size distributions of the religious groups across the areas studied" (Voas, Olson, and Crockett 2001: 1). If they are right that existing cross-sectional comparisons are meaningless, then germane evidence can only be produced by comparing the fate of religion in one setting over time.

Britain

The best way to see the effects of competition is to take a single setting in which the degree of competition changes and examine the resulting effects on religion. Hence it is worth considering the history of religion in particular countries. The supply-side model fails to fit the history of religion in Britain. Before the Reformation there was one church, organized on a national parish structure, which glorified God on behalf of, and provided religious offices for, the entire people. With the Reformation, the religious cultures of Scotland, Wales, and England diverged. Each national church also fragmented internally, to create a large number of competing organizations. By the middle of the nineteenth century, about half the population worshipped outwith the state churches of England, Wales, and Scotland. Since then pluralism has increased further with the growth of non-Trinitarian sects and Pentecostalism. There are interesting technical arguments about exactly how one measures diversity[4] but no one questions that the last two hundred years have seen a considerable increase in its extent. Few Britons are far from a major urban area and for most of the twentieth century it has been possible to find almost every imaginable variant of Christianity on offer in British cities. The increase in diversity and the gradual removal of such constraints on competition as supporting the state churches with public funds and denying government office to dissenters should have created an increase in religious vitality. Britain of the 1990s should be more religious than Britain of the 1890s or 1790s or 1690s. It is not.[5]

The same point could be made for the rest of Europe. In the nineteenth and twentieth centuries, state regulation of religion was relaxed, competition increased, and the religious life became more diverse. Whether the religious market of Finland or Greece is as free as that of the United States is neither here nor there. All we need to establish is that it is freer now than it was in 1798 or 1898 and that in all such countries religious participation has declined.

Dubious Connections

Large-scale statistical data sets are important in the social sciences but putative correlations cannot be allowed to support explanations that are not reasonable at the level of the acting individual. Correlation, even at the hitherto-unknown level of constant concomitance, is not itself explanation. To understand why two variables are related, we must be able to unpack the correlation to plausible stories about individual actors, groups, and institutions. A persistent difficulty I have with the supply-side approach is that while I can think of historical examples that well fit its basic assumptions, I can also think of very many exceptions and qualifications. The following three points are at the heart of the macro story.

1. In a free market, start-up costs for new religions are low: hence more innovation, more diversity, and more chance of people finding a religion they like.
2. In a competitive market, clergy have an incentive to evangelize and recruit a congregation. If they do not spread the faith, they do not eat. Hence the clergy work harder and tailor their product to what the customers want.
3. State monopolies encourage wasteful inefficiency because there is no competition. So state churches will be ornate, elaborate, extravagant, and permit such high costs as lengthy training periods for clergy.

Each of these points seems at first intuitively plausible but then crumbles as one considers the historical record. Take the point of low start-up costs. It seems sensible that a regulated religious economy will stifle innovation until one remembers that the "upstart sects" whose success in America forms such a central part of the supply-side case were founded in the then-regulated economy of Britain and did rather well there *before* they were carried to America. And persecution did the British Quakers or the Swiss Anabaptists no harm at all. Their decline started at the point where the growing climate of religious toleration removed the penalties on nonconformity.

Of state churches, Iannaccone says:

> One might expect state churches to cost more per practising member and to produce members with lower than average levels of religious knowledge and belief. One of the sources of higher costs is likely to be higher than normal wages for the state church's clergy and higher than normal required levels of seminary training (1991: 161).

As with so many of the supply-side generalizations, this is only partly true. Taking the points in reverse order, the length (and hence cost) of clerical training will have more to do with religious and class questions than with legal status and the religious economy. The importance it gives to the *organization* as the carrier of truth means that the Catholic Church has very long training periods (at least for its core clergy; the ordinary priest may require less knowledge) and this is the case in nineteenth-century France, where the church was dominant and in Scotland, where it was tiny. In some countries the church has run boarding schools to start priestly training in the pre-teen years. In addition to wishing to instill a great deal of knowledge in its functionaries it also wishes to ensure loyalty, especially from its geographic outposts. Hence the practice of drawing the brightest young ordinands from the provinces into Spain or Rome.

Whether a religion stresses knowledge of texts over experience is also germane. Scottish Presbyterianism is typical of those brands of Protestantism that require detailed knowledge of scripture and insist that their clergy be trained in the biblical languages of Greek and Hebrew. Note that this is the case for the Presbyterian Church of Ireland (which is a dissenting, nonstate, and minority church) and for the Presbyterian Church of Scotland (which is a state-established and hegemonic church). However, the Pentecostal variety of Protestantism places greater emphasis on the piety and spiritual experiences of the clergy and hence typically calls for less formal training.

The nature and extent of clerical training also has much to do with the social class from which the clergy is drawn and the levels of ambient religiosity in the wider society. At the extremes of high and low class, there is little training. When it was common for the younger sons of the nobility and the gentry to take holy orders in the Church of England little formal instruction was given because it was not necessary. The education of a gentlemen was sufficient. In the eighteenth century the sole test for admission to holy orders was a series of questions asked by the bishop's chaplain, questions that any educated Christian could have answered. It was only when the middle classes began to replace the lesser gentry that the Church of England established theological colleges.

Likewise there seems no simple connection between establishment and overall wage levels. Prior to the reforms of the mid-nineteenth century, English bishops lived like princes but many vicars and curates were extremely ill-paid. Furthermore, we find state church regimes varying considerably in the mechanisms for determining the levels of taxation to be used to pay for religious offices. The established Church of Scotland in the eighteenth century was often in a parlous condition because it was funded by a tax on the property of "heritors" who themselves made decisions about clerical salaries, church building, school building, and poor relief. Those heritors who had little sympathy for the Kirk and little sense of their own social and religious obligations kept assessments down and the cost of religious provision low.

There is a further complication of which the supply-siders seem unaware. Not all legally established churches are funded by the state. In Britain, the Church of Scotland and the Church of England retained their legal status but had their funding base significantly altered. Their rights to land taxes were commuted into capital sums and for most of the twentieth century they have been on the same financial footing as the dissenting denominations: reliant on a combination of contemporary donations and the income from invested capital.

Iannaccone's claim about average levels of religious knowledge is probably untestable. First, it is impossible to separate what people learn in church from what they gain elsewhere. Second, there is the historically specific obstacle to comparison: religious monopolies tend to be characteristic of premodern societies where illiteracy meant that levels of knowledge about everything (and not just religion) were low. However, we do know one thing that should make us cautious of accepting Iannaccone's claim. As many surveys have discovered, present-day Americans—the beneficiaries of a religious free market—are often woefully ignorant of the basic tenets of their faith (Gallup and Jones 1989). In contrast Finns, subject to compulsory religious education, have proved themselves reasonably well-informed about things they do not much believe. In a study in the early 1960s, 94 percent could recite accurately the Lord's Prayer (Seppanen 1972).

Iannaccone may inadvertently have hit upon an important observation and then missed the point. It is likely that levels of religious knowledge are connected to one particular kind of competition: bitter conflict. In a world of consensus, especially where the religion gives high place to ritual rather than to belief, a great deal of knowledge is not required. A few simple phrases and actions will suffice for salvation. But in settings of considerable ethnic conflict (for example in Liverpool or Belfast or Glasgow in the nineteenth century), one group of believers may feel obliged to learn more about why they are superior. Hence the popularity of anti-popery evening classes in which students mastered such publications as the *Hand-Book for the Study and Discussion of Popery with Special Reference to its Political Relations*. However, this seems some way from the general claim and does not fit well the modern U.S. situation where a plethora of organizations compete for members within a largely tolerant culture and by advertising peripheral virtues (such as the friendliness of the services) rather than by directly criticizing others for heresy.

To return to the general claim that monopolies are inefficient, the example of the Catholic Church offers an obvious problem. Far more often a monopoly than any Protestant competitor, it is arguably a model of efficiency. By insisting on celibate clergy, it can maintain its staff with only living expenses and pocket-money. Three or four priests can be accommodated in a single clergy house and serviced by women who work for well below the market rate because they see that service as a religious vocation. There are no families to provide for and (a considerable burden from the mid-twentieth century onwards) no expensive pension schemes to maintain. Catholic efficiency can be seen in the ratio of church attenders to clergymen. In Australia in 1996, the Baptists, Presbyterians, and Churches of Christ had 74 attenders per cleric and the Anglicans 76, but the Catholic Church had 349 (Hughes

1998: 4). The work-rate of Catholic clergy poses a problem for the general supply-side assumption that a direct link between earnings and popularity has a positive effect on the motives of the clergy. There have been exceptions but generally Catholic priests are, by the standards of the wider society, extremely poorly paid. Yet this had not prevented them working extremely hard to serve the perceived needs of their people.

The Protestant requirement for democratic participation in services and accountability meant a national structure of local congregations. Thus in the growing cities, Protestant national churches and the dissenting organizations tried to recreate the rural parish structure. In contrast the Catholic Church often built one large central church and repeated its masses as often as was necessary to accommodate the Catholics of the area. Thus while Protestant organizations invariably offered more seats than they had participants, in large towns and cities, the Catholic Church often had more participants than it had seats. Their failure to understand this led some of the enumerators of the 1851 Census of Religious Worship to alter the returns for Catholic churches because they assumed that attendance rates higher than the number of seats were a clerical error! The point missed by the rational choice theorists is that the differences between the Catholic Church and Protestant sects and denominations owe far more to theology and ecclesiology than to market situation.[6]

Stark has repeatedly given clerical sloth as one of the primary defects of establishment. At first sight, the observation seems plausible. Depending on their own efforts to recruit a following gave the Methodists of nineteenth-century America an incentive to evangelize. Doubtless being funded by land taxes allowed many eighteenth- and nineteenth-century Anglican clerics to become unmindful of their duties. Some Presbyterian ministers in the North of Scotland in the eighteenth and early nineteenth centuries were indolent. Many depended on farming their glebe lands for income but some took the injunction to be shepherds rather too literally. The minister of Farr, who rented three large farms, repeatedly ignored injunctions from the Presbytery of Tongue to attend more to his spiritual duties. The Synod of Caithness judged that he "seems to be obstinately determined to entangle himself with worldly affairs and to have no regard to the command of the [Presbytery]" (McInnes 1951: 107). The minister of Applecross celebrated communion only four times in twenty years, kept a boat for his fishing, and "has a considerable land property and money stocked otherwise" (McKay 1980: 4). It is said of the minister of Duthill that he had only two sermons but for variety changed the passages of scripture that were a pretext for them. We might note from the Caithness Synod's criticism of the minister of Farr that, however common was inattentiveness to duty, it was not tolerated by the clergy in general.

Taken to the extreme which it must be by the supply-siders if it is to explain the contrasting fates of whole denominations and even entire countries, the claim that the structure of reward determines levels of commitment is implausible. As they are paid by the state irrespective of their popularity, Stark says of Lutheran pastors: "the German clergy are better off with empty churches, which place little demand on their time, than with full ones" (1997: 185). What is assumed of the character of the typical Lutheran pastor is made clear if we apply the same logic to Stark. I presume that for most of his long and distinguished career Stark was paid by his university irrespective of how many students took his courses. Would he count himself "better off" if he was unpopular? As he is not paid for his journal articles, I can only suppose he writes so much because he wishes to persuade us to accept his beliefs. Of course, there will be exceptions, but it seems a reasonable principle to say we should hesitate to impute to a group of people an attitude to their values and beliefs we would not readily apply to ourselves.

HUMAN CAPITAL

Although the supply-side model is described in propositions about individual decision-making, most of the evidence provided concerns correlations between various indices in large-scale data sets. The presumed connections between the rational choices of actors and the resulting societal patterns are laid out in Iannacconne's "Religious practice: a human capital approach" (1990). He claims that an economistic approach can explain denominational mobility, the typical age of converts, the typical pattern of inter-religious marriage, and the levels of participation found in different sorts of marriages.

The notion of "investment" is used to explain why most Americans stay in the churches in which they were raised, return to that church if they have drifted away (as they typically do in early adulthood), and, if they move, ideologically travel only short distances. People who have invested a certain amount of human capital (time and effort) in acquiring the beliefs of one tradition and mastering its liturgical or ritual procedures will be reluctant to lose that capital. To move a long way requires a lot of new investment and wastes previous effort. Hence there are not many Baptists becoming Catholics.

Here we have the common phenomenon of a body of data fitting an alternative explanation every bit as well as its fits a human capital approach. We could suppose, as most sociologists of religion have done previously, that beliefs *sediment* so as to shape our receptivity to future alternatives and that beliefs are associated with enduring identities and supporting communities. That you have held for some time a Baptist view of religion may not stop you ceasing to be religious but makes it likely that, if you remain religious or wish to return to a supernatural faith at some later stage of your life, you will find most *plausible* beliefs that accord with the residues of the earlier stage of belief. Having been a Baptist for a while is likely to make you feel like a Baptist and to be emotionally attached to that identity and community. Using conventional sociological ideas, we can explain the pattern identified by Iannaccone perfectly well without recourse to the contentious idea that people's religious attachments are shaped by a wish to maximize the return on their investment of human capital.

Iannacconne believes that data on the typical age at which people experience religious conversion also supports his model:

> The human capital model predicts that religious switching, like job changing, will tend to occur early in the life cycle as people search for the best match between their skills and the context in which they produce religious commodities. Across time, the gains from further switching will diminish as the potential improvement in matches diminishes and the remaining years in which to capitalize on that improvement decrease (1990: 298).

Again, the presented data fit the "prediction" but the prediction does not test the theory because the same data are readily compatible with a quite different explanation: that the plausibility of beliefs is a product of social interaction with other like-minded believers and the extent to which those beliefs produce a satisfactory understanding of the world and one's place in it. Both of these are likely to produce increased plausibility over time. Fifty-year-old Scottish Presbyterians do not become Moonies, not because they have few years left in which the recoup their new investment but because their long involvement with Presbyterianism and Presbyterians makes them ill-disposed to believe Moon and his representatives.

Like so much of the rational choice approach, the human capital propositions sound plausible in the abstract and unlikely when put into claims about specific people and actions. Iannaccone assumes that beliefs and liturgical practices are hard to learn. Mastering the entire Shorter Catechism will take time but most Christian churches are similar and, as researching sociologists regularly prove, their rituals can very quickly be picked up by imitating the person in the pew in front. Furthermore, Iannaccone regards learning as a cost, which misses the point that it can be viewed as an enjoyable challenge. After all, the main consumers of evening classes are the elderly and retired. Knowing that they do not have enough life left to become another Picasso or Constable does not prevent thousands of old people taking up painting.

The explanation of data on the effects of inter-religion marriages is even less persuasive. We know from a variety of sources that where a couple belong to the same church or religious tradition, they are more likely than "mixed" marriages to be regular church attenders, to give money to religious work, to raise their children in the faith, and so on. Iannaccone claims:

> A household can produce religious commodities more efficiently when both husband and wife share the same religion. Single-faith households benefit from

> "economies of scale": the same car drives everyone to church; there is no question as to how time and money contributions will be allocated to different religions; it is not necessary to debate the religion in which one's children will be reared (1990: 301).

There is no doubt that conflict between spouses about religious beliefs and affiliation can be painful and hence no surprise in the data Iannaccone presents to show that people tend to marry within the same denomination. People can imagine the disputes and act to avoid them. But a much simpler explanation of the pattern is that churches provide an excellent venue for meeting young people who are similar not only in religion but in social class, culture, and ethnic background.

Better evidence for Iannaccone's model are data that show that shared-faith marriages have higher rates of church attendance than interdenominational marriages but again, nothing in this especially supports the claim that the pattern arises because "partners of the same religion can produce religious commodities more efficiently." There is an alternative that Iannaccone dismisses when he says that "a shared faith should have only indirect effects on individual beliefs" (1990: 303). An axiom of sociology is that reality is socially constructed, maintained, and changed. To add to one's own internalized beliefs a significant other who reinforces such beliefs will have a profound impact on the strength of one's faith and hence on the enthusiasm with which one participates in collective expressions of such beliefs. Contrary to Iannaccone's assertion, the sharing of a faith is very likely to have sufficient effect on the strength of belief to explain why the church involvement of same-faith marriages is higher than that of cross-faith marriages.

Furthermore, there is a problem with the direction of causality. Iannaccone's data do not establish which of (a) couples sharing the same faith, and (b) extensive religious involvement, comes first. For his model to work (a) must precede (b) but the reverse is equally, if not more, likely. It is precisely those people who are most committed to their faith who will make a point of considering only fellow believers as suitable marriage partners.

GENERAL CRITICISMS

I would now like to identify some very general weaknesses in the rational choice approach.[7] First the specificity is often more apparent than real. There are lots of hypotheses and theorems and regression equations, which seems terribly scientific, and then you discover that this superficial rigor disguises a great deal of indeterminacy. Anomalous cases cause one sort of problem but equally problematic are cases that are accommodated too easily. For example, in explaining the virtue of the free market, the supply-siders argue that low costs are good because people will consume more.

But in trying to explain why demanding conservative sects often seem more robust than mainstream liberal denominations, they say that high costs are good because the more people invest in an enterprise the less likely they are to abandon it.

The resolution of this paradox is that the demands churches make of their members cannot exceed the benefits members receive from participating in such churches. Thus demanding churches must provide more or better rewards. True. But as we have no way of knowing the best balance of costs and rewards, and hence cannot say in advance where *utility* lies, what appears to be an explanation is reduced to tautology. If people stay in a church we say that the balance of costs and rewards is right; if they leave, we say it is wrong.

This leads us to a general problem of economic or rational choice models: *comparisons*. Maximizing is possible only in so far as the rewards of two different activities can be compared. When we find soap powders at different prices, we can compare the weight in the box or the strength of the powder and thus decide which really offers the better deal. How do we do this with religion? How can we compare the rewards of being religious with the rewards of not being religious? Of course, some secondary aspects of church-going have their secular alternatives. If one of the reasons you go to church is to meet members of the opposite gender, then you can compare church and the bowling alley as mating arenas. But the core part of religion—getting right with God—has no secular counterpart against which it can be compared to see what is the rational choice.

Furthermore, it should be stressed that even another religion is not an alternative to a religion in the sense that a Ford is an alternative to a Chrysler. Like some secular ideologies (but unlike consumer goods), religions generally demand (and get) the complete faith of their adherents. With the exception of Buddhism and modern liberal Protestantism, the great religions claim a unique grasp of the salvational truth. To the guardians of Roman Orthodoxy, the Catholic Church is the unique repository of religious truth. Other religions are not plausible alternatives that can be examined for maximizing opportunities; they are errors, falsehoods, and heresies. In the most charitable description, non-Catholic Christians are "our separated brethren." Or to put it another way, one cannot hedge one's bets by buying only a small amount of a religion. One may temporize and many believers do their best to experiment with their involvement in various churches but the absence of certainty about the ultimate returns for such involvement means that we cannot regard religious promiscuity as a form of rational diversification of investment.[8]

Even if we leave aside the problem of alternatives, we run into the difficulty that the second requirement for maximizing—the existence of a neutral means of comparing costs—is absent. To one potential member of a Pentecostal church, a two-hour prayer meeting may be a price to be paid while to another it may be the answer to prayer. Whether something is a cost or a reward depends on whether one believes, and it changes at the point of conversion. But becoming a believer is precisely the thing we are trying to explain.

I now come to the greatest weakness in the rational choice approach. In the very first essay I wrote on rational choice (Bruce 1992) I pointed to a small technical flaw that goes to the heart of the matter. In measuring diversity, Stark and his colleagues counted different ethnic, racial, and linguistic variants of the same tradition. I argued then that it was a mistake to suppose that a black Pentecostal church and a white Pentecostal church gave two choices to the inhabitants of a southern U.S. town. In a racist country (as the United States most certainly was in 1906 and in many places still is today) a black church does not offer an alternative to whites or vice versa. A Spanish Pentecostal church is not an option for a monolingual English-speaker. Even the Anglo who speaks Spanish is unlikely to feel at home in an overwhelmingly Mexican church.

The obvious point is that maximizing opportunities are constrained by noneconomic considerations. In the case of religion, they are constrained by two sorts of forces. As in the example of race, choices are limited by other sources of identity. But choices are also constrained by religious affiliation itself.

A distributor of Massey-Ferguson tractors who finds he is selling a duck can change to a John Deere dealership. If agriculture declines, he can get out of tractors altogether, sell his land for housing development, and invest his surplus in e-commerce shares. Churches and evangelists have a long history of economic irrationality because there are huge cultural constraints on what ideological organizations with their historical roots in organic communities can do to become more popular. In the U.S., the mainstream Lutheran churches may feel envious of the success of their more conservative brethren but they cannot readily change their beliefs. Western European Protestant churches may envy the stability of the Catholic Church but, unlike the tractor distributor, they cannot change to the more popular line.

To be more precise, the rational choice model ignores cultural norms and, until recently, so too did Stark and his associates. Then in a 1995 paper they added a new "proposition 4a" to the already extensive list: "To the degree that competitive forces are constrained within a religious economy, pluralism will not be related to religious participation" (1995: 443). As religious economies are almost always constrained, either by ethnic and national loyalties, or by the loyalties engendered by religion itself, that refinement pretty well demolishes the free market model.

Where we most clearly see the limits of economistic models is in the way that people *respond to failure*. The adherents of minority religions and deviant political ideologies very often persist with unpopular products and seek a silver lining by claiming that their lack of success is itself proof that they are right. It is just that most people are too sinful or too deep in false consciousness or too stupid to know a good thing when they see one. When the management of Ford realized that the Edsel was a disaster, they did not continue to produce it and console themselves with the belief that the lack of customers just proved that it was too good a car for the ordinary folks. They dropped it and started again.

Let me add an important aside. The narrowness of my target should be noted. This is not an attack on the view that most behavior is rational. It is perfectly proper that we should assume action to be minimally rational until we have very good grounds for arguing that, in any particular case, it is not. I would go even further and argue that, were social action not minimally rational, we would not be able to describe or comprehend, let alone explain, it. What I am taking issue with here is the very specific claim that *economic* (as distinct from social, legal, or political) rationality provides a useful model for understanding religious belief and behavior.

That aside apart, my conclusion is simple. Economic or rational choice models of behavior depend on us knowing what is the rational choice. When faced with the possibility of buying the same breakfast cereal from two outlets, it would be irrational not to compare the prices and buy the cheaper. But "To the extent that we cannot tell, or cannot tell uniquely, what the rational choice would be, the theory fails. . . . In a word rational-choice theory can fail because it does not tell us what rationality requires" (Elster 1986: 17).

WHEN WOULD IT WORK?

In a general evaluation of the rational choice approach, it is useful to ask in what circumstances the economistic model might work. Following the point about social constraints, we might reasonably conclude that the model should work for a field where demand for the product in general is high but brand loyalty is low, and where there are mechanisms for assessing costs and rewards. The consumption of refrigerators and cars would seem to fit. Almost all of the costs and most of the rewards are clear. Assessing future reliability and hence maintenance costs may be difficult but we know the price of the Volvo and the Ford. Demand for personal transport is high and brand loyalty is typically very low. People do not get shot for preferring a Volvo to a Ford. Men in white sheets do not burn crosses in front of the houses of people who switch car brands.

If we transfer this to the case of religion we come to a curiously ironic conclusion. The sort of culture in which people feel free to switch between alternative religions would be one in which religion was not embedded in important social identities. The sort of people who would switch in search of reduced costs and increased rewards would be people who were not fully won over to any of the religions they sampled (for if they were, they would see competitors as selling false Gods, not offering maximizing opportunities). In brief, a world in which people behaved as Stark and his associates assume we do would be a fairly secular one. If the economistic model is ever applicable it is not to traditionally religious people in religious societies. It is to lightly committed people in societies that do not set much store by religion.

AN ALTERNATIVE

Olson concludes one discussion by asking "if pluralism has a negative effect on religious involvement, why is church membership and attendance so high in the U.S., probably the most religiously pluralistic of industrialized nations?" (1999: 171). There is not space here to do any more than sketch a reply but, because there is a tendency to forget that sociologists explained religious behavior before the rational choice approach, I will list parts of the answer to Olson's question. First, the religious life of the U.S. continues to be invigorated by migrants from more traditionally religious countries. In the 1990s, one in ten inhabitants of the U.S. were born outside the country. Second, as Hadaway and colleagues have shown, U.S. church attendance rates are based on self-report and are exaggerated (Hadaway, Marler, and Chaves 1993; Marler and Hadaway 1999). Third, pluralism at the national level disguises considerable hegemony at the local level. Fourth, and this is perhaps the most important point, the U.S. is unusual in the extent to which its federal and diffuse structure permits committed believers to construct distinctive subsocieties to preserve subcultures. Most European societies are small, centralized, and densely populated; hence such cultural diversity as there is imposed upon very many people in ways that are hard to avoid. A few examples will make the point. In the U.K. until very recently most people had access to only 4 television channels and each felt obliged sometimes to cater to ethnic, religious, and cultural minorities. Many U.S. cities have so many channels serving distinct audiences that any segment of the population can consume just the programming that fits its existing identity. U.K. schools teach a national curriculum, U.S. schools have considerable freedom to tailor their teaching to their catchment population. The U.S. has such a variety of higher-education institutions that a fundamentalist can study for a law degree in a fundamentalist law school which employs fundamentalist faculty. A Scottish conservative evangelical who wishes to study law has to do so in a secular law school. In brief the structure of politics, the law, public administration, and mass communication in the U.S. permits minorities to construct micro-worlds in which their values and beliefs can be constantly reinforced and can acquire a taken-for-granted status that is impossible in most European societies.

CONCLUSION

In his brief, the editor of this collection asked the critics of the rational choice approach to consider how it might be amended to make it acceptable. My conclusion is that it is beyond redemption. It rests on a simple mistake. It accepts Gary Becker's claim that economics offers a viable model for understanding all social action. There is rather a good case for saying that economics does not explain economic action terribly well but, leaving that aside, it provides little or no purchase on religious action. Most religious behavior is traditional. Poles are not Catholics because that is the rational choice; they are Catholics because they are Poles. Even in fluid situations, religious behavior is shaped by social norms that prevent maximizing: class, race, ethnicity, nationality, and language all limit choice. But religion itself limits choice. To the extent that people are successfully socialized into a particular religion they are not able to see other religions as utility-maximizing opportunities. And even if they could, the mechanical requirements for making an economistic rational choice are missing; we cannot compare costs and rewards.

The basic principles do not work. Two things disguise the poverty of economism. First, because it has so many of them, its propositions sometimes coincide with the truth. But, as with the example of mixed-marriage couples and church attendance, those observations that are well founded are not dependent on economism nor do they test it. They can be at least as well or better explained by less contentious approaches.

To be persuasive a theory of human behavior must rest on a believable character. Can we really believe in Stark's pastor who welcomes the decline of his church because shrinking congregations means that he maximizes his utility with an improved effort-to-reward ratio? Do we know couples whose decisions about church attendance are influenced by gasoline costs?

It might be worth entertaining a theoretical approach that requires implausible story lines if it is supported by strong historical or comparative statistical evidence. Rational choice is not.

NOTES

1. The themes presented here are developed at length and supported by a wide variety of evidence in Bruce (1999).

2. Olson has correctly pointed out that the supply-siders mistakenly take diversity to be evidence of competition. It may be that but it may also reflect a situation where diverse populations support their own churches while making little or no attempt to recruit members of other populations. I made a related point about racial divisions in the U.S. in Bruce (1992).

3. Stark, Finke, and Iannaccone (1995) had a similar problem when they tried to make a case from the 1851 Census of Religious Worship in England and Wales. Their first analysis failed to produce the desired result so, on not particularly persuasive grounds, they dropped the much larger case of England and concentrated on Wales.

4. Before I published this criticism (in Bruce 1992) I pointed out to Finke that the Herfindahl index of diversity had a subtle and potentially fatal flaw: it actually measures the evenness of distribution across a range of options rather than the extent of choice in that it awards a "more diverse" score to a place with four equally popular alternatives than to one with ten alternatives where one or two are very large and others are very small. Finke never replied. Crockett (1998) identified another weakness with the index. It is scale-specific. Using the registration districts rather than the parishes to analyze the 1851 Census of Religious Worship produces a 10 percent increase in diversity. Given the weak correlations in many of the contested analyses this effect cannot be ignored.

5. The supply-side view of religion in Britain is presented in Stark, Finke, and Iannaccone (1995). A critical response and an alternative set of data is presented in Bruce (1995a) and (1995b). For a view from a leading British historian who disagrees with my explanation of secularization in Britain but has no doubts as to its reality, see Brown (2001).

6. Interestingly, few people have considered the other side of the supply-side claim. While we have debated the supposed inefficiencies of religious hegemonies, serious attention has not yet been given to the inefficiencies of competition. The most obvious is unnecessary duplication. As Robin Gill has persuasively argued, denominational rivalry in nineteenth-century Britain caused massive overprovision of places, saddled congregations with an albatross of debt, and ensured that even well-supported churches were half-empty, thus making them rather unwelcoming to possible newcomers (Gill 1993).

7. Very similar points are made by Bryant (2001) in a detailed critical review of the essays in Young (1997).

8. We should also note that promiscuity is rare and is typical only of the cultic religion typified by New Age spirituality. In more orthodox religions, most switchers regard each new position as the true and best church. That is, most of such experimenting as there is, and it is relatively little, is done in the spirit of serial monogamy rather than promiscuity.

REFERENCES

Blau, Judith R., Kenneth C. Land, and Kent Rudding. 1991. "The Expansion of Religious Affiliation: An Explanation of the Growth in Church Participation in the United States, 1850–1930," *Social Science Research* 21: 329–352.

Breault, Kevin D. 1989a. "New Evidence on Religious Pluralism, Urbanism, and Religious Participation," *American Sociological Review* 54: 1048–1053.

———. 1989b. "A Re-Examination of the Relationship Between Religious Diversity and Religious Adherents: Reply to Finke and Stark," *American Sociological Review* 54: 1056–1059.

Brown, Callum. 2001. *The Death of Christian Britain*. London: Routledge.

Bruce, Steve. 1992. "Pluralism and Religious Vitality," in Steve Bruce, ed. *Religion and Modernization: Sociologists and Historians Debate the Secularization Thesis*. Oxford: Oxford University Press, 170–194.

———. 1995a. "The Truth about Religion in Britain," *Journal for the Scientific Study of Religion* 34: 417–430.

———. 1995b. "A Novel Reading of Nineteenth Century Wales: A Reply to Stark, Finke and Iannaccone," *Journal for the Scientific Study of Religion* 34: 520–522.

———. 1999. *Choice and Religion: A Critique of Rational Choice Theory*. Oxford: Oxford University Press.

Bryant, Joseph M. 2001. "Cost-benefit Accounting and the Piety Business: Is Homo Religiosus, at Bottom, a Homo Economicus?" *Method and Theory in the Study of Religion* 12: 520–548.

Chaves, Mark and Philip S. Gorski. 2001. "Religious Pluralism and Religious Participation," *Annual Review of Sociology* 27: 261–281.

Crockett, Alasdair. 1998. "A Secularising Geography? Patterns and Processes of Religious Change in England and Wales, 1676–1851," unpublished Ph.D. thesis, University of Leicester.

Elster, Jon. 1986. *Rational Choice*. Oxford: Basil Blackwell.

Finke, Roger and Rodney Stark. 1988. "Religious Economies and Sacred Canopies: Religious Mobilization in American Cities, 1906," *American Sociological Review* 53: 41–49.

Gallup, George H., Jr. and Sarah Jones. 1989. *101 Questions and Answers: Religion in America*. Princeton, N.J.: Princeton Religious Research Center.

Gill, Robin. 1993. *The Myth of the Empty Church*. London: SPCK.

Hadaway, C. Kirk, Penny Long Marler, and Mark Chaves. 1993. "What the Polls Don't Show: A Closer Look at U.S. Church Attendance," *American Sociological Review* 58: 741–752.

Hughes, Philip. 1998. "Clergy: A Major Part of the Church's Workforce," *Pointers: Bulletin of the Christian Research Association* 8: 1–5.

Iannaccone, Laurence. 1990. "Religious Practice: A Human Capital Approach," *Journal for the Scientific Study of Religion* 29: 297–314.

———. 1991. "The Consequences of Religious Market Structure," *Rationality and Society* 3: 156–177.

Land, Kenneth C., Glenn Deane, and Judith Blau. 1991. "Religious Pluralism and Church Membership: A Spatial Diffusion Model," *American Sociological Review* 56: 237–249.

McInnes, John. 1951. *The Evangelical Movement in the Highlands of Scotland 1688–1800*. Aberdeen: The University Press.

McKay, Margaret M., ed. 1980. *The Revd John Walker's Report on the Hebrides of 1764 and 1771*. Edinburgh: John Donald.

Olson, Daniel V. A. 1999. "Religious Pluralism and U.S. Church Membership: A Reassessment," *Sociology of Religion* 60: 149–173.

Seppanen, Paavo. 1972. "Finland," in *Western Religion,* Hans Mol, ed. The Hague: Mouton, 143–173.

Stark, Rodney. 1997. "German and German-American Religiousness," *Journal for the Scientific Study of Religion* 36: 182–193.

Stark, Rodney, Roger Finke, and Laurence Iannaccone. 1995. "Pluralism and Piety: England and Wales 1851," *Journal for the Scientific Study of Religion* 34: 431–444.

Voas, David, Daniel V. A. Olson, and Alasdair Crockett. 2001. "Religious Pluralism and Participation: Was Everybody Wrong?" Paper presented at the annual meeting of the Society for the Scientific Study of Religion, October, Columbus, Ohio.

Young, Lawrence A. 1997. *Rational Choice Theory and Religion.* London: Routledge.

8

Reflections on the "New Paradigm": Unfinished Business and an Agenda for Research

Ted G. Jelen

Readers who have read the essays in this volume from beginning to end have experienced (as I have) a first-rate and fascinating intellectual exchange. The contributors to this volume have raised a number of important issues and questions relating to the "market model" of religious adherence (an inadequate term, but one of my own choosing), which will provide the basis for an exciting research agenda. It is my enviable, yet daunting, task, to attempt to tie together some of the major themes discussed in the earlier chapters.

The complexity of these issues is perhaps best exemplified by the difficulty in finding a name for what R. Stephen Warner has termed "the New Paradigm." Some analysts, such as Laurence Iannaccone (as well as the pieces by Gill, and Stark and Finke in this volume) have emphasized the "rational choice" aspect of the research under consideration, while others (such as Steve Warner's chapter in this volume and Thomas Robbins [2001]) have sought to de-emphasize this aspect of the emerging research program. Others, such as Daniel Olson, have emphasized the importance of religious pluralism, but, as Stark and Finke point out, pluralism does not necessarily lead to competition between religious organizations. Thus, I have opted for the term "market model" for the sake of clarity, recognizing that this term does not capture the richness and complexity of the research program to which it refers. Nevertheless, these differences in description suggest that the market approach is complex and multifaceted, with numerous points of description and of contention.

The essays in this volume make clear that intellectual inquiry into, and opposed to, the market model is an ongoing process. While Stark and Finke (who are, of course, the leading proponents of the market program) appear at times to regard works such as *Acts of Faith* (2000) and *The Churching of*

America (1992) as representing a nearly complete research program, the other essays in this volume make clear that there are several important issues still outstanding. If, as Thomas Robbins (2001) has suggested, the market model has no serious contemporary competitors as a comprehensive theory, it remains the case that aspects of the theoretical approach remain controversial.

My intention in this concluding chapter is to highlight some of these ongoing issues, and to offer some tentative directions for future research. One thing I do *not* intend to do is to assess the myriad and extensive empirical evidence which has been brought to bear on these controversies. Numerous studies in journals such as *American Sociological Review, American Journal of Sociology, Journal for the Scientific Study of Religion, Sociology of Religion*, and *Review of Religious Research* contain data relevant to claims made by proponents and opponents of the market model. Alternative summaries of the empirical evidence are offered by Stark and Finke (2000) and by Chaves and Gorski (2001). Rather, I hope to shed some light on more general, conceptual issues which appear to divide scholars on matters relating to the market approach to religious adherence.

Another goal of this concluding chapter is to attempt a preliminary assessment of "progress" in what Warner has termed "the new paradigm," using a concept provided by Thomas Kuhn (1970). While there is much to admire in Kuhn's classic work, *The Structure of Scientific Revolutions*, my own sense of scientific progress is guided by the work of Imre Lakatos (1970). Lakatos has suggested that scientific "research programs" resemble paradigms in the Kuhnian sense, with two important differences. First, while Kuhn suggests that, in periods of "normal science," one paradigm is generally dominant, Lakatos allows for the co-existence of multiple research programs. Second, Kuhn suggests that scientific "progress" can best be assessed within a particular paradigm, and comparisons between paradigms are, at best, problematic. By contrast, Lakatos argues that, although differences between research programs are never settled by simple empirical tests (such as "crucial experiments"), it is possible to compare the progress of competing research programs, or to use extrinsic criteria for the assessment of single research programs. Lakatos's main criterion for progress is the ability of the research program to predict novel facts. That is, if an "approach," a "research program," or a "paradigm" is to be judged successful, it must extend its reach to subsume novel phenomena, or comparable phenomena in diverse settings.

What this means for the current set of issues raised in this book is that, if proponents or critics of the market research program are to make their case, they must broaden the scope of the program to include other religious settings, or other dependent variables. To put the matter as bluntly as I can, if the market model of religious economies is simply a theory of religious participation, it is ultimately stagnant, and perhaps destined for intellectual obsolescence. However, if the program can successfully be expanded to include other social phenomena, the prospects for economic approaches to the study of religion appear to be much more promising.[1] As I will argue in the concluding section of this chapter, one possible justification for continued work in the religious market program is the program's initial success, and apparent promise, in explaining variations in the political role of religion within and across national settings.

My first task, then, is to highlight and examine some of the outstanding issues raised by the contributors to this collection, and to offer some preliminary suggestions as to how intellectual progress might be revitalized or sustained.

UNIVERSALITY

One of the themes which has emerged from the essays in this volume is that the scope of the market model of religious participation remains controversial. Stark and Finke have made it quite clear, both in their earlier writings and in their chapter in this volume, that they regard their approach as at least an approximation of a general theory, which can be applied to many (perhaps even all) human societies in which religion is practiced. The parsimony and rigor of the Stark–Finke analysis in this volume suggests that, for the most part, variations in historical and cultural context are either irrelevant, or can be subsumed under more general axioms of the formal theory.

However, most of the other essays in this volume (including both supporters and critics of the market model of religious adherence) suggest that the scope of the theory is either limited, or that the approach requires specification as to the circumstances under which the market process is thought to apply. The most obvious example is the chapter contributed by R. Stephen Warner, in which he suggests that the "New Paradigm" (market based) differs from the older, "sacred canopy" approach by regarding the American experience, rather than the European, as "normative" (in the sense of providing a baseline for comparison with other cases). While the comparability of the American and European cases is admittedly an empirical question, Warner's essay makes it clear that, in his view, similarities between the causes and consequences of religious competition on both sides of the Atlantic are to be discovered, rather than assumed. Moreover, several of the chapters cite work by Laurence Iannaccone (1991), in which he suggests that the effects of religious monopoly may be different for Protestant and Catholic nations. While the validity of "Catholic exceptionalism" thesis is again controversial (see Olson 1999; Finke and Wittberg 2000; Finke and Stark 1992, for different reactions to this claim), Iannaccone's analysis does suggest that there may be limits to the scope of the market model.

Several of the contributors to this volume have also questioned the conceptual equivalence of several phenomena which the market model purports to explain. For example, Steve Bruce has questioned the utility of a metaphor of "capital investment" to describe the stabilizing effects of intensive religious socialization, preferring instead a social learning model. While both the economic and social-psychological descriptions both account for the positive relationship between strong childhood socialization and adult loyalty to one's religious denomination, the hypothesized processes underlying these descriptions are quite different.

More generally, the essays by Bruce and Olson in this volume draw attention to a moderately controversial claim made by Stark and Finke, namely, that religious *conflict* is equivalent to religious *competition*. At one level, of course, the processes are quite different. The notion of religious competition involves an assumption that there will exist several plausible competitors in a pluralistic religious market. We are invited to imagine religious "shoppers" (see Roof and McKinney 1990) choosing among alternative religious organizations which are sufficiently similar to appeal to members of the same religious economy, yet which are different enough to permit the religious consumer to distinguish among them.

Do religious organizations actually compete with one another? Yes. In my own fieldwork in rural Indiana (Jelen 1991, 1993), I was able to observe pastors associated with different denominations taking great pains to differentiate their denominations from those who were theologically "adjacent" on a hypothetical left-right scale. Several of these pastors made the case for attracting new members and retaining continuing members on (occasionally arcane) theological grounds. For example, I devoted one particularly memorable afternoon to listening to a Baptist minister explain to me in exhaustive (and exhausting) detail why the GARBC (General Association of Regular Baptist Churches) was the "authentic" spiritual heir to John the Baptist, and why the corresponding claims of American Baptists, Southern Baptists, and Independent Baptists were not to be believed. This case was made primarily on theological and historical grounds. However, pastors in the highly competitive religious market of Putnam County, Indiana, also competed on more mundane, "secular" grounds as well. Contrary to Steve Bruce's supposition, these market considerations including availability of parking spaces, childcare for the parents of young children, and transportation for the elderly. In particular, the local Assembly of God had an elaborate (and highly effective) system of youth services and organizations, which used aspects of the popular culture to attract teenagers from other denominations (nicely anticipating Warner's point about the religious unreliability of the young). I am hard pressed to imagine that Putnam County is in any way atypical of numerous other communities throughout the United States.

That having been said, it seems plausible to suppose that other manifestations of religious pluralism involve cognitive processes which are much different. One suspects that, regardless of the intensity of dinner-table conversation between a Baptist parent and a teenage child who has just joined the Assemblies of God, this sort of interaction is qualitatively different than the role of the Catholic Church in providing non-Communist national identities in Poland during the Cold War, or the exacerbation of Hindu-Muslim conflict on the Indian subcontinent. Recent research (Aras 2000) has shown that support for Hindu nationalism in India is directly related to the individual Hindu's proximity to Muslims.[2] It seems unlikely that very many Indian Hindus actually contemplate converting to Islam. Rather, the presence of a visible, alien religious force makes certain aspects of one's identity more salient than they would be in a more religiously homogeneous environment. In both the central Indiana and Indian subcontinent cases, the hypothesized relationship between religious diversity and religious participation is confirmed. In most other respects, it is difficult to accept that the processes are in any way equivalent. This is not to say that some argument or evidence could not be advanced to show that the contexts have similarities which have eluded my attention. It is merely to suggest that, to my knowledge, such arguments and evidence have not yet been provided.

Thus, the appropriate scope of the market model of religious economies remains controversial. An important reason for this is that there are several phenomena which yield similar empirical predictions, but may represent quite different social processes. Most importantly, the similarities and differences between religious competition and religious conflict would appear to require further sustained investigation.

SECULARIZATION

In *Acts of Faith*, Stark and Finke devote a good deal of attention to debunking the claim made by many adherents of the "old paradigm" that secularization is a natural and inevitable consequence of modernity. The hypothesis relating modernization to a decline in religious belief and participation has received, at best, mixed support, and no longer seems plausible to many sociologists of religion. If we understand "secularization" to mean a diminishing of individual religious commitment, "secularization theory" has been seriously undermined, if not refuted, by empirical evidence.

However, as Casanova (1994) has suggested, "secularization" is a multifaceted concept, and it seems likely that religious pluralism and competition can accelerate the process by which the public life of a particular nation or community can be "de-sacralized." In particular, the emergence of a competitive religious economy may undermine the use of religion as a public resource.

Any discourse, public or private, requires the existence of *warrants*, or shared premises on which participants in a conversation can agree (Toulmin 1974; Greenawalt 1988; Segers and Jelen 1998). Such warrants can be epistemological (for example, scientific discourse requires at least general agreement on what constitutes evidence), linguistic (words have meanings shared by participants in a discourse), or moral (certain acts are generally considered morally reprehensible). An element of Berger's (1969) "sacred canopy" is that shared religious beliefs and values can contribute to a set of shared meanings within which public life can be conducted.[3] This is, of course, a very old insight. Alexis de Tocqueville (1945) noted that, in the mid-nineteenth century, "Christianity rules by universal assent," and that "*Christian morality is everywhere the same*" (1945: 314–315, emphasis added).

In a religiously pluralistic setting, it is difficult to use shared religious values as a warrant for public discourse. If a society is characterized by religious competition between similar, yet distinguishable, denominations, religious suppliers have incentives to engage in "product differentiation," which seems likely to undermine the political use of religious beliefs as rhetorical devices. Conversely, if religious diversity is occasioned by immigration, or some other process by which genuinely distinctive religious traditions are part of the religious economy, shared religious premises may be difficult, if not impossible, to employ in public or political discourse.

An example may clarify this point. In his book, *Listen, America!* (1980), Jerry Falwell attempted to use biblical and historical warrants to condemn homosexuality, and, more particularly, the legal acknowledgment of gay rights. Characterizing the United States as a "Christian Nation," which had achieved superpower status because of divine approval of our shared Christian heritage, Falwell advanced his opposition to the legal and cultural acceptance of homosexuality by citing biblical passages (primarily from Exodus and Leviticus), and reminding his readers that the Roman Empire had fallen at the point at which (and, presumably, because) homosexuality had become accepted.

For present purposes, what is of most interest here are the warrants Falwell uses in his argument. Falwell's case is only plausible to the extent that he and the reader share a belief in the inerrancy of the Bible, as well as a particular view of the dynamics of world history.[4] Falwell *assumes* a great deal of common ground on which to base his condemnation of homosexuality.

A decade or so later, the futility of invoking a shared Christian (or "Judeo-Christian") heritage had become apparent even to activists within the Christian Right. In *The Culture of Disbelief* (1993), Stephen Carter argues that the enactment and enforcement of laws designed to protect the civil liberties of gays constituted a violation of the right of religious free exercise. Carter argued that the religious values held by some Americans proscribed social interaction with those whose lifestyles constituted "abomination." If citizens who held such beliefs were legally obligated to provide goods and services, housing, and employment to gay people, the free exercise rights of religious conservatives would be violated. The point is not that we should all agree that homosexuality is wrong. Rather, we are simply asked to believe that some people believe homosexuality is wrong, and the rest of us are constitutionally and morally obligated to respect those beliefs.

Note the shift in emphasis here. In *The Culture of Disbelief*, Carter explicitly and specifically denies that a "Christian America" is either possible or desirable. Carter suggests that the United States is too religiously diverse to make such a vision even conceivable. However, Carter reaches the same conclusion as Jerry Falwell, not by invoking religious beliefs or concepts, but by using the language of individual rights[5] and an explicit warrant from the First Amendment of the U.S. Constitution.

As a political scientist, I perhaps take changes in the public consequences of religious consensus and competition more seriously than the other contributors to this volume. However, Anthony Gill (not coincidentally, another political scientist) makes virtually the same point in his chapter on the economics of religious freedom. Although Gill uses the formal language of rational choice theory, he suggests that political leaders can use shared religious imagery to gain political power, and to justify policies made using that power. Conversely, political outsiders (who oppose either a particular government or an entire regime) may have incentives to undermine the religious basis of political legitimacy, or to reactivate such shared religious values in opposition. The latter process may well have occurred in Iran in the late 1970s (when Khomeini came to power) and in Poland in the 1990s (ending Communist rule in Poland).

Thus, Stark and Finke have suggested in several places that the magnificent cathedrals which dot the European landscape do not reflect a period in which religious belief and participation were generally widespread, and they are very likely correct in that claim. However, the fact that political leaders were able to invoke authoritative religious values doubtlessly contributed to the maintenance and stability of secular political power. After all, European monarchs did often rule by divine right, and the fact that relatively few commoners actively worshiped the deity which conferred such earthly power may be of limited importance. Of course, the insights of Stark and Finke pose another question; namely, *why* did ordinary citizens attach legitimacy to regimes justified by religious beliefs they did not share? One possibility is that the public affirmation of authoritative religious beliefs by powerful elites may have suppressed the public expression of alternatives (see especially Noelle-Neuman 1993). Regardless of the correct answer to this puzzle, it seems clear that medieval Christianity had political effects which were not limited by the existence of widespread disbelief.

This point can be generalized. Religious pluralism, through some social process or processes, may indeed increase the extent of religious belief, and the amount of religious practice in a particular society. However, pluralism may also tear the fabric of the "sacred canopy," by reducing the utility of religious warrants in public discourse, and consigning religious belief to a "private sphere" of activity. Thus, even if individuals are not becoming more "secular" in pluralistic religious economies, the public face of social and political discourse may become desacralized as the result of religious competition.

TOWARD A THEORY OF RELIGIOUS DEMAND

In their essay in this volume, and in *Acts of Faith,* Stark and Finke assume that individual religious preferences are quite stable, and that such preferences, in the aggregate, form stable and distinctive "market niches." They further assume that the groups which result from these preferences form a unidimensional continuum, defined as "an axis of tension between the group and the socio-cultural environment" (Stark and Finke this volume, and 2000; see also Wilson 2001). While these assumptions are perhaps useful, in that they draw our attention away from overemphasis on drastic shifts in religious demand being the primary causes of religious change (Bankston 2001), they are nevertheless very strong and controversial axioms. While "paradigms" (in the classic, Kuhnian, sense) direct attention toward certain problems, and away from others, treating religious preferences as exogenous to the dynamics of religious markets is a potentially serious limitation (Wilson 2001).

Two of the essays in this volume are addressed specifically to variations in the demand side of the equation. William Bainbridge's insightful ethnohistorical description of the development of religious "compensators" in a particular family serves to remind us that the desire (or "demand") for religious goods can be quite idiosyncratic at the individual level, and resistant to more general theorizing. Bainbridge's study is instructive to both proponents and critics of the market model. Proponents of the market approach stand reminded that the stability and exogeneity of religious demand cannot plausibly be assumed, but must be described empirically, and ultimately explained. Similarly, some critics of the market approach to religion are admonished by Bainbridge's insights not to attribute variations in religious demand exclusively to macro-level forces leading inexorably (or otherwise) toward "modernization" or individual-level "secularization."

An important theoretical question for future inquiry in the market research program is the extent to which individual variations in religious demand can be explained within the parameters of the formal theory, and which require explanatory structures which are not subsumed by Stark and Finke's axiomatic system. Iannaccone (1990) has described certain variations in religious demand in terms of "capital investment," while, in the present collection, Steve Bruce has suggested that other, noneconomic approaches to religious socialization provide more parsimonious and more plausible explanations for stable variations in the demand for religious goods.

Another item for the growing research agenda within the religious markets research program is more empirical in nature. How can individual variations in the demand for religious goods be described, empirically measured, and ultimately explained? Indeed, it is somewhat surprising that there has been so little ethnographic or survey-based work done on the development and distribution of religious preferences, given that the market model entails some very strong, and very explicit, assumptions about the values and behavior of religious consumers. In *Acts of Faith*, Stark and Finke use the distribution of membership in different churches and sects to approximate a measurement of religious demand along a "high-tension–low tension" dimension, but such indirect measurements can only be suggestive. It is at least potentially circular to argue that the distribution of religious memberships constitutes evidence of the distribution of religious preferences, unless one is willing to assume that the religious market in the United States is completely free of legal or cultural constraints, and that the religious goods offered to American consumers perfectly reflect their preferences. Needless to say, such an assumption is very controversial, and is addressed to some extent in Anthony Gill's essay in this volume.

Second, the essay by Hamberg and Pettersson point out the importance of variation in religious demand across cultural (in this case, national) contexts. While their attempt to measure national variations in religious demand is quite preliminary (if extremely resourceful), it seems plausible to suppose that variations in the attitudinal constraint of religious values across nations may well reflect differences in individual preferences. It is intriguing, for example, to consider the question of why diversity of religious demand seems stronger in religiously homogeneous Norway than in either religious homogeneous Spain or religiously heterogenous Netherlands. By way of explanation, one might reasonably consider differences in religious doctrine (does Spain represent another instance of a possible "Catholic exceptionalism" phenomenon?) or in religious regulation (are there important differences between religious monopolies established *de facto* or *de jure*?)

More generally, accounts of religious markets have attempted to fill this void, by treating religious preferences as dependent variables to be explained rather than as independent variables whose values are to be assumed. Darren Sherkat (1997) has proposed a sketch of a general model of religious preferences, in which individual preferences are regarded as responsive to societal constraints and variations in the availability of religious goods. As such, Sherkat's account provides the basis of a nonrecursive model of religious supply and demand, in which the religious commodities provided by the providers of religious goods and the consumers of religious products are considered to have reciprocal influence on each other.

Of course, if the causal relationships between variations in religious supply and religious demand are completely reciprocal, it is impossible to determine whether the "supply-side" or the "demand side" of religious markets contains the crucial causal variable(s). Dynamic accounts of religious sociology, like the Creation, require an "unmoved mover" before they can be rendered nontautological. How can we account for changes in either the supply of or demand for religious goods from outside the relationships embedded in religious markets? While such a question is well beyond the scope of this chapter, one possible source of variation is in the practice of government regulation. Governments can affect (sometimes drastically) the contexts within which religious markets operate. Indeed, it is partially the generally unregulated religious market in the United States which has occasioned Warner's observation that, in the "new paradigm," American religious practice is to be considered normative. More recently, John Wybraniec and Roger Finke (2001) have analyzed the market consequences of the U.S. Supreme Court's decision in *Employment Division v. Smith*. Wybraniec and Finke show that this decision, which was widely regarded as a strong restriction on the free exercise rights of religious minorities, had immediate and profound effects on religious freedom in the United States. Over time, of course, such regulation of unconventional religions could well restrict the religious market in the U.S., and have predictable effects on religious membership and participation.

Anthony Gill's chapter in this volume shows further that the process by which governments decide whether and how to regulate religious practice may be subject to the same cost-benefit analyses which Stark and Finke attribute to religious suppliers and consumers. Gill's analysis suggests the possibility that there may exist stable equilibria in religious and political markets which are relatively closed. For example, while there clearly exist meaningful variations in the extent of religious regulation in the United States over time, neither major party has an incentive to support substantial increases in religious regulation, and neither party can legitimately be considered the "anti-religion" party, or the party opposed to the practice of particular religions.[6] It is perhaps no accident that the restriction of religious liberty occasioned by the *Smith* decision was created by an unelected judiciary, rather than by the elected branches of government. By contrast, Gill has shown here and elsewhere (1998) that religious markets in Latin America have changed rather dramatically over the past generation, with the Catholic Church having lost its religious monopoly, and the church having to compete with a growing number of evangelical Protestant churches. Gill makes clear that the initial impetus for this change was external, and occasioned by extensive missionary activity from North America. Gill shows that, while the impetus for change in the religious markets of Latin America came through disturbances on the supply-side, it is likely that the changes in popular religious preferences will provide risks and opportunities for Latin American political leaders in the future. Gill's account, which strikes me as very plausible, suggests that changes in religious markets (on either the supply or the demand sides) may indeed depend on forces exogenous to the market theory. It does the market program no serious damage to acknowledge the dependence of religious markets on external forces.

The more general point, of course, is that religious demand is an important component of any religious market. Religious demand appears to vary meaningfully across individuals, across cultures, and over time. It is neither necessary nor desirable for proponents of the market approach (Stark and Finke 2000; Iannaccone 1997) to assume away these important and fascinating questions. Religious demand is *both* an independent and dependent variable, and a complete understanding of the dynamics of religious markets must take both aspects of demand into account.

PROGRESS IN THE NEW PARADIGM

Having suggested a few areas in which future scholarly work in the religious markets research program seems warranted, it remains to assess the actual and potential payoff of the market approach. As noted at the outset of the essay, progress in a research program is assessed, at least in part, by the explanatory power of the core assumptions of that program. That is, does a research program, such as the market model of religious behavior, enable us to explain an increasing number of aspects of human behavior? In this section of the chapter, I plan to describe three different problems in the social scientific study of religion which the market model helps to make intelligible. These examples are merely intended to be illustrative, rather than exhaustive, and, by an amazing coincidence, are problems in the social sciences which I address in my own published work. I make no apology for the personal nature of these examples, since they help describe rather nicely how one scholar has found the Stark–Finke approach to religious phenomena quite useful, if not entirely definitive.

First, research in the market program has occasioned a de-emphasis on the notion of a "sacred canopy," understood as widely shared religious beliefs within which social and political life can be conducted. However, declaring the demise of the canopy metaphor may be premature. Religious pluralism, and the resulting competition between religious bodies, can reduce the utility of religious values as public rhetorical resources, which can in turn lead to a public secularization even in the face of high levels of individual religious commitment.

An example might make this point clearer. Michele Dillon (1996) has compiled an impressive comparison of Catholic anti-abortion rhetoric in several countries. For present purposes, it is instructive to compare Dillon's analysis of the rhetoric of Catholic leaders in Poland and the United States. In Poland, Dillon reports that Catholic bishops and pastors who seek to advance a pro-life agenda do so using the Aquinian language of natural law. That is, when Polish Catholic leaders seek to subsume the abortion issue under a more general rubric of Catholic theology. This might seem a reasonable strategy given the Church's *de facto* religious monopoly in Poland. Conversely, Dillon shows that, in the religiously pluralistic United States, the anti-abortion discourse of Catholic leaders is much more secular, and engages the arguments of pro-choice advocates. For example, much Catholic abortion discourse in the United States addresses the concerns of feminists, and attempts to show that being "pro-life" is also being "pro-woman." Similarly, Laura Grindstaff (1994) has shown that abortion discourse in the popular press has become progressively less religious, and increasingly "scientific." Thus, even religious leaders addressing the issue of abortion are likely to make arguments based on genetics (the fetus is a biologically unique being), or developmental physiology.

The point can be generalized: in pluralistic religious markets, there may not exist a set of shared religious symbols and beliefs which can be used as warrants in public debate. To this extent, religious people and organizations who seek to apply their religious values to public policy must couch their arguments in more secular, "publicly accessible" form (Greenawalt 1988). Effectively, religious diversity may deprive political actors with religious motivations of their most distinctive arguments (see especially Segers and Jelen 1998). Thus, while tearing the fabric of the "sacred canopy" does not seem to have resulted in a decline in religious devotion in the United States, and, indeed, may be the principal cause of the high levels of religious commitment in the U.S., the effects of religious pluralism have had consequences for public discourse in this country.

Second, the market model provides some insight into another puzzle of American politics; namely, in a nation with levels of religious commitment as are found in the United States, and in which evangelical Protestantism is a strong and growing component of the American religious mosaic, why has the Christian Right been so unsuccessful in mobilizing more than a small fraction of its potential membership, and so ineffective in achieving its policy goals? Studies of the earlier, Falwell–Robertson manifestation of the Christian Right (Green 1993; Jelen 1991, 1993; Wilcox 1992) have emphasized the divisive effects of religious particularism on religio-political mobilization of cultural conservatives. That is, differences over doctrinal issues such as glossolalia, faith healing, and anti-Catholicism have effectively prevented the formation of a potentially formidable political coalition. Indeed, more recent spokespersons for the Christian Right, such as former Executive

Director of the Christian Coalition Ralph Reed, have taken pains to address the issue of particularism, and to de-emphasize theological elements of efforts to promote "family values" (Reed 1994).

Given the high level of agreement on many social issues among all types of evangelical Protestants (and, indeed, between many Protestants and conservative Catholics), why should religious differences be so important? The market model of religious economies provides the basis for a very plausible explanation. In genuinely competitive religious markets, in which religious "firms" actually compete for potential members, religious entrepreneurs may find it advantageous to engage in "product differentiation." Just as advertisers devote substantial resources to convincing us that there exist meaningful differences between Coke and Pepsi, or between McDonald's and Burger King, so too might Assemblies of God, Baptist churches of all stripes, and other doctrinally conservative religious bodies seek to distinguish themselves from their nearest competitors. Indeed, I was able to observe this process in some detail (Jelen 1993) in a rural midwestern community, and noted that such particularism was most prevalent on the theological right.

If church members are hearing a message of differentiation in the pews, it may be difficult for them to overcome these attitudes in the political arena. Thus, we have observed that Pat Robertson's frequent discussion of spiritual gifts made his candidacy relatively unattractive to adherents of Jerry Falwell's more austere brand of fundamentalism, or that socially conservative Catholic candidates may have difficulty attracting support from Christian Right supporters (Jelen 2000b).

Thus, religious pluralism may have the paradoxical effect of enhancing religious activity at the individual level, but inhibiting the public assertion of religiously based values. At a minimum, the diversity of the theological right in the United States (which can plausibly be regarded as a consequence of religious competition in the U.S.) has directed the activities of religious conservatives away from specifically religiously based interest groups, and toward mobilization within political parties (see especially Green, Rozell, and Wilcox 2001). Genuinely ecumenical coalitions of social and religious conservatives seem easiest to form within organizations specifically designed to aggregate diverse interests and preferences (such as the Republican Party).

Finally, several studies have noted that religious socialization seems most effective when the religious body in question constitutes a minority. For years, I had been puzzled by the fact that religious values seemed to be transmitted more effectively when the church was situated in the "wrong" settings. My colleagues and I have found the Catholic Church to be a more effective agent of social learning on abortion and women's rights in primarily Protestant European nations than in nations with large Catholic populations (Jelen and Wilcox 1993, 1998; Jelen, O'Donnell, and Wilcox 1993) and that the Catholic Church is generally more effective at inculcating pro-life attitudes in American states in which the church constitutes a numerical minority. Further, a strong Catholic presence in certain states appears to occasion a pro-choice countermobilization among non-Catholics (Cook, Jelen, and Wilcox 1993).[7]

Again, the market model of religious competition provides a promising basis of an explanation for these phenomena. If one imagines the Catholic Church as a "high-tension" church in such inhospitable settings as Denmark or the American South, Catholic pastors in these areas might seek to raise the costs of belonging to enhance the distinctiveness self-identification as a Catholic. Again, this sort of evidence does not constitute unequivocal support for the market model. One might imagine increasing the church-society tension as a means of addressing the "free rider" problem (Iannaccone 1994), or, alternatively, as providing a source of subnational identity in an alien environment. In the latter explanation, people who remain in the church in the face of countervailing social pressure might simply wish to embrace their Catholicism as completely as possible. Regardless, the market approach provides a theoretical starting point for understanding what had previously struck me as an anomalous set of empirical findings.

IN LIEU OF CONCLUSION

The essays in this volume suggest that, whatever the current state of intellectual exchange, the religious markets research program merits our continued scholarly attention. There are two principal reasons for this. First, the critics and supporters of the approach have shown that there is indeed a great deal more to do. While it is tempting to regard the rigorous, consistent, and elegant theory offered by Stark and Finke as a nearly completed intellectual project, it seems clear that several of the assumptions and consequences of that theory require further examination. Second, the market model does seem to provide a framework within which other phenomena relating the social to the sacred can be explained. Whether we regard religious bodies such as churches as religious "firms," or as God's representatives on earth, it is clear that churches have many social functions besides providing sites for public worship. The extent to which the economic model of human behavior which provides the basis for the market model of religious economies can account for the multifaceted activities of religious organizations is a matter which will undoubtedly occupy the attention of scholars for some time to come.

NOTES

1. Of course, macro-level descriptions of scientific progress are, to an important extent, context dependent. One could argue that the "rational choice" approach constitutes the general research program, and that the extension of economic modes of analy-

sis to religion ultimately represents what Lakatos would term a "progressive problem shift." However, it seems reasonable to suppose that the adaptability or lack of adaptability of the market approach to other problems in the social scientific study of religion will determine whether this research program merits further scholarly attention.

2. Aras also reports that membership in the Brahmin caste is also related to support for Hindu nationalism. Since Brahmins are generally regarded as the caste most likely to benefit from observance of the caste system, it may be that this finding constitutes evidence of some extremely "rational" cost-benefit analysis.

3. The title of Richard Neuhaus's book, *The Naked Public Square* (1984), refers precisely to the tearing of the "sacred canopy," and the resulting difficulty in conducting public debate.

4. In his chapter on "The Rise and Fall of Empires," Falwell goes to some lengths to persuade the reader of his view of history as involving the varying fortunes of great powers, which in turn are attributable to the respective nation's relationship with God.

5. I have suggested elsewhere (Jelen 1999) that the language of individual rights constitutes a "political Esperanto" in the United States. See also Glendon (1991).

6. Supporters of the Christian Right may dispute this claim. I have also suggested elsewhere (Jelen 2000a) that the fragmentation of governmental powers in the U.S. (via federalism and the separation of powers in the federal government) may create electoral incentives for certain officials to raise issues relating to religious freedom.

7. It should be noted that we were not able to find a similar contextual effect when the units of analysis were Canadian provinces. See Chandler, Cook, Jelen, and Wilcox (1994).

REFERENCES

Aras, Nandita S. 2000. *The Social Bases of Support for Hindu Nationalism and Hindu Nationalist Parties.* Unpublished Ph.D. dissertation, Columbia University.

Bankston, Carl L., III. 2001. Review of *Acts of Faith: Explaining the Human Side of Religion.* In *Review of Religious Research* 42: 332–334.

Berger, Peter. 1969. *The Sacred Canopy: Elements of a Sociological Theory of Religion.* Garden City, N.Y.: Anchor.

Carter, Stephen L. 1993. *The Culture of Disbelief: How American Law and Politics Trivializes Religious Devotion.* New York: Basic Books.

Casanova, Jose. 1994. *Public Religions in the Modern World.* Chicago: University of Chicago Press.

Chandler, Marthe A., Elizabeth Adell Cook, Ted G. Jelen, and Clyde Wilcox. 1994. "Abortion in the United States and Canada: A Comparative Study of Public Opinion." In *Abortion Politics in the United States and Canada: Studies in Public Opinion.* Ted G. Jelen and Marthe A. Chandler, eds. Westport, Conn.: Prager: 131–143.

Chaves, Mark and Philip S. Gorski. 2001. "Religious Pluralism and Religious Participation," *American Review of Sociology* 27: 261–281.

Cook, Elizabeth Adell, Ted G. Jelen, and Clyde Wilcox. 1993. "Catholicism and Abortion Attitudes in the American States: A Contextual Analysis," *Journal for the Scientific Study of Religion* 32: 223–230.

Dillon, Michele. 1996. "Cultural Differences in the Abortion Discourse of the Catholic Church: Evidence from Four Countries," *Sociology of Religion* 57: 25–36.
Falwell, Jerry. 1980. *Listen, America!* Garden City, N.Y.: Doubleday.
Finke, Roger and Rodney Stark. 1989. "Evaluating the Evidence: Religious Economies and Sacred Canopies," *American Sociological Review* 53: 41–49.
———. 1992. *The Churching of America, 1776–1990.* New Brunswick, N.J.: Rutgers University Press.
Finke, Roger and Patricia Wittberg. 2000. "Organizational Revival from Within: Explaining Revival and Reform in the Roman Catholic Church," *Journal for the Scientific Study of Religion* 39: 154–170.
Gill, Anthony. 1998. *Rendering Unto Caesar: The Catholic Church and State in Latin America.* Chicago: University of Chicago Press.
Glendon, Mary Ann. 1991. *Rights Talk.* New York: The Free Press.
Green, John C. 1993. "Pat Robertson and the Latest Crusade: Religious Resources and the 1988 Presidential Campaign," *Social Science Quarterly* 74: 157–168.
Green, John C., Mark J. Rozell, and Clyde Wilcox. 2001. "Social Movements and Party Politics: The Case of The Christian Right," *Journal for the Scientific Study of Religion* 40: 413–426.
Greenawalt, Kent. 1988. *Religious Convictions and Political Choice.* New York: Oxford University Press.
Grindstaff, Laura. 1994. "Abortion in the Popular Press: Mapping Media Discourse From *Roe* to *Webster*." In *Abortion Politics in the United States and Canada: Studies in Public Opinion.* Marthe A. Chandler and Ted G. Jelen, eds. Westport, Conn.: Praeger: 57–88.
Iannaccone, Lawrence R. 1991. "The Consequences of Religious Market Structure," *Rationality and Society* 3: 156–177.
———. 1994. "Why Strict Churches Are Strong," *American Journal of Sociology* 99: 1180–1211.
———. 1997. "Rational Choice: Framework for the Scientific Study of Religion." In *Rational Choice Theory and Religion: Summary and Assessment.* Lawrence A. Young, ed. New York: Routledge: 25–44.
Jelen, Ted G. 1991. *The Political Mobilization of Religious Beliefs.* Westport, Conn.: Praeger.
———. 1993. *The Political World of the Clergy.* Westport, Conn.: Praeger.
———. 1999. "On the Hegemony of Liberal Individualism: A Reply to Williams," *Sociology of Religion* 60: 35–40.
———. 2000a. *To Serve God and Mammon: Church-State Relations in American Politics.* Boulder, Colo.: Westview.
———. 2000b. "Illinois: Moral Politics in a Materialist Political Culture." In *Prayers in the Precincts: The Christian right in the 1998 Elections.* John C. Green, Mark J. Rozell, and Clyde Wilcox, eds. Washington, D.C.: Georgetown University Press, 243–256.
Jelen, Ted G., John O'Donnell, and Clyde Wilcox. 1993. "A Contextual Analysis of Catholicism and Attitudes Toward Abortion in Western Europe," *Sociology of Religion* 54: 375–383.
Jelen, Ted G. and Clyde Wilcox. 1993. "Catholicism and Opposition to Gender Equality in Western Europe," *International Journal of Public Opinion Research* 5: 40–57.

———. 1998. "Context and Conscience: The Catholic Church as an Agent of Political Socialization in Western Europe," *Journal for the Scientific Study of Religion* 37: 28–40.

Kuhn, Thomas. 1970. *The Structure of Scientific Revolutions*. Chicago: University of Chicago Press.

Lakatos, Imre. 1970. "Falsification and the Methodology of Scientific Research Programmes." In *Criticism and the Growth of Knowledge*. Imre Lakatos, ed. New York: Cambridge University Press.

Neuhaus, Richard John. 1984. *The Naked Public Square*. Grand Rapids, Mich.: Eerdmans.

Noelle-Neuman, Elisabeth. 1993. *The Spiral of Silence: Public Opinion—Our Social Skin*. Chicago: University of Chicago Press.

Olson, Daniel V. A. 1999. "Religious Pluralism and U.S. Church Membership: A Reassessment," *Sociology of Religion* 60: 149–173.

Reed, Ralph. 1994. *Politically Incorrect*. Dallas: Word.

Robbins, Thomas. 2001. "The Elementary Firms of Religion," *Review of Religious Research* 42: 334–336.

Roof, Wade Clark and William McKinney. 1990. *American Mainline Religion: Its Changing Shape and Future*. New Brunswick, N.J.: Rutgers University Press.

Segers, Mary C. and Ted G. Jelen. 1998. *A Wall of Separation? Debating the Public Role of Religion*. Lanham, Md.: Rowman & Littlefield.

Sherkat, Darren E. 1997. "Embedding Religious Choices: Integrating Preferences and Social Constraints into Rational Choice Theories of Religious Behavior." In *Rational Choice Theory and Religion: Summary and Assessment*. Lawrence A. Young, ed. New York: Routledge, 66–86.

Stark, Rodney and Roger Finke. 2000. *Acts of Faith: Explaining the Human Side of Religion*. Berkeley: University of California Press.

Tocqueville, Alexis de. 1945. *Democracy in America*, 2 volumes. Phillips Bradley, ed. New York: Vintage Books.

Toulmin, Stephen. 1974. *The Uses of Argument*. London: Cambridge University Press.

Wilcox, Clyde. 1992. *God's Warriors: The Christian Right in 20th Century America*. Baltimore: Johns Hopkins University Press.

Wilson, John. 2001. Review of *Acts of Faith: Explaining the Human Side of Religion*. In *Review of Religious Research* 42: 336–339.

Wybraniec, John and Roger Finke. 2001. "Religious Regulation and the Courts: The Judiciary's Changing Role in Protecting Minority Religions From Majoritarian Rule," *Journal for the Scientific Study of Religion* 40: 427–444.

Index

About the Contributors

ABOUT THE EDITOR:

Ted G. Jelen is professor and chair of political sience at the University of Nevada at Las Vegas. He has published extensively in the areas of religion and politics, the politics of abortion, and public attitudes toward a variety of social issues. He is the former book review editor of the Review of Religious Res*earch*, and is currently the editor of the *Journal for the Scientific Study of Religion*.

ABOUT THE CONTRIBUTORS:

Steve Bruce is professor of sociology at the University of Aberdeen, Scotland. He is the author of thirteen books on the sociology of religion, including God Save *Ulster: Religion and the Politics of Paisleyism*; *The Rise and Fall of the New Christian Right: Conservative Protestant Politics in America, 1978–1988*; *Pray TV: Televangelism in America*; *Religion in Modern Britain*; *Religion in the Modern World: From Cathedrals to Cults*; and *Choice and Religion: A Critique of Rational Choice Theory*.

Roger Finke is professor of sociology and religious studies at Pennsylvania State University, and the director of the American Religion Data Archive (www.thearda.com) at Purdue University. His recent book with Rodney Stark, *Acts of Faith: Explaining the Human Side of Religion: A Social Science Paradigm* received the 2001 Distinguished Book Award from the American Sociological Association's Section on the Sociology of Religion.

Anthony Gill is associate professor of political science at the University of Washington, and is the author of *Rendering Unto Caesar: The Catholic Church and the State in Latin America*. He has written articles appearing in the *American Journal of Political Science, Rationality and Society, Politics and Society*, and the *Journal of Church and State*, as well as numerous book chapters. Professor Gill is currently studying the political origins of religious liberty in Latin America and other parts of the world.

Eva M. Hamberg is professor of sociology of religion and chair of immigration studies at Lund University, Sweden. She has published books and articles in several fields, including works on secularization and value changes in Scandinavia, religious market structures and the effects of religious pluralism, economic aspects of international migration, and changes in religiosity, world views, and values among immigrants. Among many other works, she is the author of *Studies in the Prevalence of Religious Beliefs and Religious Practice in Contemporary Sweden*.

Daniel V. A. Olson is associate professor of sociology at Indiana University, South Bend. He has published numerous scholarly articles on religion and politics, religiously based friendship networks, congregational growth and financial giving, and religious pluralism and invovlement. His work has appeared in such journals as *Social Forces, American Sociological Review, Sociology of Religion, Review of Religious Research*, and the *Journal for the Scientific Study of Religion*.

Thorleif Pettersson is professor of sociology of religion at Uppsala University, Sweden. Previously, he had served as a Research Fellow at the Swedish Collegium for Advanced Studies in the Social Sciences, The Stockholm Institute for Future Studies, and the Stockholm Institute for the Sociology of Religion. He is currently working on comparative studies at the micro-level, as a member of the Steering Committees of the European Value Study and the World Values Study, and in the area of Church sociology.

Rodney Stark is professor of sociology and comparative religion, University of Washington. His work forms the core of what has become known as the "new paradigm" in the social scientific study of religion, and appears in 22 books and nearly 150 scholarly articles. Among his recent books are *The Rise of Christianity* (1996), *Religion, Deviance, and Social Control* (coauthored with William Sims Bainbridge, 1997), and *Acts of Faith: Explaining the Human Side of Religion* (coauthored with Roger Finke, 2000).

R. Stephen Warner is professor of sociology at the University of Illinois at Chicago, and a past president of the Association for the Sociology of Religion. In addition to his agenda-setting article on the new paradigm (*American Journal of Sociology,* 1993) he is the author of numerous articles and chapters on varieties of religion in contemporary America, and is the co-editor (with Judith G. Wittner) of *Gatherings in Diaspora: Religious Communities and the New Immigration* (1998). Warner's congregational case study, *New Wine in Old Wineskins*, was the recipient of the 1989 Distinguished Book Award of the Society for the Scientific Study of Religion.